essential
DESSERTS

essential
DESSERTS

MURDOCH BOOKS

Published in 2011 by Murdoch Books Pty Limited

Murdoch Books Australia
Pier 8/9
23 Hickson Road
Millers Point NSW 2000
Phone: +61 (0) 2 8220 2000
Fax: +61 (0) 2 8220 2558
www.murdochbooks.com.au

Murdoch Books UK Limited
Erico House, 6th Floor
93–99 Upper Richmond Road
Putney, London SW15 2TG
Phone: +44 (0) 20 8785 5995
Fax: +44 (0) 20 8785 5985
www.murdochbooks.co.uk

Publisher: Kylie Walker
Project Editor: Melody Lord
Food Editor: Anneka Manning
Editor: Melissa Penn
Concept Design: Vivien Sung
Designer: Susanne Geppert

Photographer: Jared Fowler
Stylists: Cherise Koch, Emma Ross
Food preparation: e'cco, Alan Wilson

Text copyright © Murdoch Books Pty Limited 2011
Based on The essential Dessert cookbook, first published by Murdoch Books in 1998.
Recipes developed in the Murdoch Books Test Kitchen.
Design copyright © Murdoch Books Pty Limited 2011

National Library of Australia Cataloguing-in-Publication Data

Title:	Essential desserts.
ISBN:	978-1-74266-092-9 (pbk.)
Series:	New essential.
Notes:	Includes index.
Subjects:	Desserts.
Dewey Number:	641.86

A catalogue record for this book is available from the British Library.

Printed by 1010 Printing International Limited, China.
Reprinted 2011.

IMPORTANT: Those who might be at risk from the effects of salmonella poisoning (the elderly, pregnant women, young children and those suffering from immune deficiency diseases) should consult their doctor with any concerns about eating raw eggs.

CONVERSION GUIDE: Cooking times may vary depending on the oven you are using. For fan-forced ovens, as a general rule, set the oven temperature to 20°C (35°F) lower than indicated in the recipe. We have used 20 ml (4 teaspoon) tablespoon measures. If you are using a 15 ml (3 teaspoon) tablespoon add an extra teaspoon for each tablespoon specified. We have used 60 g (Grade 3) eggs in all recipes.

On the cover: Pavlova with fresh fruit (page 57)

a mere trifle

Sweet food is one of life's primeval joys. We all know that dessert isn't strictly necessary — life isn't going to end without it — but then who among us would choose to live on bread and water? Dessert gives us something to look forward to as a child while we plough through our worthy meat and vegetables. It brings a lovingly prepared meal to a close with a fanfare, not a whimper. While salty food sparks the appetite, sweet food soothes and caresses it, leaving us warm and contented. It is a luxury, an exquisite indulgence, something that gives us true pleasure but in a duller, greyer world is completely expendable. The names of older desserts reflect this … the unimportant trifle, the silly syllabub, the flummery and the fool. Yet these charming concoctions of sugar, cream, eggs and fruit live on through the ages to defy their names and prove their worth. Desserts are not mere trifles, they are truly, essentially life-enhancing … as you are about to find out.

contents

special features

black forest gateau (page 196)

just
desserts

It could be said that dessert is the mark of a truly civilised society. As our ancestors gathered round the fire at the end of a hard day's hunting, there is one thought we can be certain did not cross their minds: 'now, are we having cheesecake or pavlova for dessert?' Desserts are rarely eaten to satisfy hunger, but to provide a sweet finish, a closing fanfare to a meal. They are meant for pleasure, not sustenance.

Antonin Carême, the artistic French chef who served for princes, kings and emperors, including the future King George IV and Tsar Alexander I, is said to have remarked that there were five fine arts, one of which was architecture, and that the main branch of architecture was confectionery. Many of his creations were based on ideas he copied from architectural drawings.

Man has been eating luxurious sweet food for a long time. In Asia thousands of years ago, cane syrup was being used as a sweetener and in Europe, fruit and honey were used. Sugar is the backbone of desserts and its increasing availability as a more refined sugar and a less expensive product has given rise to the invention of a million recipes.

Sugar, like spices, reached the Western world via the Arab trade routes and, when it first appeared, was available only in tiny quantities and used medicinally. Known as white gold, it was prohibitively expensive. During the next few centuries, the rich used sugar, like spices, indiscriminately as a sign of wealth, sprinkled on everything they ate. It wasn't until the 15th century that Italians went back to Arabic traditions of using sugar in a select few dishes.

The rich may have been enjoying sweet foods for hundreds of years but, in the Western world, the idea of dessert as a separate course is relatively modern. Sweet dishes were originally served on the banqueting table with the savoury: a typical example of one 'course' might be veal, tongue, chicken, blancmange, vol-au-vent, a cake and a fish. Many desserts actually evolved from savoury dishes to sweet. For example, one of the oldest known desserts is blancmange, which started life as a dish of pounded chicken breasts and almonds. Pies often included both sweet (fruit) and savoury (meat) fillings together.

Jelly began as a savoury decorative dish at banquets — gelatin boiled from animal bones and moulded creatively would be the centrepiece of the table, displaying the chef's great talents and control of his raw ingredients. This gelatin then began to be sweetened. When the Victorians invented the copper jelly mould, the idea took off with a vengeance, leading to a frenzy of moulded blancmanges, creams and cakes (often named simply 'shapes'). Powdered gelatin was created in the 1840s but did not really become popular until much later with the advent of ice boxes and home refrigeration.

The sweet pudding has only existed for the past couple of centuries — before that the pudding was a savoury mixture of grains and dried fruit stuffed into animal guts and boiled in the same broth as the meat and vegetables. (Fortunately for our squeamish modern palates, today's only reminder of this is the beef suet in a traditional Christmas plum pudding.) This manner of cooking, using nothing but an open hearth, was available to all, while cakes and other desserts requiring ovens were still only enjoyed by the rich. The invention of the pudding cloth in the 17th century coincided with an increased importation of dried fruit to England and a drop in the price of sugar, making it available to the not-so-rich. Hence the sweet pudding was born.

A well-stocked table, with a multitude of dishes set out, had always been a graphic way of displaying wealth, but in the 16th century the banqueting tables began to be cleared for dessert. The word itself derives from the French *desservir*, the cleared or de-served table. Plates were removed and the table swept clear of crumbs. Sometimes the guests would retire to another room (or another building!) for dessert. In Victorian England the tradition arose of removing the tablecloth before serving dessert.

Although there are obviously many old and traditional desserts, the past couple of centuries have seen a plethora of newer recipes. The development of transportation, the invention of refrigeration, and the exploration of the world, which transplanted hundreds of different types of fruit from one place to the next and introduced new ingredients such as chocolate, spices and sugar to the Western world, have created myriad wonderful recipes.

Ice cream, now taken entirely for granted, was, as a commercially available product, the direct result of the invention of refrigeration techniques. Cold food was originally thought to be poisonous or dangerous to eat and was a novelty served at special occasions and eaten with some bravado. Food and drinks were usually taken tepid (hot drinks such as tea and coffee were equally frowned upon when they first arrived on the scene). Ice, until the first ice-making machines appeared in the 1860s, was a natural commodity that had to be gathered, transported and stored in insulated ice houses. The advent of ice boxes changed the face of what could be stored at home. It was also now possible to set jelly and freeze ice cream at home.

All over the world different cultures have their own versions of desserts and it is surprising how similar they can be. Rice puddings come in many forms, from hot, creamy and oven-baked in the West to sticky black varieties in the East. Puddings made with bread and noodles are common in many cuisines, and ice creams are fairly universal, from the gelati of Italy to the kulfi of India. Migrants from Europe who settled in America and

Australia took with them the desserts from their own cultures as well as inventing new ones with ingredients now available. Many countries took on their own national desserts: pavlova is as Australian as a kangaroo, and ice cream became a national symbol in America — it was deemed an essential foodstuff and indispensable to the morale of the army. (Ironically, in 1942 ice cream was banned as part of the war effort in Britain where it was named a 'luxury' item.) The British themselves are associated with steamed and baked puddings.

As well as the favouritism of nationality, desserts fall in and out of fashion: Jell-o made its all-encompassing appearance in the 1940s and 1950s, baked Alaska and black forest gateaux wowed the 1970s, tiramisu was the dessert of the 1980s, and the 1990s gave us sticky date pudding and the ubiquitous crème brûlée. We enjoyed the simple delight of panna cotta at the beginning of the 21st century. Who knows what the future will bring?

Our star rating:

When we test recipes, we rate them for ease of preparation. The following cookery ratings are used in this book:

☀   A single star indicates a recipe that is simple and generally quick to make, perfect for beginners.

☀☀   Two stars indicate the need for a little more care or a little more time.

☀☀☀ Three stars indicate special dishes that need more investment in time, care and patience, but the results are worth it. Even beginners can make these dishes as long as the recipe is followed carefully.

before you start

basics

- Read the recipe through and take note of any soaking, standing and overnight refrigeration times, and necessary equipment.
- Cooking times will vary, so if your pudding is sloppy or your soufflé not puffed, and the specified time is up, leave it a little longer.
- Many recipes can be varied by substituting or adding your favourite flavours.

measurements

- Always follow one set of measurements — metric or imperial, or cups. We have included cup measurements for ingredients such as flour, sugar and liquids, and weights for everything else.
- For accuracy, cups and spoons should be levelled with the back of a knife if possible.
- For liquid measures, plastic and glass jugs with the calibrations visible both inside and outside are easiest to use.
- Electronic scales have a digital display and can be programmed for metric and imperial weights. They are the most accurate way of measuring by weight.
- Balance scales can be used with most metric and imperial weights. The scale pans hold the weights on one side and the ingredients on the other, and weights are measured by evenly balancing both sides.

- Spring weights have a scale pan on top of a calibrated scale. Choose one with an adjustable tension screw as they will need to be adjusted to keep them true.

ingredients

- The sweetness of recipes can be varied where sugar is not an integral part of the recipe. Sugar in pies, jellies and fruit desserts is generally variable, whereas if it is part of a liquid:dry ratio in a pudding, it cannot be changed without altering the texture of the dish.
- Butter should be fresh and unsalted but if you only have salted butter, the flavour of the dish will only be slightly different. Keep butter well wrapped in the fridge and away from anything strong smelling. Grate butter into a bowl to soften it more quickly.
- Eggs are taken to be 60 g (2¼ oz) in weight. Eggs should be refrigerated and used as soon as possible after purchase.
- Eggs should be brought to room temperature before use in cooking.
- Very fresh egg whites and old egg whites do not beat as well as those a few days old. Fresh eggs are easier to separate as the white is stronger and more viscous and the yolk holds its shape better.
- When beating egg whites, bowls and beaters must be completely clean and dry. There must be no yolk in the whites.
- Cream for whipping has a minimum of 35% fat. Thick (double/heavy) cream

refers to cream with a minimum of 45% fat and is not thickened with gelatin.
- Whip cream slowly at first, then speed up. Start with cold cream and a chilled bowl in hot weather. Whipped cream should be white and form a stiff peak which droops slightly at the top. Cream is overwhipped if it starts to turn grainy and yellowish.
- Cream for piping from a piping bag should be slightly under-whipped as the heat from your hand and the continued working of the cream will cause it to thicken further.
- Flour may be dry or slightly damp according to the humidity and will absorb more or less liquid accordingly.
- Doughs and pastries may need a little more flour on a sticky day, but avoid adding too much as it will make them tougher.
- Nuts keep best if frozen in airtight bags. Toasting nuts gives them a fresh flavour.
- Grind cold nuts in a food processor, with a tablespoon of sugar and flour from the recipe to help absorb any excess oil.
- Vanilla extract or essence should be pure as it gives a much better flavour.
- A humid day will not be kind to caramel or meringues, so choose something else to make.
- Lemon and lime juice should be freshly squeezed for the best flavour.

equipment

- A few pieces of good equipment will go a long way towards successful results. Choose carefully to get something that really lasts.
- If you don't have exactly the right size tin, it may not matter. A 1 cm (½ inch) difference will not ruin a pie or tart — you may just have a little too much, or not quite enough filling and the pastry will be a bit thinner or thicker. Any more than 2 cm (¾ inch) may change things too much, so use your judgement.
- Ovens do not all behave in the same way. Fan-forced ovens will cook more quickly and can be used to cook more than one thing at a time as they have a more overall heat.
- Not all ovens are accurate so use an oven thermometer placed in the centre of the oven to check the temperature.
- Pastry that needs a quick exposure to heat to set it is best cooked near the oven element, whereas dishes cooked in a water bath should be placed awat from the element.
- Bakeware should respond quickly and evenly to the oven temperature. Shiny metal bakeware will deflect heat and prevent scorching, whereas dark, matt, non-stick bakeware will absorb and hold heat and may need a slightly lower cooking temperature or a little less cooking time. Baking trays should be solid so they don't buckle.
- Good-quality saucepans work best. Stainless steel pans with a heavy 'sandwiched' base are best for even heat distribution. Non-reactive pans will not react with food acids and cause discolouration. Choose pans with comfortable handles, rounded edges and lids with a tight seal.
- Non-stick pans are good for custards but caramelising sugar should be done in a stainless steel pan where you can see the colour changes. Do not use metal utensils with non-stick pans.
- Glass heatproof bowls are useful for whisking egg whites and melting chocolate. Stainless steel bowls also work well for these functions, as well as heating up and cooling down quickly when required. A large ceramic bowl is invaluable for mixing large quantities.
- Buy a good-quality food processor with a bowl large enough to cope with large quantities. A spice grinder will take care of any small quantities.
- Blenders should have a good motor and blades which sit both up and down in the goblet, otherwise small amounts will simply go round and round.
- Beating to aerate and combine ingredients can be done with a balloon whisk or electric beaters. Run a spatula down the bowl occasionally. Don't use a food processor for beating as it will not aerate the ingredients.
- If your heat source does not turn down very low, use a heat diffuser. These are small mats that spread the heat over the base of saucepans to prevent them getting too hot.
- Freezer thermometers are used for accurate freezer temperature readings. Food that is stored at -18°C (0°F) will be free from bacterial and enzyme activity. A few degrees higher at -10°C (14°F), enzymes take effect. Ice cream should be frozen at -18°C (0°F).
- Deep-frying thermometers are essential for accurate oil measurements. Oil at the correct temperature will cook the food and seal in the flavours with a minimum of absorption.
- Sugar thermometers are essential for accurate sugar solution temperature measurements. Sugar syrup also has a series of critical temperatures for soft and hard-ball stages until it begins to caramelise.
- A kitchen timer is essential for accurate timing and to prevent burning food.
- Baking paper or parchment should be non-stick to be most effective. Greaseproof paper is not non-stick but is useful for making piping bags.

1

2

3

4

5

6

7

8

9

10

11

in the kitchen

A few basic utensils will simplify the creation of superb, enticing desserts. The better quality ones will last longer.

1. cutters
Cutters come in various shapes and sizes. Graded sets of plain and fluted round cutters have a sharp cutting edge and a blunter, rolled-top edge for pressing down on. Metal cutters have a better edge. Fancy cutters should be stored carefully as they can easily get squashed.

2. chinoise
Stainless steel chinoise or cone-shaped sieves are more effective for puréeing. The purée can be forced through the holes in the cone with the back of a ladle or a wooden spoon.

3. canelle knife or citrus zester
Zesters have a row of holes with sharpened edges running across the top. When they are firmly drawn across a citrus fruit, they peel off the zest in long thin shreds. Many zesters have a canelle knife on one side that removes a larger v-shaped piece of zest. Both leave the bitter pith behind.

4. baking beads
Small reusable ceramic or metal beads used for blind baking pastry. Rice or dried beans can be substituted.

5. flour sifter/dredger
Useful for dusting work surfaces with flour, this container can also be filled with icing (confectioners') sugar/unsweetened cocoa powder for dusting over desserts.

6. measuring cups and spoons
All spoons and cup measures in this book are level, not heaped. Dry ingredients should be leveled off with a knife.

7. cream horn moulds
Useful for shaping biscuits and moulding ice creams. Available in different sizes.

8. spoons
Large metal spoons are best for folding in dry ingredients or combining one mixture with another without losing too much air.

9. whisks
Whisks beat air into ingredients and lumps out. Balloon whisks consist of loops of stainless steel joined by a large handle. They range from large ones for egg white through to small ones for sauces and dressings. Flat whisks, which consist of a wire coiled around a loop, are useful for whisking in saucepans or containers without rounded bottoms and can also be used on flat plates.

10. melon baller, corer, fruit knife
Used for coring and cutting fruit. The sharp, serrated edges of the corer cut the fruit without squashing. Melon ballers can also be used for coring halved fruit, as can the sharp tip of fruit knives.

11. decorating equipment
These nozzles, made from metal or plastic, vary in size from large for cream and pastry, to small for intricate decoration (as shown). You can buy special patterned nozzles for stars, shells, and so on.

14

12

15

13

14

16

17

18

19

20

21

22

23

12. wooden spoons

Wooden spoons are useful for stirring, mixing and beating as they do not conduct heat or scratch non-stick surfaces. Some spoons have a flat edge and corner to help you get into the sides of saucepans. Choose spoons made of hard, close-grained wood for durability.

13. lemon squeezer

Available in glass, ceramic, plastic and wood, the squeezers that have a container underneath to catch the juice are the most useful.

14. rubber spatulas

These can scrape a bowl completely clean and are useful for getting residue out of food processors. Tiny versions are available for scraping jars clean. Hand wash to make them last longer. They tend to absorb colour and flavour, so keep separate ones for sweet and savoury use.

15. lattice cutter

For topping pies and tarts, this will cut a lattice pattern into rolled out pastry with a minimum of fuss. Usually made from plastic so it will not mark work surfaces.

16. metal moulds

Dariole, baba and mini pudding basins are used for baked and steamed puddings or moulding set puddings and jellies.

17. jelly moulds

Moulds are used for shaping jellies and other set desserts. They are available in different shapes and sizes. Metal moulds are the most commonly available. These are good conductors of cold, which helps set the jelly and are easier to heat when unmoulding. Moulds are also available in glass or ceramic. All moulds should be filled right to the top to give the full effect of the pattern. Some moulds can be used for baked desserts but may be difficult to unmould if the pattern is too detailed.

18. rolling pin

This should be large enough to roll out a full sheet of pastry, ensuring a smooth surface. Good-quality rolling pins are made of hard wood with a close grain and very smooth finish. Wood is preferable to ceramic and marble as its surface collects and holds a fine layer of flour. Rolling pins are available in various shapes and sizes; different cultures use different thicknesses of rolling pin. Those used for large sheets of pastry such as strudel can be as long and thin as curtain rods.

19. tart/flan tins

These can be fluted or plain. Loose-bottomed ones enable you to remove the tart easily. Metal is better for pastry. Tart rings are used on a baking tray and give a straight edge. To prevent rust, dry well (in the warm oven) before storing.

20. palette knife

These have long flexible blades for spreading. Available in different sizes, smaller ones are useful for more fiddly jobs and larger ones for cake fillings. as they can slide across the whole surface in one smooth motion. They can also be used for turning food (flipping pikelets in frying pans, for example).

21. pastry wheel

Metal or plastic wheels used for cutting fluted edges on pastry.

22. pastry brush

Made with natural or nylon bristles, these can be flat or round. Also used for glazing and oiling. Be careful when using nylon bristles with hot liquids or hot surfaces, as they may melt. Dry brushes thoroughly before storage. A separate brush should be used for oil.

23. ceramic heatproof moulds

Heart-shaped moulds with draining holes for coeur à la crème, petit pots and ramekins are required for baked and set desserts and soufflés.

custards & other creamy things

The starting point for any comprehensive book of desserts has to be the custard. The basis for so many favourite desserts is this gentle and nourishing mixture of eggs and cream, sweetened with sugar. And from the custard it is but a magical flick of the whisk to soufflés and mousses, syllabubs and flummeries — creamy creations that tantalise on the spoon and literally melt in the mouth.

perfect custard

Custard forms the basis of many desserts, either in its purest form as crème anglaise, with a wine base such as zabaglione or sabayon, or thickened as crème patisserie. Custard can create a base for soufflés, ice creams, baked puddings, and desserts set with gelatin, like bavarois.

As the name crème anglaise suggests, custard is of English origin. There are two types of custard, pouring (made on the stovetop) and baked. The main ingredients of both are eggs, which are better if brought to room temperature first, and milk. To make a perfect smooth, velvety custard, of whichever type, the golden rule is to keep the heat low. Never let custard overcook or you will end up with a pan full of scrambled eggs. Custards made with whole eggs will set more quickly, as the egg white sets at a lower temperature.

pouring custard

To make a perfect pouring custard, separate 3 eggs, put the yolks in a bowl with 2 tablespoons caster (superfine) sugar and beat with a balloon whisk until light and fluffy. When properly beaten, the mixture will fall in a ribbon that will hold its shape for a few seconds. Pour 375 ml (13 fl oz/1½ cups) milk into a saucepan and bring to scalding point — small bubbles will appear around the edge. Stir if a skin appears to be forming. Pour into the egg mixture, stirring with the balloon whisk until well combined.

If there is any milk protein on the base of the saucepan, rinse it out as this may cause the custard to catch on the bottom. Return the custard to the pan and stir over low heat.

For a more gentle heat, if you have a double boiler, you can use it for custard making. Alternatively, use a metal bowl set over a pan of simmering water (don't let the bowl touch the water).

Heat the custard very gently so the egg yolks will thicken evenly. To prevent lumps forming, stir continuously. There is even a technique for efficient stirring. Make sure the wooden spoon passes through the middle of the pan and around the edge, where the custard is hottest, so will thicken quickest. Keep stirring to ensure the custard thickens evenly and keep it below simmering point to prevent it from curdling. (If the custard curdles a little, try removing it from the heat, adding a teaspoon of chilled water and beating well. This will prevent further curdling but will not make a smooth custard.) The custard is ready when it forms a coating on the back of a spoon, which you can draw a line through and will hold its shape.

When ready, either pour it quickly through a sieve into a bowl or plunge the base of the saucepan into chilled water to stop the cooking process. If chilling the custard, lay a piece of baking paper or plastic wrap directly over the surface to prevent a skin forming. If keeping the custard warm, put it in a bowl over a pan of hot water.

For a vanilla custard, add a split vanilla bean to the milk when you scald it and leave to infuse for 5–30 minutes, depending on the strength of flavour required. Remove the bean before adding the milk to the eggs. Alternatively, add 2 teaspoons of natural vanilla extract to the finished custard.

baked custard

Baked custard should be cooked in a bain-marie or water bath to ensure a gentle heat, so the mixture does not curdle. The ramekins or moulds should be placed in a baking dish with enough water to come halfway up their sides. To prevent water bubbling around the edges, you can sit the moulds on a tea towel (dish towel) inside the baking dish. The custard is cooked when the centre is set but still wobbles when the mould is shaken. The custard will set as it cools. The texture should be smooth and creamy.

vanilla bavarois

Preparation time: 40 minutes + overnight
   chilling time
Cooking time: 10–15 minutes
Serves 4

685 ml (23½ fl oz/2¾ cups) milk
1 vanilla bean, split lengthways
1 cinnamon stick
6 egg yolks
150 g (5½ oz/⅔ cup) caster
   (superfine) sugar
3 teaspoons powdered gelatin
185 ml (6 fl oz/¾ cup) pouring
   (whipping) cream
raspberries, to serve

1 Gently heat the milk, vanilla bean and cinnamon stick in a saucepan until almost boiling. Remove from the heat and set aside to infuse for 5 minutes. Remove the cinnamon stick and vanilla bean.
2 Whisk together the egg yolks and sugar until thick and pale. Gradually whisk in the milk. Pour into a large clean pan and stir continuously over low heat until the mixture thickens. Do not boil. Remove from the heat. Cover the surface with plastic wrap to prevent a skin forming.
3 Place 2 tablespoons water in a small heatproof bowl, sprinkle the gelatin in an even layer over the surface and leave to go spongy. Bring a large pan filled with about 4 cm (1½ inches) water to the boil, remove from the heat, carefully lower the gelatin bowl into the water (it should come halfway up the side of the bowl) and stir until dissolved. Whisk into the custard. Cover as before and leave to cool.
4 Beat the cream until soft peaks form and fold into the cold custard. Spoon into four 250 ml (9 fl oz/1 cup) ramekins or moulds, tap the bases gently on a worktop to remove air bubbles, then refrigerate overnight.
5 To unmould, tilt each ramekin slightly on its side. Use your finger to gently pull the bavarois away from the edge, allowing air to enter and break the suction. Turn the bavarois out onto a plate. If it does not come out straight away, wipe a cloth dipped in hot water over the outside of the mould. Serve with raspberries.

Whisk the egg yolks and sugar together until thick and pale.

When the bavarois is set, use your index finger to gently pull it away from the edge of the mould.

crème brûlée

Crème brûlée is taken from the original English dish 'burnt cream', said to have been invented at Trinity College, Cambridge. It is traditionally made in a large, shallow dish, thus giving as much surface area for the toffee as possible. You can use any type of sugar for a brûlée topping, but the results will be different. Granulated sugar melts well and brown sugar gives a stronger caramel flavour.

vanilla brûlées

Preparation time: 30 minutes + 4 hours chilling time
Cooking time: 30 minutes
Serves 6

750 ml (26 fl oz/3 cups) pouring (whipping) cream
2 vanilla beans, split lengthways
8 egg yolks
110 g (3¾ oz/½ cup) sugar
3 teaspoons sugar, extra, for topping
fresh fruit (such as blueberries) (optional), to serve

1 Gently heat the cream and vanilla beans in a large, heavy-based saucepan until almost boiling. Remove from heat and leave to infuse for 30 minutes. Remove the beans. Whisk the egg yolks and sugar in a large bowl until thick and pale. Add the cream, then pour into a clean saucepan over low heat and stir until the mixture thickens slightly. Do not boil or you may curdle the mixture. Remove from heat and divide among six 170 ml (5½ fl oz/⅔ cup) ramekins or dariole moulds. Cover and refrigerate for at least 3 hours.

2 Before serving, preheat the grill (broiler) to very hot. Sprinkle a thin layer of sugar over the surface of the brûlées. Put the ramekins in a large ovenproof dish, packing ice around them to prevent the custards being heated. Grill (broil) the brûlées until the sugar caramelises into an even sheet. Keep watching or you may burn the caramel. The sugar needs to caramelise quickly so that the custard doesn't have time to melt. Chill the crème brûlées until you serve them but not for longer than 1 hour or the crust will soften. If desired, serve with fresh fruit.

panna cotta with ruby sauce

gently while stirring. Remove from the heat. Whisk the gelatin into the cream mixture. Pour into the moulds and chill for 2 hours, or until set. Unmould by wiping a cloth dipped in hot water over the mould and upending it onto a plate.
3 While the panna cotta is chilling, make the ruby sauce. Stir the sugar with 250 ml (9 fl oz/1 cup) water in a saucepan over medium heat until the sugar dissolves. Add the cinnamon stick and simmer for 5 minutes. Add the raspberries and wine and boil rapidly for 5 minutes. Remove the cinnamon stick and push the sauce through a sieve. Discard the seeds. Cool, then chill before serving with the panna cotta. Serve with raspberries.

baked custard

Preparation time: **5 minutes**
Cooking time: **35 minutes**
Serves **4**

3 eggs
95 g (3¼ oz/½ cup) soft brown sugar
375 ml (13 fl oz/1½ cups) milk
125 ml (4 fl oz/½ cup) pouring
    (whipping) cream
1 teaspoon natural vanilla extract
freshly grated nutmeg, to dust

1 Preheat the oven to 180°C (350°F/ Gas 4). Brush a 1 litre (35 fl oz/4 cup) ovenproof dish with melted butter.
2 Whisk the eggs, sugar, milk, cream and vanilla in a bowl for 1 minute. Pour into the greased dish and place the dish in a shallow baking dish. Pour enough boiling water into the baking dish to come halfway up the side of the ovenproof dish.
3 Place on the oven shelf, sprinkle the top of the custard with nutmeg and bake for 15 minutes. Reduce the heat to 160°C (315°F/Gas 2–3) and bake for a further 20 minutes, or until the custard is set. It should no longer be liquid but should wobble slightly when the dish is shaken lightly. Remove the dish from the water bath immediately. Serve warm or cold.

panna cotta with ruby sauce

✳ ✳

Preparation time: **20 minutes + 2 hours**
    chilling time
Cooking time: **20 minutes**
Serves **6**

750 ml (26 fl oz/3 cups) pouring
    (whipping) cream
3 teaspoons powdered gelatin
1 vanilla bean, split lengthways
80 g (2¾ oz/⅓ cup) caster (superfine) sugar

RUBY SAUCE
235 g (8½ oz/1 cup) caster (superfine) sugar
1 cinnamon stick
125 g (4½ oz) fresh or frozen raspberries,
    plus extra, to serve
125 ml (4 fl oz/½ cup) red wine

1 Lightly grease six 150 ml (5 fl oz) ramekins or moulds with flavourless oil. Place 60 ml (2 fl oz/¼ cup) of the cream in a small bowl, sprinkle the gelatin in an even layer over the surface and leave to go spongy.
2 Put the remaining cream in a saucepan with the vanilla bean and sugar and heat

vanilla bean cream pots with tamarillos

✹ ✹

Preparation time: 1 hour + 30 minutes
    standing time and 4 hours chilling time
Cooking time: 1 hour
Serves 6

700 ml (24 fl oz) pouring (whipping) cream
1 vanilla bean, split lengthways
2 eggs
2 egg yolks
2 tablespoons caster (superfine) sugar

POACHED TAMARILLOS
6 tamarillos with stalks
375 g (13 oz/1½ cups) caster (superfine) sugar
5 cm (2 inch) piece of orange zest
2–3 tablespoons Kirsch or cherry liqueur

1 Put six 125 ml (4 fl oz/½ cup) ramekins in a large baking dish. Put the cream and vanilla bean in a saucepan, bring slowly to the boil then reduce the heat and simmer for 5 minutes. Remove from the heat, split the bean, scrape out the seeds and return the bean and seeds to the cream. Cover and set aside for 30 minutes. Strain.

2 Preheat the oven to 160°C (315°F/ Gas 2–3). Whisk the eggs, egg yolks and sugar in a jug. Whisk in the cream, pour into the ramekins and cover each securely with foil. Pour hot water into the baking dish to come halfway up the ramekins. Bake for 30 minutes, or until just set. Refrigerate, covered, for 4 hours, or overnight.

3 Plunge the tamarillos into boiling water for 10 seconds, then put in chilled water and peel away the skins, leaving the stalks attached. Put the sugar in a saucepan with 750 ml (26 fl oz/3 cups) water and the orange zest. Stir to dissolve the sugar. Bring to the boil and boil for 3 minutes. Reduce the heat to a simmer and add the tamarillos. Poach for 6–8 minutes, depending on their ripeness. Turn off the heat, add the liqueur and leave the fruit in the syrup to cool. When ready to serve, remove the fruit from the pan, then bring the syrup to the boil and boil for 5–10 minutes, until reduced and thickened. Pour into a jug, cover and cool. Cut each tamarillo in half, leaving the stalk end intact, and serve with the sauce and vanilla bean cream.

NOTE: You can use 1 teaspoon of natural vanilla extract instead of the bean if you wish. Add it to the finished custard.

eggs

Eggs are extremely versatile. Egg yolks enrich and thicken custards and creamy desserts. Beaten egg whites are the foundation of meringues, soufflés and mousses. Eggs are used in cheesecakes, pastries and steamed puddings and make shiny glazes for puff pastry. Fresh eggs have a bright whole yolk surrounded by a thick, viscous white. Stale egg whites do not beat to a foam as successfully. To test an egg for freshness, place it in a glass of water: a fresh egg will stay horizontal at the bottom. As eggs age, the air cell at the round end becomes larger and the eggs will stand up or float.

chocolate

Chocolate was originally taken as a drink or used in recipes. It was sold as a paste or in solid bars and was very expensive. Milk was added to chocolate in England, but it was the Swiss who made the first commercial milk chocolate. Cocoa beans were known to Europeans from the time of Colombus, but it wasn't until 1519 when Hernando Cortes tasted chocolate drink, given to him by the Aztecs, that Europeans knew how to use the beans. Chocolate drink was thought to be energy-giving and was used as a restorative. It was also taken up with enthusiasm by temperance societies in the 19th century, as an alternative to alcohol.

petit pots au chocolat

Preparation time: 20 minutes + 6 hours chilling time
Cooking time: 1 hour
Serves 8

170 ml (5½ fl oz/⅔ cup) thick (double/ heavy) cream, plus extra, to serve
½ vanilla bean, split lengthways
150 g (5½ oz/1 cup) chopped dark chocolate
80 ml (2½ fl oz/⅓ cup) milk
2 egg yolks, at room temperature
55 g (2 oz/¼ cup) caster (superfine) sugar
unsweetened cocoa powder, to serve

1 Lightly brush eight 80 ml (2½ fl oz/ ⅓ cup) ramekins with melted butter and put them in a roasting tin. Preheat the oven to 140°C (275°F/Gas 1). Heat the cream in a small saucepan with the vanilla bean until the cream is warm. Leave to infuse for 10 minutes then scrape the seeds out of the vanilla bean into the cream, and discard the empty bean.
2 Mix the chocolate and milk together in a saucepan. Stir constantly over low heat until the chocolate just melts.
3 Place the egg yolks in a bowl and slowly whisk in the sugar. Continue whisking until the sugar dissolves and the mixture is light and creamy. Add the vanilla cream and the melted chocolate to the beaten egg yolks and mix well.
4 Pour into the ramekins, filling approximately two-thirds of the way up. Pour enough boiling water into the roasting tin to come halfway up the sides of the ramekins. Bake for 45 minutes, or until the chocolate pots are puffed up slightly and feel spongy.
5 Remove from the roasting tin and set aside to cool completely. Cover with plastic wrap and refrigerate for 6 hours before serving. Serve with a dollop of extra cream and a sprinkle of sifted cocoa.

chocolate bavarois

Preparation time: 30 minutes + 4 hours
   chilling time
Cooking time: 10 minutes
Serves 6

200 g (7 oz/1⅓ cups) chopped dark chocolate
375 ml (13 fl oz/1½ cups) milk
4 egg yolks
80 g (2¾ oz/⅓ cup) caster (superfine) sugar
1 tablespoon powdered gelatin
310 ml (10¾ fl oz/1¼ cups) pouring
   (whipping) cream
chocolate flakes, to garnish

1 Combine the chocolate and milk in a small saucepan. Stir over low heat until the chocolate melts and the milk just comes to the boil. Remove from the heat.
2 Beat the egg yolks and sugar until combined, then gradually add the hot chocolate milk, whisking until combined. Return to a clean pan and cook over low heat until the mixture thickens enough to coat the back of a wooden spoon. Do not allow it to boil. Remove from the heat.
3 Put 2 tablespoons water in a small heatproof bowl, sprinkle the gelatin in an even layer over the surface and leave to go spongy. Stir into the hot chocolate mixture until dissolved. Refrigerate until cold but not set, stirring occasionally.
4 Beat the cream until soft peaks form, then fold into the chocolate mixture in two batches. Pour into six 250 ml (9 fl oz/1 cup) glasses and refrigerate for 4 hours or overnight, or until set. To serve, garnish with chocolate flakes.

blancmange

Preparation time: 40 minutes + 6–8 hours
   chilling time
Cooking time: 10 minutes
Serves 6

100 g (3½ oz) blanched almonds
250 ml (9 fl oz/1 cup) milk

chocolate bavarois

125 g (4½ oz/½ cup) caster
   (superfine) sugar
3 teaspoons powdered gelatin
310 ml (10¾ fl oz/1¼ cups) pouring
   (whipping) cream

1 Grease six 125 ml (4 fl oz/½ cup) fluted moulds or ramekins. Process the almonds and 60 ml (2 fl oz/¼ cup) water in a small food processor until finely chopped and paste-like. With the motor running, gradually add the milk. Pour into a small saucepan, add the sugar and stir over low heat until the sugar dissolves. Allow to cool.
2 Strain the milk through a strainer lined with muslin (cheesecloth). Twist the muslin tightly to extract as much milk as possible—you should have 310 ml (10¾ fl oz/1¼ cups) of almond milk.

3 Place 60 ml (2 fl oz/¼ cup) cold water in a small heatproof bowl, sprinkle the gelatin in an even layer over the surface and leave to go spongy. Do not stir. Bring a small pan filled with about 4 cm (1½ inches) water to the boil, remove from the heat and place the bowl into the pan. The water should come halfway up the side of the bowl. Stir the gelatin until clear and dissolved, then stir it through the almond milk. Allow to cool completely.
4 Whip the cream into firm peaks, then fold the almond mixture through. Pour into the moulds and refrigerate for 6–8 hours, or until set. To unmould, loosen the edge with your fingertip and turn out onto a plate. If they do not unmould easily, wipe the outside of the moulds with a cloth dipped in hot water.

crème caramel

cover the base. The caramel will continue cooking in the pan so work quickly and be careful not to burn yourself.

3 To make the custard, heat the milk in a pan over low heat until almost boiling. Remove from the heat. Whisk together the sugar, eggs and vanilla for 2 minutes, then stir in the warm milk. Strain the mixture into a jug and pour into the ramekins.

4 Place the ramekins in a baking dish and pour in enough boiling water to come halfway up the sides of the ramekins. Bake for 30 minutes, or until the custard is set. The custards should no longer be liquid and should wobble slightly when the dish is shaken lightly. Allow to cool, then refrigerate for at least 2 hours, or until set.

5 To unmould, run a knife carefully around the edge of each custard and gently upturn onto serving plates. Shake gently to assist removal, if necessary. Can be served by itself or with fresh berries, whipped cream and wafers.

NOTE: This recipe can be varied by flavouring the custard with spices such as cardamom, cinnamon or nutmeg, lemon or orange zest, or with a little of your favourite spirit or liqueur. Crème caramel appears in France as crème renversée, in Italy as crema caramella and in Spain, South America and Mexico as a flan.

banana custard

Preparation time: 15 minutes
Cooking time: 5 minutes
Serves 4

1 egg, lightly beaten
2 tablespoons custard powder
2 tablespoons sugar
250 ml (9 fl oz/1 cup) milk
125 ml (4 fl oz/½ cup) thick (double/heavy) cream
2 bananas, sliced diagonally

1 Combine the beaten egg, custard powder, sugar, milk and cream in a heatproof bowl and whisk until smooth.

crème caramel

Preparation time: 25 minutes + 2 hours chilling time
Cooking time: 35 minutes
Serves 8

185 g (6½ oz/¾ cup) sugar

CUSTARD
750 ml (26 fl oz/3 cups) milk
90 g (3¼ oz/⅓ cup) caster (superfine) sugar

4 eggs
1 teaspoon natural vanilla extract

1 Preheat the oven to 160°C (315°F/Gas 2–3). Brush eight 125 ml (4 fl oz/½ cup) ramekins or moulds with melted butter.

2 Place the sugar and 60 ml (2 fl oz/¼ cup) water in a saucepan. Stir over low heat until the sugar dissolves. Bring to the boil, reduce the heat and simmer, without stirring, until the mixture turns golden and starts to caramelise. Remove from the heat immediately and pour enough hot caramel into each ramekin to

2 Pour into a saucepan and stir constantly over low heat for 5 minutes, or until the custard thickens slightly and coats the back of a wooden spoon.
3 Remove the bowl from the heat and gently stir in the banana. Serve hot or cold.

spicy coconut custard

☀

Preparation time: **20 minutes**
Cooking time: **1 hour**
Serves **8**

2 cinnamon sticks
1 teaspoon freshly grated nutmeg
2 teaspoons whole cloves
310 ml (10¾ fl oz/1¼ cups) pouring (whipping) cream
90 g (3¼ oz) chopped palm sugar (jaggery) or soft brown sugar
270 ml (9½ fl oz) coconut milk
3 eggs, lightly beaten
2 egg yolks, lightly beaten
toasted flaked coconut, to serve

1 Preheat the oven to 160ºC (315ºF/ Gas 2–3). Combine the cinnamon, nutmeg, cloves, cream and 250 ml (9 fl oz/1 cup) water in a saucepan. Bring to simmering point, reduce the heat to very low and leave for 5 minutes to allow the spices to infuse the liquid. Add the sugar and coconut milk, return to low heat and stir until the sugar dissolves.
2 Whisk the eggs and egg yolks in a bowl until combined. Stir in the spiced mixture, then strain, discarding the whole spices. Pour into eight 125 ml (4 fl oz/ ½ cup) ramekins or dariole moulds. Place in a baking dish and pour in enough hot water to come halfway up the sides of the ramekins. Bake for 40–45 minutes until set. The custards should wobble slightly when the dish is shaken lightly. Remove the custards from the baking dish. Serve warm or chilled with toasted coconut sprinkled over the top.

rice custard

Preheat the oven to 150°C (300°F/Gas 2). Lightly grease a 1 litre (35 fl oz/4 cup) ovenproof dish, then add 185 g (6½ oz/1 cup) cooked rice and 3 tablespoons sultanas and put the dish inside a baking dish half filled with water. Combine 3 lightly beaten eggs, 600 ml (21 fl oz) milk, 1 teaspoon natural vanilla extract and 3 tablespoons caster (superfine) sugar. When thoroughly mixed, pour it over the rice and sultanas. Bake for 30 minutes, stir gently with a fork and cook for another 30 minutes. Stir again and, if desired, sprinkle the surface with freshly grated nutmeg. Bake for another 20 minutes, or until the custard is just set. Serve warm or cold.

coconut

Indigenous to India, coastal Southeast Asia and the Caribbean, the coconut is a versatile fruit. It has a fibrous husk, a hard brown shell and soft white flesh that changes from a jelly-like consistency when young to a harder and oilier texture when mature. The coconut milk contained within the nut is not the type used in cooking — this is derived from pressing the flesh of the coconut to extract first the cream and then the milk. Coconut milk is sold in tins, as a powder and in solid blocks. In its desiccated form, coconut flesh appears on lamingtons and in coconut ice. Coconut marries especially well with lime.

orange spanish cream

✳ ✳

Preparation time: 20 minutes + 4 hours
    chilling time
Cooking time: 10 minutes
Serves 6

3 eggs, separated
165 g (5½ oz/⅔ cup) caster (superfine)
    sugar
2 teaspoons finely grated orange zest
125 ml (4 fl oz/½ cup) fresh orange
    juice
1½ tablespoons powdered gelatin
750 ml (26 fl oz/3 cups) milk
orange segments (optional), to serve

1 Beat the egg yolks, sugar and orange zest in a small bowl with electric beaters or a balloon whisk for about 5 minutes, or until thick and creamy.
2 Pour the orange juice into a small heatproof bowl, sprinkle the gelatin in an even layer over the surface and leave to go spongy. Do not stir. Bring a large saucepan filled with about 4 cm (1½ inches) water to the boil, remove from the heat, carefully lower the gelatin bowl into the water (it should come halfway up the side of the bowl), then stir the gelatin until it dissolves.
3 Combine the gelatin mixture with the milk in a saucepan and bring almost to the boil — do not boil or the gelatin will lose its setting properties. Remove from the heat and gradually pour onto the egg yolk mixture, mixing continually as you pour.
4 Beat the egg whites in a metal or glass bowl until stiff peaks form, then gently fold them into the milk mixture with a large metal spoon. Pour carefully into a 1.5 litre (52 fl oz/6 cup) glass serving dish or six 250 ml (9 fl oz/1 cup) dishes and cover with plastic wrap. Refrigerate for 4 hours, or overnight, until set. Serve with orange segments.

NOTE: Spanish cream is also known as honeycomb mould, snow cream and New England quaking custard. This recipe appears in old English and American recipe books including Shaker recipes. It is a custard that separates into two or three layers — a bubbly layer on top and smooth layers underneath, created by folding the egg whites into a warm mixture rather than a cold one. If the custard mixture is cold when the egg whites are folded in, they will stay suspended by the gelatin.

lemon posset

✳

Preparation time: 5 minutes + 2 hours
    chilling time
Cooking time: 5 minutes
Serves 4

110 g (3½ oz) caster (superfine)
    sugar
310 ml (10¾ fl oz/1¼ cups) thick
    (double/heavy) cream
juice of 2 lemons (about 100 ml/
    3½ fl oz)

1 Place the sugar and cream in a saucepan over low heat and bring to the boil slowly, stirring so the sugar dissolves and the cream does not boil over. Boil for 2–3 minutes, then add the lemon juice and mix well.
2 Pour the mixture into four 100 ml (3½ fl oz) ramekins, cover with plastic wrap and chill for 2 hours or overnight. Serve with tuile biscuits (cookies).

orange spanish cream

mont blanc

The dessert Mont Blanc is supposed to resemble the snow-capped peak of the French mountain Mont Blanc. It is flavoured with chestnuts, sweetened and puréed before being pressed through a ricer to form strands. The cap is made from sweetened whipped cream. Italians call it Monte Bianco and they add chocolate to the recipe.

mont blanc

Preparation time: 10 minutes + cooling time
Cooking time: 25 minutes
Serves 4

250 ml (9 fl oz/1 cup) pouring (whipping) cream
1 teaspoon natural vanilla extract
90 g (3¼ oz/⅓ cup) caster (superfine) sugar
435 g (15¼ oz) plain chestnut purée
2 teaspoons icing (confectioners') sugar

1 Combine half of the cream with the vanilla, sugar and chestnut purée in a saucepan. Stir over low heat until combined. Increase heat to medium and stir for 15–20 minutes, or until thickened. Cover with plastic wrap. Cool completely.
2 Divide the mixture into four, then push each portion through a ricer (or a metal strainer) held over a serving dish. Leave the mounds untouched as the threads are fragile and will crumble easily.
3 Whip remaining cream and icing sugar together, until soft peaks form. Spoon over the chestnut mixture and serve.

soufflé secrets

Soufflés are held up by beaten egg whites and hot air. As the soufflé cooks, the air within it expands and pushes it upwards, sometimes as much as doubling its height.

Soufflés are, technically, always hot. Although sometimes called soufflés, iced or cold soufflés are actually mousses — they are held up by gelatin and beaten egg whites and will not collapse like hot soufflés. The lightness in a cold soufflé comes from the whisked egg whites themselves, rather than the expansion of hot air. Soufflés can be made on a custard-type base, a roux base (such as is used for chocolate soufflés), or, for a really light result, a fruit purée.

making a perfect soufflé

To get the best rise out of a soufflé, you will need a straight-sided ovenproof glass or ceramic soufflé dish (a metal dish will give a quicker cooking time, but be careful if you are making a fruit soufflé, as some fruits react with metal and turn the soufflé grey around the edge). If the mixture comes more than two-thirds of the way up the dish, you will need to make a collar (see step 1).

The following instructions are for a soufflé based on a fruit purée. You will need about 250 g (9 oz) of fruit (for example, 2 mangoes and the pulp from 4 passionfruit), 4 egg whites and 3 tablespoons caster (superfine) sugar. Separate the eggs one by one into a smaller bowl, just in case one of them breaks.

1 To make a collar, wrap a double layer of non-stick baking paper around a 1.5 litre (52 fl oz/6 cup) soufflé dish so that it extends 5 cm (2 inches) above the rim. Tie with a piece of string.

2 Lightly grease the inside of the dish and collar with melted butter or flavourless oil and sprinkle with a little caster (superfine) sugar. Turn the dish so the sugar coats the entire surface of the dish and collar, then turn the dish upside down and tap to loosen any excess sugar. The sugar will help the soufflé grip and climb up the side of the dish as it cooks. Preheat the oven to 220°C (425°F/Gas 7) and put a baking tray on the middle shelf.

3 Purée the mango flesh in a food processor and then add the passionfruit (leave the seeds in if you wish but do not process).

4 Place the egg whites in a large, very clean, dry stainless steel or glass bowl — any hint of grease will prevent them foaming. (Traditionally, egg whites are beaten in copper bowls, as the copper and whites react to form a more stable foam. You must clean the bowl with 2 tablespoons salt mixed with 2 tablespoons lemon juice or vinegar, and rinse and dry it thoroughly JUST before you use it.) Leave the whites for a few minutes to reach room temperature, then whisk with a balloon whisk or electric beaters. A balloon whisk gives better volume than electric beaters, but make sure you use a large enough whisk — a small one will not give you enough volume. Whisk slowly until the whites start to become a frothy foam, then increase your speed until the bubbles in the foam are small and evenly sized. When the foam forms stiff peaks, add the sugar little by little. Continue whisking until the mixture is glossy — don't overwhisk or it will become grainy and will not rise well.

5 Fold two spoonfuls of the whites into the fruit purée and mix well to loosen and lighten the mixture. Fold in the remaining whites with a large metal spoon, being careful not to lose any volume. Pour into the dish and run your finger around the edge to loosen the mixture from the side of the dish. Place on the baking tray in the oven — unless it's an emergency, don't open the oven door until the cooking time is up. It should take 20–25 minutes to cook. If the soufflé is rising more on one side than the other, rotate the dish. Some fruit with a higher sugar content may cause the top of the soufflé to brown too quickly. If so, rest a piece of foil on top of the soufflé to prevent over-browning. When the soufflé is ready, it should have a pale gold crust and not wobble too much. Serve immediately.

hot mocha soufflé

Preparation time: 25 minutes
Cooking time: 45 minutes
Serves 20

3 tablespoons caster (superfine) sugar
40 g (1½ oz) unsalted butter
2 tablespoons plain (all-purpose) flour
185 ml (6 fl oz/¾ cup) milk
1 tablespoon instant espresso-style coffee
    granules
100 g (3½ oz) good-quality dark chocolate,
    melted
4 eggs, separated
icing (confectioners') sugar, to dust

1   Preheat the oven to 180°C (350°F/
Gas 4). Wrap a double layer of baking
paper around a 1.25 litre (44 fl oz/
5 cups) soufflé dish, to come 3 cm
(1¼ inches) above the rim. Secure with
string. Brush with oil or melted butter,
sprinkle 1 tablespoon of the sugar into the
dish, shake the dish to coat the base and
side evenly, then tip out excess.
2   Melt the butter in a saucepan, add
flour and stir over low heat for 2 minutes,
or until lightly golden. Add milk gradually,
stirring until smooth. Stir over medium
heat until the mixture boils and thickens;
boil for another minute, then remove
from the heat. Transfer to a large bowl.
3   Dissolve the coffee in 1 tablespoon hot
water, add to the milk with the remaining
sugar, melted chocolate and egg yolks,
then beat until smooth.
4   Whisk the egg whites in a clean dry
bowl until stiff peaks form and then fold a
little into the chocolate mixture to loosen
it slightly. Gently fold in the remaining
egg white, then spoon the mixture into
the soufflé dish and bake for 40 minutes,
or until well risen and just set. Cut the
string and remove the collar. Serve
immediately, dusted with icing sugar.

hot chocolate soufflé

Preparation time: 30 minutes
Cooking time: 20 minutes
Serves 6

caster (superfine) sugar, to coat
175 g (6 oz) good-quality dark chocolate,
    chopped
5 egg yolks, lightly beaten
60 g (2 ¼ oz/¼ cup) caster (superfine)
    sugar
7 egg whites
icing (confectioners') sugar, to dust

1   Preheat the oven to 200°C (400°F/
Gas 6). Wrap a double layer of baking
paper around six 250 ml (9 fl oz/1 cup)
ramekins, to come 3 cm (1¼ inches)
above the rim. Secure with string. Brush
the insides with melted butter, sprinkle
with the sugar, shake to coat evenly, then
tip out excess. Place on a baking tray.
2   Put the chocolate in a heatproof bowl.
Half fill a saucepan with water and bring
to the boil. Remove from the heat and
place the bowl over the pan — don't let
it touch the water. Stir occasionally until
the chocolate melts. Stir in the egg yolks
and sugar. Transfer the mixture to a large
bowl. Whisk the egg whites in a large
bowl until firm peaks form.
3   Fold a third of the beaten egg white
through the chocolate mixture to loosen
it. Use a metal spoon to fold through the
remaining egg white until just combined.
Spoon the mixture into the ramekins
and bake for 12–15 minutes, or until
well risen and just set. Cut the string and
remove the collars. Serve immediately,
dusted with icing sugar.

hot mocha soufflé

Sprinkle the greased soufflé dish with sugar, then shake to coat evenly and tip out excess.

To help the soufflé rise evenly, run your thumb or a knife around the inside edge to make a small gap between the soufflé and the dish. This gives a 'hat' effect when the soufflé is cooked.

hot fruit soufflé

✹ ✹

Preparation time: **15 minutes**
Cooking time: **25–30 minutes**
Serves **4**

caster (superfine) sugar, to coat
60 g (2¼ oz) unsalted butter
60 g (2¼ oz/½ cup) plain
   (all-purpose) flour
375 ml (13 fl oz/1½ cups) puréed fruit
60 g (2¼ oz/¼ cup) caster (superfine)
   sugar
4 egg whites
icing (confectioners') sugar,
   to dust
cream (optional), to serve

1 Brush a 1.25 litre (44 fl oz/5 cup) soufflé dish with melted butter, sprinkle with the sugar, shake to coat evenly, then tip out excess. Preheat the oven to 200°C (400°F/Gas 6) and put a baking tray on the top shelf to heat.
2 Melt the butter in a saucepan, add the flour and mix well. Remove from the heat, stir until smooth, then stir in the fruit purée. Return to the heat, bring to the boil and simmer for 2 minutes. Add the sugar and stir until dissolved (taste in case it is too tart). Leave to cool.
3 Whisk the egg whites in a large clean bowl until soft peaks form, add 1 tablespoon to the fruit mixture and mix well. Fold in the remaining whites, being careful not to lose too much volume. Fill

the soufflé dish to three-quarters full and run your thumb or a knife around the inside edge to create a small gap between the soufflé and the dish—this will help the soufflé rise evenly.
4 Put the soufflé on the hot baking tray and bake for 20–25 minutes. Serve immediately, dusted with icing sugar. Served with cream, if desired.

NOTE: Suitable fruit to use in soufflés are those that make a good purée, such as raspberries, strawberries, mango, peaches, apricots and passionfruit. Bananas are a little too heavy. You could use apples or plums, or dried fruit, but you'd have to cook them into a purée first.

chilled lime soufflé

✳ ✳

Preparation time: 35 minutes + chilling time
Cooking time: nil
Serves 4

caster (superfine) sugar, to coat
5 eggs, separated
230 g (8 oz/1 cup) caster (superfine)
    sugar
2 teaspoons finely grated lime zest
185 ml (6 fl oz/¾ cup) lime juice,
    strained
1 tablespoon powdered gelatin
310 ml (10¾ fl oz/1¼ cups)
    pouring (whipping) cream
finely shredded lime zest, to serve

1 Cut four strips of foil or baking paper
long enough to fit around 250 ml
(9 fl oz/1 cup) soufflé dishes or ramekins.
Fold each in half lengthways, wrap one
around each dish, extending 4 cm
(1½ inches) above the rim, then secure
with string. Brush the inside of the collar
with melted butter, sprinkle with the
sugar, shake to coat, then tip out excess.
2 Use electric beaters to whisk the egg
yolks, sugar and lime zest in a small bowl
for 3 minutes, or until the sugar dissolves
and the mixture is thick and pale. Heat
the lime juice in a small saucepan, then
gradually add the lime juice to the yolk
mixture while whisking, until well mixed.
3 Pour 60 ml (2 fl oz/¼ cup) water into
a small heatproof bowl, sprinkle the
gelatin in an even layer over the surface
and leave to go spongy. Bring a large
saucepan filled with 4 cm (1½ inches)
water to the boil, remove from the heat
and carefully lower the gelatin bowl into
the water (it should come halfway up the
side of the bowl). Stir until dissolved.
Cool slightly, then add gradually to the
lime mixture, beating on low speed until
combined. Transfer to a large bowl,
cover with plastic wrap and refrigerate
for 15 minutes, or until thickened but
not set.

4 In a small bowl, lightly whip the cream.
Use a metal spoon to fold the cream into
the lime mixture until almost combined.
Use electric beaters to whisk egg whites in
a clean, dry bowl until soft peaks form.
Fold egg white quickly and lightly into the
lime mixture, using a large metal spoon,
until just combined with no lumps of egg
white remaining. Spoon gently into the
soufflé dishes and chill until set. Just
before serving, remove the collars. Serve
topped with lime zest.

Wrap the foil or baking paper
around the soufflé dishes,
extending above the rims. Secure
with string.

Use a large metal spoon to fold
the whisked egg white quickly and
lightly into the lime mixture.

chocolate rum mousse

✳ ✳

Preparation time: 20 minutes + 2 hours
   chilling time
Cooking time: 5 minutes
Serves 4

250 g (9 oz) good-quality dark
   chocolate, chopped
3 eggs
60 g (2¼ oz/¼cup) caster
   (superfine) sugar
2 teaspoons dark rum
250 ml (9 fl oz/1 cup) pouring (whipping)
   cream, softly whipped

1 Put the chocolate in a heatproof bowl. Half fill a saucepan with water and bring to the boil. Remove from the heat and place the bowl over the pan, making sure it is not touching the water. Stir occasionally until the chocolate melts. Set aside to cool.
2 Use electric beaters to whisk the eggs and sugar in a small bowl for 5 minutes, or until they are thick, pale and have increased in volume.
3 Transfer the mixture to a large bowl. Use a metal spoon to fold in the melted chocolate with the rum, leave the mixture to cool, then fold in the whipped cream until just combined.

4 Spoon into four 250 ml (9 fl oz/1 cup) ramekins or dessert glasses. Refrigerate for 2 hours, or until set.

caramel mousse

✳ ✳ ✳

Preparation time: 20 minutes + 2 hours
   chilling time
Cooking time: 10 minutes
Serves 6

2 tablespoons lemon juice
1 tablespoon powdered gelatin
250 g (9 oz/1 cup) sugar
5 eggs
60 g (2¼ oz/¼ cup) caster (superfine) sugar
220 ml (7½ fl oz) pouring (whipping) cream

1 Put lemon juice in a bowl, sprinkle gelatin in an even layer over the surface and leave it to go spongy. Bring a saucepan filled with about 4 cm (1½ inches) water to the boil, then remove from the heat. Stand the gelatin bowl in the pan and stir until the gelatin is completely dissolved.
2 Put the sugar in a heavy-based saucepan and place over low heat. Melt the sugar, swirling the pan as it melts, and then turn up the heat and cook the sugar until it turns to caramel. As soon as it turns a dark golden brown, plunge the base of the pan into a sink of cold water to stop the caramel colouring any further. Place the pan back on the heat, add 125 ml (4 fl oz/½ cup) water, then melt the caramel gently until it is a smooth liquid. Leave to cool a little.
3 Whisk the eggs with the caster sugar until they are fluffy and lighter in colour, add the caramel and gelatin and continue whisking until everything is mixed. Cool the mixture in the refrigerator, stirring every few minutes. When it begins to thicken, whisk the cream until it reaches soft peaks and fold it into the mixture. If the caramel has settled at the bottom, make sure you fold it through well.
4 Spoon the mixture evenly into six dessert glasses or ramekins. Refrigerate for 2 hours, or until set.

caramel mousse

fruit gratin

Slice some fresh peaches and strawberries and layer evenly in four small gratin dishes. Sprinkle with a few raspberries, making the surface reasonably flat. Coat the fruit with an even, thick layer of zabaglione and place the dishes under a preheated grill (broiler). Grill (broil) under low heat until the surface turns golden brown, then serve immediately. You can also sprinkle up to a tablespoon of brandy or liqueur over the fruit if you wish. Serves 4.

zabaglione

Preparation time: **5 minutes**
Cooking time: **10 minutes**
Serves **6**

4 egg yolks
80 g (2¾ oz/⅓ cup) caster (superfine) sugar
80 ml (2½ fl oz/⅓ cup) Marsala

1 Combine all the ingredients in a large heatproof bowl set over a saucepan of barely simmering water. Make sure the base of the bowl does not touch the water. Whisk with a balloon whisk or electric beaters for 5 minutes, or until the mixture is smooth and foamy and triples in volume. Do not stop whisking and do not allow the bowl to become too hot or the eggs will scramble. The final result will be creamy, pale and mousse-like.
2 Pour the zabaglione into four glasses and serve immediately.

NOTE: Sometimes zabaglione is served chilled. If you want to do this, cover the glasses with plastic wrap and refrigerate for at least 1 hour. You must make sure the zabaglione is properly cooked or it may separate when left to stand.

Combine the egg yolks, sugar and Marsala in a heatproof bowl set over a pan of simmering water.

Whisk the ingredients together until the mixture is smooth and foamy and triples in volume.

lemon passionfruit syllabub with berries

✳ ✳

Preparation time: 50 minutes + 1 hour
   chilling time
Cooking time: nil
Serves 8–10

2 teaspoons finely grated lemon zest
80 ml (2½ fl oz/⅓ cup) lemon juice
125 g (4½ oz/½ cup) caster (superfine)
   sugar
125 ml (4 fl oz/½ cup) dry white wine
8 passionfruit
500 ml (17 fl oz/2 cups) thick (double/
   heavy) cream
500 g (1 lb 2 oz) blueberries
500 g (1 lb 2 oz) raspberries
2 tablespoons icing (confectioners') sugar,
   plus extra, to dust
500 g (1 lb 2 oz) strawberries, halved

1   Stir the lemon zest, juice, sugar and
white wine together in a jug and set
aside for 10 minutes. Cut the passionfruit
in half and push the pulp through a
sieve to remove the seeds. Add half the
passionfruit pulp to the lemon, sugar and
wine mixture.
2   Whisk the cream with electric beaters
until soft peaks form. Gradually whisk in
the lemon and passionfruit syrup until all
the syrup is added (the mixture will have
the consistency of softly whipped cream).
Stir in the remaining passionfruit, cover
and refrigerate for 1 hour.
3   Combine the blueberries, raspberries
and icing sugar and place in a 2.5–3 litre
(87 fl oz/10 cup–104 fl oz/12 cup)
serving bowl. Spoon the cream mixture
over the top, decorate with strawberries,
dust with icing sugar and serve
immediately.

NOTE: This thick, custardy dessert was
originally made by beating milk or cream
with wine, sugar, lemon juice and possibly
spices, the acid curdling and thickening
the mixture. Some versions were based on
cider while others were further fortified
with brandy. Syllabub was sometimes
used in place of cream on desserts such as
trifle, and instead of meringue for floating
islands. A thinner version was made as a
drink and served at festive occasions in
special syllabub glasses.

strawberries

These delicious red vine fruits
are related to the rose, which
accounts for the beautiful
fragrant aroma and flavour. The
strawberry is unusual in that
the seeds or small pips are on
the outside of the fruit rather
than in the centre as with other
fruits. When at the height of the
season, in spring and summer,
they are often served just as
they are or sweetened and
eaten with cream or ice cream.
Strawberries make beautiful
tart and cake fillings and, of
course, jam. Sweetened and
puréed, they make a simple
sauce called a coulis.

cappuccino mousse

with the gelatin and leave to go spongy. Bring a large pan filled with about 4 cm (1½ inches) water to the boil, remove from the heat and lower the gelatin bowl into the water. Stir until dissolved. Stir into the warm custard and mix well.

3 Allow the mixture to cool completely and thicken slightly. Use a metal spoon to fold in the whipped cream. Pour into six dessert dishes and refrigerate until firm.

cappuccino mousse

❋ ❋

Preparation time: **1 hour + 4 hours chilling time**
Cooking time: **5 minutes**
Serves **6**

250 g (9 oz) white chocolate, melted
125 g (4½ oz) unsalted butter, softened
2 eggs, lightly beaten
3 teaspoons powdered gelatin
310 ml (10¾ fl oz/1¼ cups) pouring (whipping) cream
3 teaspoons instant coffee granules
freshly grated nutmeg, to garnish

1 Stir the chocolate, butter and eggs together in a bowl until smooth. Place 2 tablespoons water in a small heatproof bowl. Sprinkle evenly with the gelatin and leave to go spongy. Bring a large saucepan filled with about 4 cm (1½ inches) water to the boil, remove from the heat and carefully lower the gelatin bowl into the water. Stir until dissolved, then cool slightly before stirring into the chocolate mixture. Mix well, then cover and chill for 30 minutes, or until just starting to set.

2 Whisk the cream to soft peaks and gently fold into the mousse. Spoon about a third of the mousse into a separate bowl and set aside. Mix the coffee powder with 3 teaspoons hot water. Allow to cool, then fold into the remaining mousse.

3 Spoon the coffee mousse evenly into six small glasses or dessert dishes and smooth the surface. Pipe or spoon the reserved white mousse over the top, cover and refrigerate for 4 hours or overnight. To serve, sprinkle with nutmeg.

orange chocolate cups

❋ ❋

Preparation time: **25 minutes + cooling and chilling time**
Cooking time: **10 minutes**
Serves **6**

125 g (4½ oz) good-quality dark chocolate, finely chopped
375 ml (13 fl oz/1½ cups) milk
5 egg yolks
2 teaspoons finely grated orange zest
90 g (3¼ oz/⅓ cup) caster (superfine) sugar
1 tablespoon powdered gelatin

185 ml (6 fl oz/¾ cup) pouring (whipping) cream, softly whipped

1 Warm the chocolate and milk in a saucepan over low heat until the chocolate melts. Whisk the egg yolks with the zest and sugar until the mixture is light and creamy. Pour the chocolate milk mixture into the egg while stirring, then return the mixture to the pan. Stir over low heat until the custard thickens slightly and coats the back of a wooden spoon — do not boil. Remove from the heat, transfer to a bowl, then allow to cool.

2 Place 60 ml (2 fl oz/¼ cup) water in a small heatproof bowl. Sprinkle evenly

coeur à la crème

Preparation time: 20 minutes + overnight
    draining time
Cooking time: nil
Serves 6

225 g (8 oz) cottage cheese, drained
60 g (2¼ oz/½ cup) icing
    (confectioners') sugar
310 ml (10¾ fl oz/1¼ cups) pouring
    (whipping) cream, whipped
passionfruit pulp, to serve

1 Process the drained cottage cheese
until smooth in a food processor or push
it through a fine sieve. Mix in the icing
sugar, then fold in the cream.
2 Line six coeur à la crème moulds
with muslin (cheesecloth) and fill with
the mixture. Cover and leave to drain
overnight in the refrigerator. Unmould
and serve with passionfruit pulp.

NOTE: If you do not have any coeur à la
crème moulds, line ramekins with muslin
and fill with the mixture. Put another
piece of muslin over each ramekin and
attach it with an elastic band. Invert each
ramekin on a wire rack and allow to drain
overnight before unmoulding.

passionfruit flummery

Preparation time: 15 minutes + 1 hour
    chilling time
Cooking time: nil
Serves 6

85 g (3 oz) passionfruit jelly crystals
250 ml (9 fl oz/1 cup) boiling water
375 ml (13 fl oz) tin evaporated milk,
    well chilled
3 passionfruit

1 Stir the jelly crystals into the boiling
water until dissolved. Pour into a shallow
metal tray and refrigerate until the
consistency of unbeaten egg white.
2 Transfer the jelly to a bowl, add the
milk and beat with electric beaters, on
high, for 5–8 minutes, or until it doubles in
volume. Use a large metal spoon to fold in
the pulp from 2 passionfruit.
3 Spoon into six 250 ml (9 fl oz/1 cup)
capacity glasses, or a serving bowl, cover
loosely with plastic wrap and chill for
1 hour, or until set. Top with pulp from
the remaining passionfruit.

flummery

Flummery is a generic term for
puddings that are thickened
with starch or gelatin.
Flummeries date back to
medieval times. Later varieties
of flummery were usually fruit
puddings thickened with starch,
a sort of fruit porridge. Modern
flummeries also include cream
and milk and use gelatin as a
thickener. They are also known
as Dutch flummery.

coeur à la crème

cheesecakes

Astonishingly, for such a modern bistro favourite, cheesecake actually hails from days of old. In fact, it is one of the earliest of all baked desserts. The moment we learnt to transform milk into curd cheese was the moment the cheesecake came into creation. The ancient Romans were baking cheese into tiny cakes on the hearth, and there is a multitude of early written recipes for cheesecakes from the Middle Ages. The modern-day version — a pastry or biscuity crumb base with a creamy topping — was perfected by the Americans, who ushered this culinary creation into their gleaming kitchens and made the New York cheesecake world famous.

baked cheesecake with sour cream

✳

Preparation time: 50 minutes + chilling time
Cooking time: 50 minutes
Serves 8–10

250 g (9 oz) plain sweet biscuits (cookies)
1 teaspoon mixed (pumpkin pie) spice
100 g (3½ oz) unsalted butter, melted

FILLING
500 g (1 lb 2 oz) cream cheese, softened
160 g (5½ oz/⅔ cup) caster (superfine) sugar
1 teaspoon natural vanilla extract
1 tablespoon lemon juice
4 eggs

TOPPING
250 g (9 oz/1 cup) sour cream
½ teaspoon natural vanilla extract
3 teaspoons lemon juice
1 tablespoon caster (superfine) sugar
freshly grated nutmeg, for sprinkling

1 Lightly grease a 20 cm (8 inch) diameter spring-form cake tin and line base with baking paper. Finely crush the biscuits in a food processor or place them in a sealed plastic bag and crush them with a rolling pin. Transfer to a bowl, add the spice and butter and stir until the crumbs are all moistened. Press firmly over the base and up the side of the tin to create an even shell. Refrigerate for 20 minutes, or until firm. Preheat the oven to 180°C (350°F/Gas 4).
2 To make the filling, beat the cream cheese with electric beaters, until smooth. Add the sugar, vanilla and lemon juice, then beat until smooth. Add the eggs, one at a time, beating well after each addition. Pour carefully over the crumbs and bake for 45 minutes, or until just firm to touch.
3 To make the topping, combine the sour cream, vanilla, lemon juice and sugar in a bowl. Spread over the hot cheesecake. Sprinkle with nutmeg and return to the oven for another 7 minutes. Turn off the oven and leave to cool with the door ajar. When cool, refrigerate until firm. Decorate with strawberries, if desired.

NOTE: Cheesecake tends to be quite dense and will be easier to cut using a knife dipped in hot water and dried between each slice.

chocolate collar cheesecake

✳ ✳ ✳

Preparation time: 1 hour 30 minutes + cooling and chilling time
Cooking time: 50 minutes
Serves 8–10

200 g (7 oz) plain chocolate biscuits (cookies), crushed
70 g (2½ oz) unsalted butter, melted
500 g (1 lb 2 oz/2 cups) cream cheese, softened
75 g (2¾ oz/⅓ cup) sugar
2 eggs
1 tablespoon unsweetened cocoa powder, sifted
300 g (10½ oz) sour cream
250 g (9 oz) dark chocolate, melted
80 ml (2½ fl oz/⅓ cup) Bailey's Irish Cream
310 ml (10¾ fl oz/1¼ cups) pouring (whipping) cream, whipped
unsweetened cocoa powder, to dust

CHOCOLATE COLLAR
50 g (1¾ oz) white chocolate, melted
150 g (5½ oz) dark chocolate, melted

1 Brush a 23 cm (9 inch) diameter spring-form cake tin with melted butter and line base and side with baking paper. Mix together the biscuit crumbs and butter, press firmly into the base of the tin and refrigerate for 10 minutes. Preheat the oven to 180°C (350°F/Gas 4).
2 Beat the cream cheese and sugar with electric beaters until smooth and creamy. Add the eggs, one at a time, beating thoroughly after each addition. Beat in the cocoa and sour cream until smooth. Beat in the cooled melted dark chocolate and then the liqueur. Pour over the base. Smooth the surface and bake for 45 minutes. The cheesecake may not be fully set, but will firm up. Refrigerate until cold.
3 Remove the cheesecake from the tin and put it on a board. To make the chocolate collar, measure the height and add 5 mm (¼ inch). Cut a strip of baking paper this wide and 75 cm (29½ inches) long. Pipe or drizzle the melted white chocolate in a figure eight pattern along the paper. When just set, spread the dark chocolate over the entire strip of paper. Allow the chocolate to set a little, but you need to be able to bend the paper without it cracking. Wrap the paper around the cheesecake with the chocolate inside. Seal the ends and hold the paper in place until the chocolate is completely set. Peel away the paper. Spread the top with cream, then dust with sifted cocoa.

flavouring with vanilla

Vanilla extract and essence are produced by steeping vanilla beans in alcohol and water and ageing the product for several months. Pure vanilla extract is very strong, requiring a smaller amount. Vanilla essence tends to have a large proportion of water. Look for products marked 'natural vanilla' or 'pure vanilla extract'. Extract should be added after the cooking process, to prevent evaporation and loss of flavour. Vanilla powder is ground dried beans. It holds flavour well and does not evaporate on heating. Synthetic vanilla flavouring is made entirely with chemicals which are a by-product of the paper-making industry. It has a harsher taste. To add to the confusion, the chemical is called 'artificial vanillin'.

chocolate collar cheesecake

When chocolate is slightly set, but still pliable, wrap the paper around the cake with the chocolate inside. Seal the ends and hold until set.

When set, carefully peel away the paper to leave the chocolate collar around the outside of the cheesecake.

tropical cheesecake

1 Lightly grease a 20 cm (8 inch) diameter spring-form cake tin and line base with baking paper. Put the biscuits in a food processor and chop until they are finely crushed. Add the coconut and butter and process until well combined. Spoon into the tin, press firmly over the base, then refrigerate.

2 Put the orange juice in a small heatproof bowl, sprinkle the gelatin in an even layer over the surface and leave to go spongy. Bring a large saucepan filled with about 4 cm (1½ inches) water to the boil, then remove from the heat. Carefully lower the gelatin bowl into the water (it should come halfway up the side of the bowl), then stir until the gelatin dissolves. Allow to cool.

3 Beat the softened cream cheese and sugar in a bowl for 3 minutes, or until smooth. Beat in the lemon juice and gently fold in the mango and crushed pineapple. Fold in the dissolved gelatin.

4 Whip the cream into firm peaks. Fold into the mixture with a metal spoon. Pour into the tin, smooth and chill overnight. Serve with extra cream and slices of fruit.

NOTE: If using fresh mangoes, use 125 g (4½ oz/½ cup) caster (superfine) sugar.

new york cheesecake

❈ ❈

Preparation time: 1 hour + 6 hours chilling time
Cooking time: 1 hour 50 minutes
Serves 10–12

60 g (2¼ oz/½ cup) self-raising flour
125 g (4½ oz/1 cup) plain (all-purpose) flour
55 g (2 oz/¼ cup) caster (superfine) sugar
1 teaspoon finely grated lemon zest
80 g (2¾ oz) unsalted butter, chopped
1 egg
375 ml (13 fl oz/1½ cups) pouring (whipping) cream, to serve

FILLING
750 g (1 lb 10 oz/3 cups) cream cheese, softened
230 g (8 oz/1 cup) caster (superfine) sugar

tropical cheesecake

❈ ❈

Preparation time: 50 minutes + overnight chilling time
Cooking time: nil
Serves 8

145 g (5 oz) plain sweet biscuits (cookies)
25 g (1 oz/¼ cup) desiccated coconut
90 g (3¼ oz) unsalted butter, melted
whipped cream and fruit, to serve

FILLING
125 ml (4 fl oz/½ cup) fresh orange juice
6 teaspoons powdered gelatin
350 g (12 oz) cream cheese, softened
90 g (3¼ oz/⅓ cup) caster (superfine) sugar
2 tablespoons lemon juice
425 g (15 oz) tin mangoes, drained and chopped, or 2 fresh mangoes, flesh chopped (see Note)
450 g (1 lb) tin unsweetened crushed pineapple, drained
310 ml (10¾ fl oz/1¼ cups) pouring (whipping) cream, extra

30 g (1 oz/¼ cup) plain (all-purpose) flour
2 teaspoons finely grated orange zest
2 teaspoons finely grated lemon zest
4 eggs
170 ml (5½ fl oz/⅔ cup) pouring
    (whipping) cream

CANDIED ZEST
finely shredded zest of 3 limes, 3 lemons
    and 3 oranges
230 g (8 oz/1 cup) caster (superfine) sugar

1   Preheat the oven to 210°C (425°F/Gas 6–7). Lightly grease a 23 cm (9 inch) diameter spring-form cake tin and line base with baking paper.

2   To make the pastry, process the flours, sugar, lemon zest and butter for about 30 seconds in a food processor, until crumbly. Add the egg and process briefly until the mixture just comes together. Turn out onto a lightly floured surface and gather together into a ball. Refrigerate in plastic wrap for about 20 minutes, or until the mixture is firm.

3   Roll the dough between two sheets of baking paper until large enough to fit the base and side of the tin. Ease into the tin and trim the edges. Cover the pastry with baking paper, then baking beads or uncooked rice. Bake for 10 minutes, then remove the baking paper and rice. Flatten the pastry lightly with the back of a spoon and bake for 5 minutes. Set aside to cool.

4   To make the filling, reduce the oven to 150°C (300°F/Gas 2). Beat the cream cheese, sugar, flour and orange and lemon zest until smooth. Add the eggs, one at a time, beating after each addition. Beat in the cream, pour over the pastry and bake for 1½ hours, or until almost set. Turn off the oven and leave to cool with the door ajar. When cool, refrigerate for 6 hours or until well chilled.

5   To make the candied zest, place a little water in a saucepan with the lime, lemon and orange zest, bring to the boil and simmer for 1 minute. Drain the zest and repeat with fresh water (this will remove any bitterness). Put the sugar in a saucepan with 60 ml (2 fl oz/¼ cup) water and stir over low heat until dissolved. Add the zest, bring to the boil, reduce heat and simmer for 5–6 minutes, or until zest is translucent. Allow to cool, drain the zest and place on baking paper to dry (you can save the syrup to serve with the cheesecake). Whip the cream, spoon over the cold cheesecake and top with candied zest.

NOTE: To make the cheesecake easier to cut, heap the zest in mounds, then cut between the mounds of zest.

Add the zest to the sugar syrup and bring to the boil.

Transfer the zest to a sheet of non-stick baking paper.

pear and ginger cheesecake

✻

Preparation time: 50 minutes + overnight
  chilling time
Cooking time: 1 hour 10 minutes
Serves 10

250 g (9 oz) plain sweet
  biscuits (cookies)
2 teaspoons ground ginger
100 g (3½ oz) unsalted butter, melted
cream, to serve

FILLING
3–4 firm ripe pears
250 g (9 oz/1 cup) caster (superfine) sugar
2 tablespoons lemon juice
500 g (1 lb 2 oz) cream cheese, softened
2 eggs
2 teaspoons ground ginger
300 g (10½ oz) sour cream

1 Lightly grease a 23 cm (9 inch) diameter spring-form cake tin and line base with baking paper. Sprinkle with flour and shake off excess.
2 Finely crush the biscuits with the ginger in a food processor. Add the butter and mix well. Spoon into the tin and press firmly onto the base and up the side. Refrigerate for 10 minutes. Preheat the oven to 150°C (300°F/Gas 2).
3 To make the filling, peel, core and thinly slice the pears and put them with half the sugar, the lemon juice and 375 ml (13 fl oz/1½ cups) water in a saucepan. Bring to the boil, lower the heat and simmer until the pears are tender but not breaking up. Strain and set aside to cool.
4 Process the cream cheese and remaining sugar in a food processor until light and smooth. Mix in the eggs and ginger. Add the sour cream and process to combine. Arrange the pears over the crust, pour the filling over the top and bake for 1 hour, or until set. Cool in the tin, then refrigerate overnight. Serve with cream.

NOTE: For a stronger ginger flavour, use ginger nut biscuits (ginger snaps) instead of plain biscuits (cookies) for the base.

pear and ginger cheesecake

raspberry swirl cheesecake

✻ ✻

Preparation time: 40 minutes + 4 hours
  chilling time
Cooking time: nil
Serves 8–10

250 g (9 oz) plain sweet biscuits (cookies)
90 g (3¼ oz) unsalted butter, melted
whipped cream, to serve
raspberries, to serve

FILLING
2 tablespoons powdered gelatin
500 g (1 lb 2 oz) light cream cheese,
  softened
80 ml (2½ fl oz/⅓ cup) lemon juice
115 g (4 oz/½ cup) caster (superfine) sugar
310 ml (10¾ fl oz/1¼ cups) pouring
  (whipping) cream, extra, whipped
250 g (9 oz) frozen raspberries
2 tablespoons caster (superfine) sugar, extra

hints and tips

CHEESE
Different types of soft cheese used in cheesecake recipes have different moisture and fat contents and are not inter-changeable. Using the wrong type of cheese may result in a cheesecake that separates or sinks.

COOLING
Baked cheesecakes should be cooled slowly, preferably in the oven with the heat switched off and the door ajar, before refrigeration. A cheesecake that is cooled too quickly may crack across the top.

TINS
Non-stick tins with a very dark coating conduct heat quickly and may cause the outside of a cheesecake to cook and darken, or burn, before the centre is cooked.

1 Lightly grease a 23 cm (9 inch) diameter spring-form cake tin and line base with baking paper.
2 Finely crush the biscuits in a food processor, then mix in the butter. Spoon into the tin and press firmly over the base and up the side. Refrigerate for 20 minutes, or until firm.
3 To make the filling, put 60 ml (2 fl oz/ ¼ cup) water in a small heatproof bowl, sprinkle evenly with the gelatin and leave

to go spongy. Bring a large saucepan filled with about 4 cm (1½ inches) water to the boil, remove from the heat, carefully lower the gelatin bowl into the water (it should come halfway up the side of the bowl), then stir until dissolved. Allow to cool.
4 Beat the cream cheese using electric beaters until creamy. Add the lemon juice and sugar and beat until smooth. Fold in the whipped cream and half the gelatin.

5 Process the raspberries and extra sugar in a food processor until smooth. Push the purée through a fine-meshed nylon sieve to remove any pips. Fold the remaining gelatin into the raspberry mixture. Put blobs of cream cheese mixture into the tin and fill the gaps with the raspberry. Swirl the two mixtures together, using a skewer or the point of a knife. Refrigerate for 4 hours, or until set. Serve with whipped cream and raspberries.

all about milk

Milk is amazing — it contains nourishing proteins, sugars, fats, vitamins and minerals. It can also be transformed into a host of other dairy products.

cream

If fresh, unhomogenised milk is left to stand, a layer of cream will form on top as the butterfat rises. So cream is simply a form of milk in which the butterfat is more concentrated. It is either skimmed off the top after rising naturally or removed by the use of centrifugal force. Cream varies in thickness and richness, according to how much butterfat it contains — the thicker the cream, the higher the percentage of butterfat. But cream labelled 'thickened cream' has had thickening agents such as gelatin added to help it hold its shape.

Cream for whipping must have at least 35% butterfat to trap the air bubbles and hold them in place. Reduced-fat cream has a maximum of 25% fat and light cream around 18%. Pouring cream has a butterfat content higher than both English single cream and American light cream, neither of which can be whipped — it varies between 35% and 48%. Thick cream ('double' in England and 'heavy' in America) has a minimum butterfat content of 48%. Clotted, scalded or Devonshire cream is the thickest and yellowest of all. All cream should be well chilled before whipping and should be refrigerated when not in use.

sour cream

Originally made by leaving cream at room temperature to sour, today sour cream is made by adding a culture to cream. It is thickened and slightly acidic because the milk sugar (lactose) converts to lactic acid. Low-fat varieties are also available.

crème fraiche

This French version of cultured sour cream is smooth, rich and slightly acidic, with a higher fat content than thick cream. Its mild acidity complements the sweetness of chocolate and fruit.

ricotta cheese

This was originally made from the whey of milk but nowadays is often made from milk. It is low in fat, has a slight sweetness and short shelf life. It should look moist and white, not dry and discoloured.

quark/fromage frais/ fromage blanc/cream cheese

These are soft-curd cheeses made from both full-fat and non-full-fat milk. Fromage frais and fromage blanc have been homogenised to give a smoother texture and have a slightly acidic edge. Cream cheese is also sold as Neufchatel.

buttermilk

Butter is produced by churning cream until the fat comes together and, traditionally, buttermilk was the liquid remaining after this process. However, cultured buttermilk is made from skim milk which has a bacterial culture added to ripen and thicken it slightly. It becomes slightly acidic as the lactose turns to lactic acid. It activates bicarbonate of soda, so is often used in baking to give a light texture.

yoghurt

This is made by adding a culture of *Lactobacillus bulgaricus*, *Lactobacillus acidophilus* or *Streptococcus thermophilus* to warm milk. The bacilli create acidity which ferments and thickens the milk and destroys some of the intrinsic bacteria, giving it a longer 'edible' life and making it an easily digested food.

mascarpone cheese

This rich, creamy cheese originated in Italy. Traditionally used in tiramisu, it also works well in cheesecakes and ice cream.

ricotta cheese

Ricotta literally means 'recooked'. This reflects its method of manufacture, in which whey and skim cows' milk are heated, thus causing the albumin or protein to collect in flakes, a process known as flocculating. As it is made from whey, ricotta is not strictly a cheese, but a by-product of cheesemaking. Ricotta is relatively low in fat, with a sweetish edge due to the presence of lactose or milk sugar. It is high in calcium. Ricotta can be whipped, eaten fresh or cooked in baked goods. It is also available in lower fat varieties. If ricotta seems wet, drain it overnight in the refrigerator in a sieve lined with muslin (cheesecloth). Ricotta is traditionally used in Italian cooking, especially cassata and cheesecakes.

chocolate ricotta tart

Preparation time: 20 minutes + 30 minutes
  chilling and cooling time
Cooking time: 1 hour
Serves 8–10

185 g (6½ oz/1½ cups) plain
  (all-purpose) flour
100 g (3½ oz) unsalted butter, chopped
2 tablespoons caster (superfine) sugar
40 g (1¼ oz) dark chocolate
½ teaspoon vegetable oil

FILLING
1.25 kg (2 lb 12 oz) ricotta cheese
125 g (4½ oz/½ cup) caster (superfine) sugar
2 tablespoons plain (all-purpose) flour
1 teaspoon instant coffee granules
125 g (4½ oz) finely chopped dark
  chocolate
4 egg yolks, at room temperature

1 To make the pastry, sift the flour into a large bowl and add the butter. Rub the butter into the flour with your fingertips, until fine and crumbly. Stir in the sugar. Add 60 ml (2 fl oz/¼ cup) cold water and cut with a knife to form a dough, adding a little more water if necessary. Turn out onto a lightly floured surface and gather into a ball.
2 Lightly grease a 25 cm (10 inch) diameter spring-form cake tin and line base with baking paper. Roll out the pastry, then line the tin so that the pastry comes about two-thirds of the way up the side. Cover with plastic wrap and refrigerate while making the filling.
3 Preheat the oven to 180°C (350°F/ Gas 4).
4 To make the filling, combine the ricotta, sugar, flour and a pinch of salt until smooth. Dissolve the coffee in 2 teaspoons hot water. Stir into the ricotta mixture, with the chocolate and egg yolks, until well mixed. Spoon into the chilled pastry shell and smooth the surface. Refrigerate for 30 minutes, or until firm.
5 Put the cake tin on a baking tray. Bake for 1 hour, or until firm. Turn off the oven

and leave the tart in the oven to cool with the door ajar (the tart may crack slightly but this will not be noticeable when it cools and has been decorated).

6 To decorate, melt the chocolate and stir in the oil. Use a fork to flick thin drizzles of melted chocolate over the tart, or pipe over for a neater finish. Cool completely then cut into wedges to serve.

frozen honey cheesecake with praline crust

✹ ✹

Preparation time: 1 hour + 8 hours freezing time
Cooking time: 25 minutes
Serves 8–10

100 g (3½ oz) flaked almonds
185 g (6½ oz/¾ cup) sugar
225 g (8 oz) plain sweet biscuits (cookies)
100 g (3½ oz) unsalted butter, melted

FILLING
250 g (9 oz) mascarpone cheese
250 g (9 oz) cream cheese, softened to room temperature
400 g (14 oz) tin condensed milk
60 ml (2 fl oz/¼ cup) honey
310 ml (10¾ fl oz/1¼ cups) pouring (whipping) cream
2 teaspoons ground cinnamon

1 Preheat the oven to 150°C (300°F/ Gas 2). To make the praline, spread the almonds on a baking tray lined with baking paper. Put the sugar in a saucepan with 125 ml (4 fl oz/½ cup) water and stir over low heat until the sugar dissolves. Bring to the boil, then simmer without stirring until toffee is golden brown. Pour over the almonds, then set aside to cool and harden before breaking into pieces.
2 Lightly grease a 23 cm (9 inch) diameter spring-form cake tin and line base with baking paper. Reserve about half the praline and finely chop the rest with the biscuits in a food processor. Stir

in the butter, spoon into the base and press firmly on the side of the tin. Bake for 15 minutes and then leave to cool.
3 To make the filling, process the mascarpone and cream cheese together until soft and creamy. Add the condensed

milk and honey. Whip the cream until soft peaks form and then fold in. Pour into the tin, sprinkle with cinnamon and swirl gently with a skewer. Do not overmix. Freeze for 8 hours, or until firm. Decorate with the remaining praline.

Pour the toffee over the flaked almonds on the baking paper-lined baking tray.

Use a skewer to swirl the cinnamon through the cheesecake filling.

buttermilk cheesecake with raspberry sauce

Preparation time: 35 minutes + 6 hours chilling time
Cooking time: 1 hour 20 minutes
Serves 8

250 g (9 oz) plain sweet biscuits (cookies)
125 g (4½ oz) unsalted butter, melted
3 teaspoons finely grated lemon zest
icing (confectioners') sugar, to dust

FILLING
750 g (1 lb 10 oz) ricotta cheese
4 eggs, lightly beaten
250 ml (9 fl oz/1 cup) buttermilk
2 tablespoons cornflour (cornstarch)
125 ml (4 fl oz/½ cup) honey
1 tablespoon lemon juice

RASPBERRY SAUCE
300 g (10½ oz) fresh or frozen raspberries
30 g (1 oz/¼ cup) icing (confectioners') sugar
1 teaspoon lemon juice

1 Grease a 23 cm (9 inch) diameter spring-form cake tin and line base with baking paper. Preheat the oven to 160°C (315°F/Gas 2–3). Finely crush the biscuits in a processor and stir in the butter and 2 teaspoons of zest, until combined. Spoon into the tin and press firmly over the base. Refrigerate while preparing the filling.
2 Beat the ricotta with electric beaters for 2 minutes, or until smooth. Add the beaten egg gradually, beating well after each addition. Whisk together the buttermilk and cornflour until smooth and add gradually to the ricotta mixture. Beat in the honey, remaining lemon zest and the lemon juice. Pour into the tin and bake for 1 hour 20 minutes, or until set. Cool, then refrigerate for at least 6 hours.
3 To make the raspberry sauce, defrost the raspberries, reserve a few as garnish, and process the rest with the icing sugar for 20 seconds, or until smooth. Add

sicilian cheesecake

lemon juice, to taste. Bring the cheesecake to room temperature and serve with raspberries and sauce. Lightly dust with icing sugar.

sicilian cheesecake

Preparation time: 45 minutes + 30 minutes chilling time
Cooking time: 1 hour 25 minutes
Serves 8

250 g (9 oz/2 cups) plain (all-purpose) flour
165 g (5¾ oz) unsalted butter, chopped
55 g (2¼ oz/¼ cup) caster (superfine) sugar
1 teaspoon finely grated lemon zest
1 egg, lightly beaten

FILLING
60 g (2¼ oz) raisins, chopped
80 ml (2½ fl oz/⅓ cup) Marsala
500 g (1 lb 2 oz) ricotta cheese
115 g (4 oz/½ cup) caster (superfine) sugar
1 tablespoon plain (all-purpose) flour
4 eggs, separated
125 ml (4 fl oz/½ cup) pouring (whipping) cream

1 Lightly grease a 26 cm (10½ inch) diameter spring-form tin. Sift the flour and a pinch of salt into a large bowl and rub in the butter, using just your fingertips. Add the sugar, lemon zest, egg and a little water, if necessary, and, using a knife, cut through until a rough dough forms. Gather the dough together into a ball.
2 Roll out the dough between two sheets of baking paper to fit the base and side of the tin, then chill for 30 minutes. Preheat

the oven to 190°C (375°F/Gas 5). Prick the pastry base, line with baking paper and fill with dried beans or rice. Bake for 15 minutes, remove the beans and paper and bake for 8 minutes, or until the pastry is dry. If the base puffs up, gently press down with the back of a spoon. Allow to cool. Reduce the oven temperature to 160°C (315°F/Gas 2–3).

3   To make the filling, put the raisins and Marsala in a small bowl, cover and leave to soak. Push the ricotta through a sieve, then beat with the sugar, using a wooden spoon, until combined. Add the flour and egg yolks, then the cream and undrained raisins and mix well. In a clean, dry bowl, whisk the egg whites until soft peaks form, then fold into the ricotta mixture in two batches.

4   Pour the filling into the pastry case and bake for 1 hour, or until just set. Check during cooking and cover with foil if the pastry is overbrowning. Cool a little in the oven with the door ajar to prevent sinking. Serve warm.

NOTE: Marsala is a fortified dark wine made in Sicily with a deep rich flavour. It is available in dry and sweet varieties. Sweet Marsala is used in desserts and as a dessert wine.

baked lime and passionfruit cheesecake

※

Preparation time: 50 minutes + overnight
   chilling time
Cooking time: 55 minutes
Serves 6–8

250 g (9 oz) plain sweet biscuits (cookies)
125 g (4½ oz) unsalted butter, melted
whipped cream, to serve

FILLING
500 g (1 lb 2 oz) cream cheese, softened
   to room temperature
80 g (2¾ oz/⅓ cup) caster (superfine) sugar

3 teaspoons finely grated lime zest
2 tablespoons lime juice
2 eggs, lightly beaten
125 g (4½ oz/½ cup) passionfruit pulp

PASSIONFRUIT TOPPING
1 tablespoon caster (superfine) sugar
3 teaspoons cornflour (cornstarch)
125 g (4½ oz/½ cup) passionfruit pulp

1   Lightly grease a 20 cm (8 inch) diameter spring-form cake tin and line the base with baking paper. Preheat the oven to 160°C (315°F/Gas 2–3). Finely crush the biscuits in a food processor and mix in the butter. Spoon into the tin and press firmly into the base and side of the tin. Refrigerate for 30 minutes.

2   Using electric beaters, beat the cream cheese, sugar, lime zest and lime juice until creamy. Gradually beat in the eggs and passionfruit pulp. Pour into the tin, put on a baking tray to catch any drips, and bake for 45–50 minutes, or until just set. Cool completely.

3   To make the passionfruit topping, combine the sugar, cornflour and 2 tablespoons water in a small saucepan over low heat. Stir until smooth, then add 2 more tablespoons water and the passionfruit pulp and stir until the mixture boils and thickens. Pour the hot topping over the cooled cheesecake, spread evenly and cool completely. Refrigerate overnight. Serve with whipped cream.

NOTE: You will need to use the pulp from about eight fresh passionfruit for this recipe.

meringue

Meringue is a quite miraculous mixture of egg whites and sugar whisked together until glossy, then baked into delicate peaks and swirls. Australia's most popular and renowned culinary creation is the timeless pavlova, named in honour of the Russian ballerina, Anna Pavlova. Meringue connoisseurs will debate over the relative merits of the crunchy, brittle variety that explodes into a thousand crumbs of sweetness when bitten into, versus 'grandmother's pavlova', with its crisp outer shell and soft, marshmallow-like centre.

kiwi fruit

The kiwi fruit is the edible berry of a woody vine. Also known as a Chinese gooseberry, it is about the size of a large hen's egg, with a thin, brown, furry skin and green flesh. A yellow-fleshed variety is also available. New Zealand is a principal source of these tangy fruits, which are high in vitamin C and potassium. It also contains an enzyme that can be used as a meat tenderiser. Kiwi fruit skin is edible, and high in dietary fibre, although most people find the furry texture unpalatable.

grandmother's pavlova

Preparation time: **30 minutes**
Cooking time: **1 hour**
Serves 6–8

4 egg whites
250 g (9 oz/1 cup) caster (superfine) sugar
2 teaspoons cornflour (cornstarch)
1 teaspoon white vinegar
250 ml (9 fl oz/1 cup) pouring (whipping) cream
strawberries and kiwi fruit, to serve
pulp from 3 passionfruit, to serve

1 Preheat the oven to 160°C (315°F/ Gas 2–3). Line a large baking tray with baking paper.
2 Place the egg whites and a pinch of salt in a large, very clean, dry stainless steel or glass bowl — any hint of grease will prevent the egg whites foaming. Leave the whites for a few minutes to reach room temperature. Use electric beaters to whisk slowly until the whites start to become a frothy foam, then increase the speed until the bubbles in the foam are small and evenly sized. When the foam forms stiff peaks, add the sugar gradually, whisking constantly after each addition, until the mixture is thick and glossy and all the sugar dissolves. Don't overwhisk or the mixture will become grainy.

3 Use a metal spoon to fold in the sifted cornflour and the vinegar. Spoon the mixture into a mound on the prepared tray. Lightly flatten the top of the pavlova and smooth the sides. (This pavlova should have a cake shape and be about 2.5 cm/1 inch high.) Bake for 1 hour, or until pale cream and crisp on the outside. Remove from the oven while warm and carefully turn upside down onto a plate. Cool completely.
4 Whip the cream until soft peaks form, then spread it over the soft centre. Decorate with hulled and halved strawberries, sliced kiwi fruit and passionfruit pulp. Cut into wedges to serve.

NOTE: The cornflour and vinegar gives the meringue a marshmallow-like centre.

pavlova with fresh fruit

❋

Preparation time: **20 minutes**
Cooking time: **40 minutes**
Serves **8**

4 egg whites
230 g (8 oz/1 cup) caster (superfine) sugar
375 ml (13 fl oz/1½ cups) pouring (whipping) cream, whipped
1 banana, sliced
125 g (4½ oz) raspberries
125 g (4½ oz) blueberries

1 Preheat the oven to 150°C (300°F/ Gas 2). Line a baking tray with baking paper. Mark a 20 cm (8 inch) circle on the paper as a guide for the pavlova base and turn the paper over.

2 Put the egg whites in a large, very clean, dry stainless steel or glass bowl— any hint of grease will prevent the egg whites foaming. Leave the whites for a few minutes to reach room temperature. Use electric beaters to whisk slowly until the whites start to become a frothy foam, then increase the speed until the bubbles in the foam are small and evenly sized. When the foam forms stiff peaks, add the sugar gradually, whisking constantly after each addition, until the mixture is thick and glossy and all the sugar dissolves. Don't overwhisk or the mixture will become grainy.

3 Spread the mixture on the paper to fill the marked circle, running a flat-bladed knife or spatula around the edge and over the top. Run the knife up the edge of the mixture, all the way around, to make furrows. This will strengthen the pavlova and give it a decorative finish.

4 Bake for 40 minutes, or until pale and crisp, then turn off the oven and cool the pavlova in the oven with the door ajar. When cold, serve decorated with whipped cream, banana, raspberries and blueberries.

NOTE: The meringue can be cooked in advance and kept overnight in an airtight container. Serve within 1 hour of decorating.

Whisk the egg whites until stiff peaks form, then add the sugar gradually and whisk until the mixture is thick and glossy.

Spread the mixture on the paper to fill the marked circle.

meringue

There are several types of meringue — ordinary, Italian, and meringue cuite. Each egg white needs at least 45 g (1¾ oz) sugar — lesser amounts give a very soft meringue suitable for pie toppings. To whisk well, egg whites need to be fresh and at room temperature, as well as free from any oil or egg yolk. For ordinary meringue, the sugar is added in at least two batches and whisked until the sugar dissolves and stabilises the whites. Meringue should be thick and shiny and hold its shape. It might not work on a humid day. Italian meringue is made by adding boiling sugar syrup to whisked egg white. Meringue cuite is made by whisking egg white and icing sugar over gentle heat. Both methods give a solid meringue that holds up well.

meringue nests

Preparation time: **20 minutes + cooling time**
Cooking time: **35 minutes**
Makes **4**

2 egg whites
125 g (4½ oz/½ cup) caster
   (superfine) sugar

1 Preheat the oven to 150° (300°F/ Gas 2). Line a baking tray with baking paper. Mark out four 9 cm (3½ inch) circles, then turn the paper over. Put the egg whites in a large clean, dry bowl and leave for a few minutes to reach room temperature. Use electric beaters to whisk the egg whites until soft peaks form. Gradually add the sugar, whisking well after each addition, until the mixture is thick and glossy. Do not overwhisk.
2 Spread 1 tablespoon of the meringue mixture evenly over each of the circles to a thickness of 5 mm (¼ inch). Put the remaining mixture in a piping bag fitted with a 1 cm (½ inch) star nozzle. Pipe the mixture around the edge of the meringue circles to make a nest 1–2 cm (½–¾ inch) high.
3 Bake for 30–35 minutes, or until just starting to colour, then turn the oven off and leave the meringues to cool completely in the oven. Once cooled, carefully remove from the trays. Transfer to an airtight container until required.

gingered custard and rhubarb filling

In a bowl, whisk 4 egg yolks and 125 g (4½ oz/½ cup) sugar together until creamy, then stir in 1 tablespoon cornflour (cornstach). In a small saucepan, combine 250 ml (9 fl oz/1 cup) milk with 2 teaspoons grated fresh ginger and bring to the boil. Remove from the heat, strain and allow to cool slightly, then gradually whisk into the egg mixture. Return to the pan and stir over low heat for 5 minutes, or until the mixture thickens. Remove from the heat and allow to cool. Cut 2 stalks of rhubarb in half lengthways, then cut into 3 cm (1¼ inch) pieces. Combine 1 tablespoon caster (superfine) sugar and 60 ml (2 fl oz/¼ cup) water in a small pan and stir over low heat until the sugar dissolves. Add the rhubarb and cook gently for 3–5 minutes, or until the rhubarb softens but still holds its shape. Spoon the cooled custard into the nests, arrange the rhubarb over it and serve. Dust with icing (confectioners') sugar or fine strips of preserved ginger.

raspberry and mascarpone filling

Combine 250 g (9 oz) mascarpone cheese with the finely grated zest of 1 lime. Stir in 60 g (2¼ oz) raspberries, if desired, mixing well so that the raspberry juices are released into the mascarpone. Divide the mixture evenly among the meringue nests and garnish with extra raspberries. Serve dusted with icing (confectioners') sugar or garnished with mint leaves.

rich chocolate mousse filling

Bring a saucepan filled with about 4 cm (1½ inches) water to the boil, then remove it from the heat. Put 60 g (2¼ oz) roughly chopped dark chocolate in a heatproof bowl and set over the pan, making sure the bowl is not touching the water. Stir until the chocolate melts. Allow to cool. Use electric beaters to whip 250 ml (9 fl oz/1 cup) pouring (whipping) cream with 60 g (2¼ oz/ ¼ cup) caster (superfine) sugar until soft peaks form. Mix one-third of the cream into the melted chocolate, stirring until well combined. Fold in the remaining cream mixture, cover and refrigerate for 2 hours. Once firm, spoon into the nests and garnish with chocolate curls (page 208). Serve immediately, dusted with icing (confectioners') sugar.

grilled fig and ricotta filling

Blend 250 g (9 oz) ricotta cheese, 2 tablespoons honey, 2–3 tablespoons orange juice, 2 teaspoons soft brown sugar, ½ teaspoon ground cinnamon and ¼ teaspoon natural vanilla extract in a food processor until smooth. Transfer to a bowl and stir in 50 g (1¾ oz) sultanas (golden raisins). Quarter 4 firm, ripe figs lengthways, place on a baking tray and sprinkle with 1 tablespoon soft brown sugar. Grill (broil) for 5–6 minutes, or until the sugar caramelises. Spoon the ricotta mixture into the nests, top with the grilled figs, sprinkle with finely chopped pistachios and serve. Any remaining fig pieces can be served separately.

mixed berry meringue stacks

✳

Preparation time: 50 minutes + chilling and cooling time
Cooking time: 35 minutes
Serves 6

2 egg whites
115 g (4 oz/½ cup) caster (superfine) sugar
250 g (9 oz) small strawberries
150 g (5½ oz) blueberries
125 g (4½ oz) raspberries
1 tablespoon soft brown sugar
375 ml (12 fl oz/1½ cups) cream, whipped
icing (confectioners') sugar, to dust

1 Preheat the oven to 150° (300°F/Gas 2). Line baking trays with baking paper and mark out eighteen 9 cm (3½ inch) circles.
2 Using electric beaters, whisk the egg whites in a clean, dry bowl until soft peaks form. Gradually add the sugar, whisking after each addition, until the mixture is thick and glossy. Spread about 1 tablespoon of the mixture evenly over each of the circles to a thickness of 5 mm (¼ inch). Bake for 30–35 minutes, or until lightly golden, then turn the oven off and leave the meringues to cool completely in the oven.
3 Hull the strawberries and combine with the other berries in a large bowl. Sprinkle with the brown sugar, then cover and refrigerate for 20 minutes.

4 To assemble, using three meringue circles for each, place one on a plate, spread with cream and arrange some of the berries over the cream. Place another circle on top, spread with cream, top with more berries and then top with the third circle. Dust liberally with icing sugar. Repeat this with all the circles to make six individual stacks. Serve immediately.

fruit covered with meringue

✳ ✳

Preparation time: 25 minutes
Cooking time: 20 minutes
Serves 4

4 ripe peaches or nectarines
40 g (1½ oz) marzipan
3 egg whites
160 g (5¾ oz/⅔ cup) caster (superfine) sugar
raw (demerara) sugar, to sprinkle

1 Preheat the oven to 200°C (400°F/Gas 6). Cut the peaches in half and remove the stone. To remove the skin, place the peaches cut-side-down on a plate, put the plate in the sink and pour boiling water over, followed by cold water. Drain immediately and peel. Roll the marzipan into four small balls, put them in the gaps left by the peach stones, then put the halves back together. Stand the peaches in a shallow ovenproof dish.
2 Bring the egg whites to room temperature in a large, clean, dry bowl, then whisk until stiff peaks form. Gradually add the sugar and whisk until thick and glossy. Cover the fruit with a layer of meringue, making sure there are no gaps. Use a fork to rough up the surface of the meringue. Sprinkle with sugar and bake for 15–20 minutes, until the meringue is lightly browned. Gently lift out. Serve with cream or ice cream.

mixed berry meringue stacks

nuts: chopping and storing

When chopping nuts in a food processor, make sure they are cold or they will become oily. You can add a tablespoon of sugar or flour to help absorb any excess oil when processing nuts. Nuts keep best frozen or refrigerated in a sealed container.

hazelnut meringue stack

Preparation time: 20 minutes + cooling time
Cooking time: 55 minutes
Serves 8

300 g (10½ oz) hazelnuts
8 egg whites
375 g (13 oz/1½ cups) caster (superfine) sugar
2 teaspoons natural vanilla extract
2 teaspoons white vinegar
600 g (1 lb 5 oz) sour cream
200 ml (7 fl oz) pouring (whipping) cream, whipped, plus extra, to serve
230 g (8 oz/1¼ cups) soft brown sugar

toffeed hazelnuts (page 218), to serve

1 Preheat the oven to 180°C (350°F/Gas 4). Roast the hazelnuts on a baking tray for 5–10 minutes, or until golden. Tip the nuts onto a tea towel (dish towel), rub vigorously in the towel to remove the skins. Transfer to a food processor and chop until finely ground.
2 Reduce the oven temperature to 150°C (300°F/Gas 2). Line four baking trays with baking paper and draw a 21 cm (8¼ inch) diameter circle on each piece, then turn the paper over.
3 Bring the egg whites to room temperature in a large, clean, dry bowl, then whisk until soft peaks form. Gradually add the sugar, whisking well

after each addition, until stiff and glossy. Fold in the ground hazelnuts, vanilla and vinegar.
4 Divide the mixture evenly among the circles and carefully spread it to the edge of each circle. Bake for 45 minutes, or until crisp. Turn off the oven and leave the meringues to cool in the oven, with the door ajar.
5 To make the filling, stir the sour cream, cream and brown sugar in a bowl until combined.
6 Sandwich together the meringue circles with the filling. Decorate with whipped cream and toffeed hazelnuts.

berries

A sweet summer explosion of glorious colour and tangy juices, berries make the perfect partner for crispy sweet meringue, but don't stop there — they have myriad other roles in the dessert world.

blackberries

This slightly tart fruit is delicious in pies, crumbles and cobblers, and is an essential ingredient in summer pudding. Refrigerate, then wash briefly just before use. Blackberries are delicious with crème fraîche, brandy and apple.

blueberries

Blueberries have a blue exterior but are white or pale green inside. Available most of the year but best in summer, they keep in the refrigerator for up to 7 days. Don't store in a metal container as they react and cause dark stains. Rinse briefly before use. Great in baked desserts, pies and cheesecakes, blueberries taste good with port, cinnamon and cream.

currants

Available in red, white and black. White currants are a variety of the red and look similar. Leave on the stalk until ready to use, then remove the stalks by gently loosening the berries between the tines of a fork. Currants are often frosted and used as a cake decoration, moulded in jellies or used in fruit tarts. Redcurrants work well with almonds, cherries and oranges. Blackcurrants are an excellent source of vitamin C and are the basic ingredient in the blackcurrant liqueur, Cassis. Blackcurrants are good with pears, apples and red wine.

mulberries

The fruit of a tree, mulberries are available in black, red and white, the black having the best flavour. They have a rich, winey flavour and their juice stains badly. Mulberries go well with cream and brandy and can be used in pastries, cakes and crumbles.

physalis (cape gooseberries)

A summer fruit that enjoys a relatively short season, this small orange or greeny yellow berry is enclosed in a papery calyx. Peel away the calyx and eat the sharp-tasting berry raw, or dipped in caramel or fondant. They make a wonderful garnish for cheesecakes, desserts and fruit platters.

raspberries

A true summer berry, the red ones are the most common but a golden variety is sometimes available. Store this delicate fruit covered in the refrigerator and get rid of any mouldy ones immediately. Eat them on their own or puréed as part of a cold mousse or hot soufflé.

strawberries

Strawberries are available all year round but vary vastly in flavour, size and colour. When they are in season, they have a wonderful aroma and flavour. Store them in the refrigerator and rinse them just before using. They are delicious on their own, with cream or ice cream, or used in traditional recipes such as strawberries romanoff, summer pudding and shortcake.

frozen praline meringue torte

frozen praline meringue torte

❋ ❋

Preparation time: 1 hour + 4 hours
   freezing time
Cooking time: 1 hour 10 minutes
Serves 8–10

4 egg whites
375 g (13 oz/1½ cups) caster
   (superfine) sugar
100 g (3½ oz) blanched almonds
2 litres (70 fl oz/8 cups) good-quality
   vanilla ice cream, softened
strawberries, hulled and sliced, to serve

STRAWBERRY SAUCE
500 g (1 lb 2 oz) strawberries, hulled
2 tablespoons lemon juice
30 g (1 oz/¼ cup) icing
   (confectioners') sugar

1   Preheat the oven to 150°C (300°F/
Gas 2). Line two baking trays with baking
paper and mark a 20 cm (8 inch) circle
on each. Brush with oil and dust with a
little caster (superfine) sugar. Bring the
egg whites to room temperature in a
large, clean, dry bowl, then whisk until
stiff peaks form, then gradually add 250 g
(9 oz/1 cup) of the sugar, a tablespoon at
a time. Whisk until thick and glossy and
the sugar dissolves. Pipe in a spiral into
the two circles. Bake for 1 hour, turn off
the oven and leave the meringues to cool
with the oven door ajar.
2   To make the praline, line a baking
tray with baking paper and sprinkle with
almonds. Combine the remaining sugar
with 80 ml (2½ fl oz/⅓ cup) water in
a saucepan and stir over low heat until
dissolved. Bring to the boil without stirring
and, when golden, pour over the almonds.
Allow to set and cool then crush finely in
a food processor or with a rolling pin.
3   Beat the ice cream until creamy and
fold in the praline. Put a meringue circle
into a lined 23 cm (9 inch) diameter
springform cake tin, spoon in the ice
cream and put the other meringue on
top. Freeze for at least 4 hours or until
ready to serve.

4   To make the sauce, process the
ingredients in a food processor until
smooth. Add a little water if too thick.
Decorate the meringue torte with sliced
strawberries and serve with the sauce.

NOTE: The torte will keep up to 4 days
in the freezer.

raspberry and white chocolate roll

❋ ❋

Preparation time: 35 minutes + 2 hours
   chilling time
Cooking time: 10 minutes
Serves 6–8

4 egg whites
185 g (6½ oz/¾ cup) caster (superfine) sugar
125 g (4½ oz) cream cheese, softened
185 g (6½ oz/¾ cup) sour cream
125 g (4½ oz) white chocolate, melted
125 g (4½ oz) raspberries

1   Preheat the oven to 180°C (350°F/
Gas 4). Line the base and long sides of
a 25 x 30 cm (10 x 12 inch) Swiss roll
(jelly roll) tin with baking paper. Bring
the egg whites to room temperature in a
large, clean, dry bowl, then whisk until
soft peaks form. Gradually add the sugar,
whisking constantly. Whisk until thick and
glossy and the sugar dissolves.
2   Spread the mixture into the tin and bake
for 10 minutes, or until lightly browned
and firm to touch. Quickly and carefully
turn onto baking paper sprinkled with
caster (superfine) sugar. Leave to cool.
3   Beat the cream cheese and sour cream
until smooth and creamy. Add the cooled
white chocolate and beat until smooth.
Spread over the meringue base, leaving a
1 cm (½ inch) border. Top with a layer of
raspberries. Carefully roll the meringue,
using the paper as a guide, from one short
end. Wrap firmly in the paper and then
plastic wrap and refrigerate for 2 hours or
until firm. Serve in slices.

baked alaska

✳ ✳

Preparation time: 40 minutes + 10 hours
    freezing time
Cooking time: 8 minutes
Serves 6–8

2 litres (70 fl oz/8 cups) good-quality
    vanilla ice cream
250 g (9 oz) mixed glacé fruit, finely chopped
60 ml (2 fl oz/¼ cup) Grand Marnier
    or Cointreau
2 teaspoons finely grated orange zest
60 g (2¼ oz) toasted almonds, finely chopped
60 g (2¼ oz) dark chocolate, finely chopped

1 sponge or butter cake, cut into 3 cm
    (1¼ inch) slices
3 egg whites
185 g (6½ oz/¾ cup) caster (superfine) sugar

1 Line a 2 litre (70 fl oz/8 cup)
pudding basin with damp muslin
(cheesecloth). Soften 1 litre (35 fl oz/
4 cups) ice cream enough to enable the
glacé fruit to be folded in with
2 tablespoons liqueur and 1 teaspoon
orange zest. Spoon into the basin, smooth
over the base and up the sides, then put
in the freezer for 6 hours or until frozen.
Soften the remaining ice cream and fold
in the almonds, chocolate, and remaining
liqueur and orange zest. Spoon into the
frozen shell and level the surface.
2 Work quickly to evenly cover the ice
cream with a 3 cm (1¼ inch) thick layer
of cake. Cover with foil and freeze for at
least 4 hours. Preheat the oven to 220°C
(425°F/Gas 7). Use electric beaters to
whisk the egg whites in a dry bowl until
soft peaks form. Gradually add the sugar,
whisking well after each addition. Whisk
for 4–5 minutes, until thick and glossy.
3 Unmould the ice cream onto an
ovenproof dish. Remove the muslin. Quickly
spread the meringue over the ice cream to
cover completely. Bake for 5–8 minutes, or
until lightly browned. Serve at once.

baked alaska

Baking ice cream inside an
insulating layer is an idea
probably invented by the
Chinese, who baked ice cream
wrapped in pastry. The French
used the same idea to make
omelette Norvegienne, using
meringue instead of pastry.
The Americans coined the
name baked Alaska.

oeufs à la neige

✹ ✹

Preparation time: 15 minutes + 1 hour
    chilling time
Cooking time: 25 minutes
Serves 4–6

4 eggs, separated
250 g (9 oz/1 cup) caster (superfine) sugar
750 ml (26 fl oz/3 cups) milk
1 vanilla bean, split lengthways
125 g (4½ oz/½ cup) sugar

1 Put the egg whites in a clean, dry bowl, leave for a few minutes to reach room temperature, then whisk until soft peaks form. Gradually add 90 g (3¼ oz/⅓ cup) sugar, whisking well after each addition, until stiff and glossy.

2 Combine the milk, 90 g (3¼ oz/⅓ cup) sugar and the vanilla bean in a large frying pan and bring to a simmer. Using two dessertspoons, mould the meringue into 16 egg shapes and lower in batches into the simmering milk. Poach for 5 minutes each batch, or until firm to touch, turning once during cooking (be careful as they are delicate and crumble easily). Remove with a slotted spoon and set aside. When they are all done, strain the milk.

3 Whisk the egg yolks with the remaining sugar until thick and pale. Gradually pour the milk into the egg yolk mixture, whisking well to combine. Remove and discard the vanilla bean. Pour the custard mixture into a pan and stir over low heat until the custard thickens and coats the back of a wooden spoon. Do not boil the custard. Pour the custard into a shallow serving dish and refrigerate for 1 hour or until chilled, stirring occasionally.

4 When the custard is completely cold, arrange the poached meringue on top. Stir the extra sugar with 2 tablespoons water in a small saucepan over low heat until the sugar dissolves completely. When the sugar dissolves, bring to the boil and simmer until the syrup turns golden brown. Working quickly and carefully, drizzle the toffee over the meringues and custard.

NOTE: Oeufs à la neige means 'snow eggs' and is sometimes known as floating islands.

chocolate coffee meringue mousse cake

✹ ✹

Preparation time: 20 minutes + 1 hour
    chilling time
Cooking time: 50 minutes
Serves 10–12

6 eggs, at room temperature,
    separated
375 g (13 oz/1⅔ cups) caster
    (superfine) sugar
2½ tablespoons unsweetened cocoa
    powder, plus extra to dust
1 tablespoon instant coffee granules
200 g (7 oz) dark chocolate
600 ml (21 fl oz) pouring (whipping)
    cream, whipped

1 Preheat the oven to 150°C (300°F/ Gas 2). Cut four pieces of baking paper large enough to line four baking trays. On three of the pieces of paper, mark a 22 cm (8½ inch) circle. On the remaining piece, draw straight lines, 3 cm (1¼ inches) apart. Line the baking trays with the paper.

2 Bring the egg whites to room temperature in a large, clean, dry bowl, then whisk until soft peaks form. Gradually add the sugar, whisking well after each addition. Whisk for 5–10 minutes, until thick and glossy and all the sugar dissolves. Gently fold the sifted cocoa powder into the meringue.

3 Divide the meringue into four portions. Spread three portions over each of the marked circles. Put the remaining meringue in a piping (icing) bag fitted with a 1 cm (½ inch) plain piping nozzle. Pipe lines about 8 cm (3¼ inches) long over the marked lines. Bake for 45 minutes, or until pale and crisp. Check the meringue strips occasionally to prevent overcooking. Turn off the oven and cool in the oven with the door ajar.

4 Put the chocolate in a heatproof bowl. Half fill a saucepan with water, bring to the boil, then remove from the heat and sit the bowl over the pan (don't let the bowl touch the water or the chocolate will get too hot and seize). Stir occasionally until the chocolate melts.

5 Dissolve the coffee granules in 1 tablespoon water. Put the melted chocolate in a bowl, whisk in the egg yolks and the coffee mixture, and beat until smooth. Fold in the whipped cream and mix the whole lot together. Refrigerate for 1 hour or until the mousse is cold and thick.

6 To assemble, place one meringue disc on a plate and spread with one-third of the mousse. Top with another disc and spread with half the remaining mousse. Repeat with the remaining disc and mousse. Cut or break the meringue strips into short pieces and pile them on top of the cake, pressing them into the mousse. Dust with cocoa and refrigerate until firm.

cocoa

Cocoa powder is made from the seeds of the cacao, a tropical tree. The seeds are roasted and ground into a pure chocolate paste. To make the powder, the vegetable fat, known as cocoa butter, is removed from the paste and the powder ground from the remaining dry solids.

Chocolate drink was fashionable in the 17th century and became known as cocoa in the 18th century. Unsweetened cocoa powder in its present form was invented by the Dutch in 1828. Cocoa labelled as Dutch, Dutched or dark cocoa, has a richer flavour than others.

fruit & jellies

In the world of food, simple certainly doesn't imply 'plain'. A piece of fresh fruit is the simplest dessert we have, and it can also be one of the most stunning. From here, it is but a tiny step to baking, grilling, poaching in a boozy syrup or serving with dollops of thick cream in a fruit salad. Simply perfection ... from the tiniest of juicy redcurrants, to the rich extravagance of a ripe fig. And what better way to show off the beauty of fruit than to suspend it in a translucent jelly?

pears

Pears are very versatile fruit. As well as being delicious by themselves, they are used in fruit salad, can be poached or baked, and cooked in tarts, puddings and crumbles. They vary in texture, shape and colour. Beurre bosc has greenish-brown skin and juicy flesh. It cooks very well for long lengths of time. Corella is smaller with a green skin streaked with red. It is equally delicious when firm or soft. Cornice has a yellow skin with a red blush. It is sweet and juicy. Nashi is an Asian variety with a crisp and juicy texture. Packham's triumph has a light yellow skin when ripe and a white juicy flesh. Williams, also known as bartlett, has a yellow skin and sometimes a red blush when ripe. Red sensation, with its bright red skin, is also available.

poached pears with ginger zabaglione

Preparation time: 20 minutes
Cooking time: 45 minutes
Makes 6

500 ml (17 fl oz/2 cups) red wine
4 pieces crystallised ginger
110 g (3¾ oz/½ cup) sugar
6 pears, peeled

GINGER ZABAGLIONE
8 egg yolks
80 g (2¾ oz/⅓ cup) caster
   (superfine) sugar
1 teaspoon ground ginger
310 ml (10¾ fl oz/1¼ cups) Marsala

1   Put the wine, ginger and sugar in a large saucepan with 1 litre (35 fl oz/ 4 cups) water and stir over medium heat until the sugar dissolves. Add the pears, cover and simmer gently, turning the pears occasionally, for 45 minutes, or until tender.
2   To make the zabaglione, about 15 minutes before the pears are ready, bring a large saucepan half-filled with water on to boil. When boiling, remove from the heat. Whisk the egg yolks, sugar and ginger in a metal or heatproof bowl, using electric beaters, until pale yellow. Set the bowl over the saucepan of steaming water, making sure the base of the bowl does not touch the water, and whisk continuously, adding the Marsala gradually. Whisk for 5 minutes, or until very thick and foamy and like a mousse.
3   Remove the pears from the pan with a slotted spoon. Arrange on plates and pour ginger zabaglione over each. Serve immediately.

mango fool

Preparation time: 20 minutes + 1 hour
  chilling time
Cooking time: nil
Serves 6

3 large, ripe mangoes
250 ml (9 fl oz/1 cup) custard
420 ml (14½ fl oz/1²⁄₃ cups) pouring
  (whipping) cream
sliced mango, to serve

1   Peel and stone the mangoes and purée
the flesh in a food processor. Add the
custard and blend to combine.
2   Whip the cream until soft peaks form,
then gently fold into the mango mixture
until just combined — do not overmix,
you want a decorative marbled effect.
3   Spoon the mixture into individual
glasses or a large serving dish. Refrigerate
for at least 1 hour before serving. Serve
topped with mango slices.

papaya lime fool

Preparation time: 15 minutes + 1 hour
  chilling time
Cooking time: nil
Serves 4

2 papaya, about 1 kg (2 lb 4 oz)
1–2 tablespoons lime juice
3 tablespoons vanilla sugar
310 ml (10¾ fl oz/1¼ cups) pouring
  (whipping) cream

1   Peel the papaya, remove the seeds
and mash the flesh until smooth. Do not
do this in a food processor or the purée
will be too runny.
2   Add the lime juice and vanilla sugar,
to taste — the amount will vary according
to the sweetness of the fruit.
3   Whisk the cream until soft peaks form,
then fold through the papaya. Spoon into
serving glasses. Chill for 1 hour or until
ready to serve.

mango fool

dates poached in earl grey syrup

Infuse 2 Earl Grey tea bags in 250 ml (9 fl oz/1 cup) boiling water for 30 minutes.
Discard the tea bags. Stir the liquid in a small saucepan with 250 g (9 oz/1 cup)
sugar over medium heat until the sugar dissolves. Bring to the boil and simmer for
10 minutes, without stirring. Add 12 fresh dates and cook for 2–3 minutes, turning
once. Serve immediately with thick (heavy/double) cream or mascarpone cheese.

72

quinces

This fruit from Asia and the Mediterranean tastes like a cross between an apple and a pear. The hard, pale yellow flesh is dry and tart when raw. Quinces require long, slow cooking, which turns the flesh to a beautiful, deep orange-pink colour.

poached quinces

Preparation time: 15 minutes
Cooking time: 4 hours
Serves 6

6 quinces
500 g (1 lb 2 oz/2 cups) sugar
2 tablespoons lemon juice
1 vanilla bean
1 cinnamon stick
2 star anise
cream (optional), to serve

1 Peel the quinces, cut them in half and core them.
2 Combine the sugar and 2 litres (70 fl oz/8 cups) water in a large saucepan and stir over low heat until the sugar dissolves.
3 Add the quinces, lemon juice and spices. Cover and simmer gently for 4 hours, or until the quinces are pink and tender. Serve warm with cream, if desired.

fruit kebabs with honey cardamom syrup

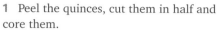

Preparation time: 20 minutes + 1 hour standing time
Cooking time: 5 minutes
Makes 8

¼ small fresh pineapple or 2 tinned pineapple rings
1 peach
1 banana
16 strawberries, hulled
pouring (whipping) cream or yoghurt (optional), to serve

HONEY CARDAMOM SYRUP
2 tablespoons honey
20 g (¾ oz) unsalted butter, melted
½ teaspoon ground cardamom
1 tablespoon dark rum or brandy (optional)
1 tablespoon soft brown sugar

1 Soak eight wooden skewers in cold water for 30 minutes to prevent them burning during cooking. Cut the pineapple into eight bite-sized pieces. Cut the peach into eight wedges and slice the banana. Thread the fruit alternately on skewers and place in a shallow dish.
2 To make the honey cardamom syrup, combine all ingredients in a bowl. Pour the mixture over the kebabs and brush to coat. Cover and leave to stand at room temperature for 1 hour.

3 Heat a barbecue or grill (broiler). Cook the kebabs on the hot, lightly greased barbecue or under the grill (broiler) for 5 minutes. Brush with the syrup occasionally during cooking. Serve drizzled with the remaining syrup, and cream or yoghurt, if desired.

baked apples

Preparation time: **20 minutes**
Cooking time: **45 minutes**
Serves **6**

6 cooking apples
60 g (2¼ oz) sultanas (golden raisins)
3 tablespoons soft brown sugar
1 teaspoon ground mixed
   (pumpkin pie) spice
40 g (1½ oz) unsalted butter, chopped
375 ml (13 fl oz/1½ cups) orange juice
cream, to serve

1 Preheat the oven to 180°C (350°F/Gas 4). Use an apple corer to core the apples. Use a sharp knife to make a shallow cut through the skin around the middle of the apples to prevent the skin bursting during cooking.
2 Combine the sultanas, sugar and spice and spoon into the apples. Put the apples in a small baking dish with the butter and juice. Bake for 45 minutes, basting occasionally. Cool for 5 minutes, transfer to plates and pour the pan juices over the top. Serve with cream.

baked apples

poached nectarines in mixed spice syrup

Preparation time: **10 minutes**
Cooking time: **20 minutes**
Serves **4**

4 nectarines
125 g (4½ oz/½ cup) sugar
4 cardamom pods
2 star anise
1 cinnamon stick
2 cloves
mascarpone cheese (optional), to serve

1 Score a cross in the base of each nectarine. Place in a large heatproof bowl and cover with boiling water for 1 minute. Drain, cool for 2–3 minutes and peel.
2 Slowly heat 500 ml (17 fl oz/2 cups) water and the sugar in a medium saucepan over medium heat until the

sugar dissolves. Lightly bruise the cardamom pods with the back of a knife and add to the pan with the star anise, cinnamon and cloves. Bring to the boil and simmer for 5 minutes.
3 Add the nectarines, cover and simmer gently for another 8–10 minutes or until soft. Remove the nectarines with a slotted spoon and transfer to serving bowls.
4 Strain the syrup, pour a little over each nectarine and serve hot or cold, with mascarpone, if desired.

papaya

Papaya is the fruit of a large tropical softwood tree. Its size bears no relation to maturity. Papaya skins range from yellowy-green to pinky-red. The flesh also varies in colour. Some are yellow and some pinky-red or orange. Ripen at room temperature until the skin loses most of its green tinge and the fruit has a pleasant aroma, then store in the refrigerator. Cut in half lengthways and spoon out the seeds. Peel, then slice or chop. Papaya makes good fools and creamy desserts. It does not work well with gelatin as it contains an enzyme, papain, which inhibits setting.

eastern fruit platter

Preparation time: **15 minutes**
Cooking time: **5 minutes**
Serves **4–6**

1 lemon grass stem, white part only, chopped
2 cm (¾ inch) piece fresh ginger, roughly chopped
1 teaspoon soft brown sugar
125 ml (4 fl oz/½ cup) coconut milk
2 mangoes
1 nashi pear, quartered
6 lychees or rambutans, stones removed
½ papaya, seeded and cut into wedges
2 star fruit, thickly sliced
1 lime, quartered

1 Simmer the lemon grass, ginger, sugar and coconut milk in a small saucepan over low heat for 5 minutes. Strain and set aside.
2 Cut down both sides of the mangoes close to the stones. Score a crisscross pattern into the flesh of each half, without cutting through the skin. Fold the outer edges under, pushing the centre up from underneath. Arrange with the rest of the fruit on a platter. Add the lime, for squeezing on the fruit.
3 Serve the coconut dressing on the side as a dipping sauce or drizzle over just before serving.

summer citrus salad

Preparation time: 15 minutes
Cooking time: 5 minutes
Serves 4–6

3 pink grapefruits, peeled and pith removed
3 large oranges, peeled and pith removed
1 tablespoon caster (superfine) sugar
1 cinnamon stick
3 tablespoons whole mint leaves

1 Cut the grapefruit and orange into segments and mix in a bowl.
2 Put the sugar, cinnamon and mint in a small saucepan with 60 ml (2 fl oz/ ¼ cup) water and stir over low heat until the sugar dissolves. Remove the cinnamon stick and mint leaves and drizzle the syrup over the fruit.

stone fruits

Preparation time: 15 minutes
Cooking time: nil
Serves 4

4 apricots, halved, stoned and thinly sliced
4 peaches, halved, stoned and thinly sliced
4 nectarines, halved, stoned and
    thinly sliced
4 plums, halved, stoned and thinly sliced
2 tablespoons apricot juice
125 g (4 ½ oz) mascarpone cheese
1 teaspoon soft brown sugar

1 Mix the fruit together and drizzle with the apricot juice.
2 Combine the mascarpone and sugar and serve with the fruit salad.

melon medley

Preparation time: 10 minutes + 30 minutes
    chilling time
Cooking time: nil
Serves 4

½ rockmelon, seeded
½ honeydew melon, seeded
¼ watermelon, seeded
pulp from 2 passionfruit

1 Cut the melons into bite-sized pieces or use a melon baller to cut them into balls. Refrigerate, covered, for 30 minutes.
2 Drizzle with passionfruit and serve.

red fruit salad

Preparation time: 30 minutes
Cooking time: 5 minutes
Serves 4

250 g (9 oz) strawberries, hulled and halved
125 g (4½ oz) raspberries
250 g (9 oz) cherries, stoned
1 tablespoon Cointreau
1 tablespoon soft brown sugar

1 Put the fruit in a bowl, drizzle with Cointreau, cover and set aside for 20 minutes.
2 Combine the sugar with 2 tablespoons water in a small saucepan over gentle heat for 3 minutes, or until dissolved. Cool, pour over the fruit and serve.

red fruit salad

soft fruit

The simple perfection of nature is impossible to surpass. When in season, a fresh ripe piece of fruit with tangy flesh and sweet juices is one of life's small joys.

apricots

These soft, sweet fruits are available late spring and summer. To ripen, leave in a paper bag at room temperature. Apricots taste good with honey, almonds, vanilla and Amaretto. Delicious raw, they can also be poached, puréed, used in desserts and ice creams or baked in pies and tarts.

cherries

Available briefly in summer, cherries can be preserved in liqueur before use in cooking, or added fresh to baked dishes such as clafoutis. Cherries are perfect with cream cheese, almonds and chocolate, and poached cherries can be used in cheesecakes, trifles and tarts, as well as in fillings for pancakes and pastries.

figs

Available in summer and autumn, figs vary from green to black. They have a delicate, sweet flesh and a soft skin that may need to be peeled. Versatile, they can be eaten raw as part of a dessert, or baked, poached and grilled. Figs taste good with vanilla, mascarpone cheese, orange and toffee.

grapes

Best known for wine-making properties, the grape is one of the first cultivated fruits and the world's largest fruit crop. Refrigerate unwashed and rinse just before serving. Grapes go with brown sugar, cream and soft cheeses. Usually eaten raw, grapes can be added to fresh fruit mince and tarts and grilled (broiled) in gratins.

mangoes

Available in many shapes and colours, ripe mangoes have a wonderful aroma and a rich, sweet delicious flesh. Ripen at room temperature, then store in the vegetable crisper in the refrigerator. They can be puréed to make ice creams and fools, or cooked in crumbles and cobblers, and taste good with lime and coconut.

nectarines

A member of the peach family, available in summer, nectarines have a smooth skin and are usually redder than peaches. Press gently along the seam to check that they are ripe. Nectarines can be used in a similar way to peaches in cooking.

peaches

Available in summer, there are more than 2,000 varieties worldwide. Peaches can be broken into two categories: clingstone or slipstone (freestone). They can be poached, baked and grilled, and complement almonds, cinnamon, vanilla and ginger. Peaches can be preserved in alcohol. Peach purée makes delicious ice creams and sorbets.

plums

Available in summer and early autumn, plums vary from white, yellow and green to dark purple. Cooking plums have a drier flesh and sharper taste than the sweet, juicy dessert plums. Plums go well with marzipan and almonds, cinnamon, vanilla, nutmeg and red wine. They are traditional in pies, cobblers and cakes, and certain varieties are divine poached in red wine.

figs with orange cream and raisins

Preparation time: 20 minutes + 1 hour soaking time
Cooking time: 12 minutes
Serves 8

250 g (9 oz) raisins
160 ml (5¼ fl oz/⅔ cup) tawny port
1 tablespoon custard powder
250 ml (9 fl oz/1 cup) skim milk
1 tablespoon sugar
100 g (3½ oz) ricotta cheese
200 g (7 oz) light French vanilla frûche or fromage frais
1 orange, peeled and zest cut into thin strips, and juiced
1 teaspoon ground cinnamon
16 fresh figs

1   Soak the raisins in the tawny port for 1 hour or until plumped up.
2   In a small saucepan, blend the custard powder with the milk, add the sugar and stir over low heat until the sugar dissolves. Increase the heat and stir continuously until the custard boils and thickens. Remove from the heat immediately, pour into a small bowl and cover the surface with plastic wrap. Cool.
3   Transfer the completely cooled custard to the small bowl of an electric mixer, add the ricotta and the frûche and beat until smooth.
4   Just before serving, add the orange zest, juice and cinnamon to the raisin mixture in a small pan and warm over low heat for 2–3 minutes. Cover and keep warm.
5   Starting from the top, cut the figs into quarters, slicing only two-thirds of the way down. Place ons erving plates. Place 2 heaped tablespoons of the orange cream into the centre of each fig, top with a tablespoon of the warm raisin mixture and serve at once.

NOTE: Frûche is a type of fromage frais and is set in the cup.

summer fruit compote

Preparation time: 40 minutes
Cooking time: 30 minutes
Serves 8

1.5 kilograms (3 lb 5 oz) mixed stone fruit, such as apricots, nectarines, plums, peaches and cherries, halved and stoned
250 ml (9 fl oz/1 cup) claret
80 ml (2½ fl oz/⅓ cup) dry sherry
170 g (6 oz/¾ cup) caster (superfine) sugar
whipped cream (optional), to serve

1   Gently plunge the fruit in small batches into boiling water for 30 seconds. Remove the fruit with a slotted spoon and put it in a bowl of iced water to stop the cooking process. Peel all of the fruit except the cherries.
2   Combine the claret, sherry, sugar and 250 ml (9 fl oz/1 cup) water in a large heavy-based saucepan. Stir over low heat without boiling until the sugar dissolves. Bring to the boil, reduce the heat and simmer for 5 minutes.
3   Add the drained fruits to the syrup in small batches and simmer each batch for 5 minutes or until just tender. Remove with a slotted spoon. Pile the fruit into a bowl. Bring the syrup to the boil, reduce the heat and simmer for a further 5 minutes. Remove from the heat and allow to cool slightly — it should be the consistency of a syrup. Pour over the fruit. Serve with a dollop of whipped cream, if desired.

summer fruit compote

strawberries romanoff

Preparation time: 20 minutes + 1 hour
  chilling time
Cooking time: nil
Serves 4

750 g (1 lb 10 oz) strawberries, hulled
  and quartered

2 tablespoons Cointreau
¼ teaspoon finely grated orange zest
1 tablespoon caster (superfine) sugar
125 ml (4 fl oz/½ cup) pouring
  (whipping) cream
2 tablespoons icing (confectioners') sugar

1 Combine the strawberries, liqueur, zest
and sugar in a bowl, cover and refrigerate
for 1 hour. Drain the strawberries,

reserving any juices. Purée one-quarter of
the berries with the reserved juices.
2 Divide the remaining berries among
four glasses. Whip the cream and icing
sugar until soft peaks form, then fold the
berry purée through the whipped cream.
Spoon over the strawberries, then cover
and refrigerate until required.

cointreau-glazed peaches

Preparation time: 10 minutes
Cooking time: 8 minutes
Serves 6

6 peaches
1–2 tablespoons soft brown sugar
80 ml (2½ fl oz, ⅓ cup) Cointreau
250 g (9 oz) mascarpone cheese
freshly grated nutmeg, to dust

1 Line a grill (broiler) tray with foil and
lightly grease the foil. Preheat the grill
(broiler) to medium. Cut the peaches in
half, remove the stones and place the
peaches, cut-side-up, on the tray.
2 Sprinkle the peaches with the sugar
and Cointreau and grill (broil) for
5–8 minutes, or until the peaches are soft
and a golden glaze forms on top.
3 Serve immediately with dollops of
mascarpone. Dust lightly with nutmeg.

pears belle hélène

Preparation time: 15 minutes
Cooking time: 15 minutes
Serves 6

375 g (13 oz/1½ cups) sugar
2 cinnamon sticks
2 cloves
6 pears, peeled and cored
6 scoops vanilla ice cream
250 ml (9 fl oz/1 cup) dark chocolate sauce
  (page 178)

strawberries romanoff

1 Combine the sugar, cinnamon and cloves in a large saucepan with 750 ml (26 fl oz/3 cups) water, stir over low heat until the sugar dissolves, then bring the syrup to the boil. Add the pears and simmer for 10 minutes, or until tender. Remove the pears with a slotted spoon and leave to cool.

2 Put a scoop of ice cream on each plate and make a hollow in each scoop with the back of a spoon. Stand the pears in the hollow and coat with the chocolate sauce.

peach melba

Preparation time: **25 minutes**
Cooking time: **10 minutes**
Serves **4**

300 g (10½ oz) fresh raspberries,
   or frozen, thawed
2 tablespoons icing (confectioners') sugar
375 g (13 oz/1½ cups) sugar
1 vanilla bean, split lengthways
4 firm, ripe peaches
vanilla ice cream, to serve

1 Purée the raspberries and icing sugar together in a food processor. Pass through a strainer and discard the seeds. Stir the sugar, vanilla bean and 600 ml (21 fl oz/2½ cups) water in a saucepan over low heat until the sugar dissolves.

2 Bring the sugar syrup to the boil and add the peaches, ensuring they are covered with the syrup. Simmer gently for 5 minutes, or until tender, then remove the peaches with a slotted spoon and carefully remove the skin.

3 Put a scoop of ice cream on a plate, add a peach, then spoon the purée over the top.

peach melba

Created by Auguste Escoffier at the Carlton Hotel in 1892, Peach Melba consisted of vanilla ice cream with peaches, set between the wings of a swan carved from ice and covered in spun sugar. In 1900, he came up with an easier version of the pudding, in which raspberry sauce is used rather than the swan. Escoffier served the dish to Dame Nellie Melba and asked if he could name his creation after her.

summer pudding

✷ ✷

Preparation time: **30 minutes**
Cooking time: **5 minutes**
Serves **6**

150 g (5½ oz) blackcurrants
150 g (5½ oz) redcurrants
150 g (5½ oz) raspberries
150 g (5½ oz) blackberries
200 g (7 oz) strawberries, hulled and
    quartered or halved
125 g (4½ oz/½ cup) caster (superfine)
    sugar, or to taste
6–8 slices good-quality sliced white bread,
    crusts removed

1 Put all the berries except the
strawberries in a large saucepan with
125 ml (4 fl oz/½ cup) water and heat
gently until the berries begin to collapse.
Add the strawberries and turn off the
heat. Add sugar, to taste (this will depend
on how ripe the fruit is). Set aside to cool.
2 Line a 1 litre (35 fl oz/4 cup) pudding
basin (steamed pudding mould) or six
170 ml (5½ fl oz/⅔ cup) moulds with
bread. For the large mould, cut a large circle
out of one slice for the base and cut the rest
of the bread into wide fingers. For the small
moulds, use one slice of bread for each,
cutting a small circle to fit the base and
strips to fit around the sides. Drain a little
of the juice off the fruit mixture. Dip one
side of each bread piece in the juice before
fitting it, juice-side-down, into the basin,
leaving no gaps. Do not squeeze or flatten
the bread or it will not absorb the juices.
3 Fill the centre of the basin with the fruit
and add a little juice. Cover the top with
the remaining dipped bread, juice-side-up,
trimmed to fit. Cover with plastic wrap.
Place a small plate, which fits inside the
dish, onto the plastic wrap, then weigh
it down with heavy tins or a glass bowl.
Place on a baking tray to catch any juices.
For the small moulds, cover with plastic
and sit a small tin, or a similar weight,
on top of each. Refrigerate overnight.
Turn out the pudding/s and serve with
any leftover fruit mixture.

Cut a circle of bread to fit the bottom of the basin and cut the rest of the bread into fingers.

Dip one side of each bread piece in the fruit juice and fit it, juice-side-down, into the mould, leaving no gaps between each piece.

When filled with fruit, cover the top with a layer of dipped bread and cover with plastic wrap.

strawberry kissel

Preparation time: **15 minutes + 3 hours chilling and 30 minutes standing time**
Cooking time: **10 minutes**
Serves 4–6

250 g (9 oz) strawberries, hulled,
   plus extra, to serve
125 g (4 ½ oz/½ cup) sugar
2 tablespoons arrowroot

1 Wash the strawberries, place in a bowl and sprinkle the sugar over. Refrigerate for 3 hours, then process in a blender or food processor and strain through a sieve.
2 Dissolve the arrowroot in 350 ml (12 fl oz/1⅓ cups) water by mixing it with 2 or 3 tablespoons of the water and then adding it to the rest. Place the dissolved arrowroot in a saucepan, bring to the boil, stirring, and add the strawberry purée. Bring to the boil again, stirring constantly, until slightly thickened. Pour into serving dishes and set aside for 30 minutes or until cooled and lightly set. Serve with extra strawberries, if desired.

macerated berries with mascarpone

Preparation time: **20 minutes**
Cooking time: **10 minutes**
Serves 4–6

125 g (4½ oz) blackberries
125 g (4½ oz) raspberries
155 g (5½ oz) blueberries
125 g (4½ oz) loganberries or similar
1–2 tablespoons caster (superfine) sugar
2 oranges
2 tablespoons sugar
mascarpone cheese, lightly stirred, to serve

1 Combine all the berries in a bowl, sprinkle the sugar over the top and toss lightly. Cover and refrigerate.

2 Peel the oranges with a vegetable peeler and remove white pith. Cut the zest into fine strips. Bring a small saucepan of water to the boil and blanch the strips, then drain. Repeat twice more to remove any bitterness from the zest.
3 Combine 80 ml (2½ fl oz/⅓ cup) water with the sugar in a small saucepan and stir over low heat until the sugar dissolves. Add the orange zest and simmer gently for 1–2 minutes, or until just tender. Cool.
4 Reserve 1 tablespoon of the orange strips and lightly mix the rest with the cooking syrup and berries.
5 To serve, spoon the berry mixture into serving glasses. Serve with mascarpone and reserved orange zest strips.

macerated berries with mascarpone

making jelly

Jellies don't have to be green and yellow and reminiscent of children's parties. Welcome to grown-up jellies — sparkling, translucent and tangy with fresh fruit.

Gelatin is best known as a setting agent for jellies, but it is also used in just about any dessert that needs to be moulded or turned out, such as light jellies, creamy bavarois or chilled cheesecakes. Gelatin is available as powder and in clear sheets or leaves. As a rule, 6 sheets of gelatin is equal to 3 teaspoons of powdered gelatin or a 10 g (¼ oz) sachet. This is enough to soft-set 500 ml (17 fl oz/2 cups) of liquid. Agar-agar, a vegetarian alternative to gelatin, is found in health food shops — use 1 teaspoon agar-agar to set 250 ml (9 fl oz/1 cup) liquid.

Jellies should be firm enough to hold their shape and be turned out without collapsing but, of course, the whole point of a jelly is that it should wobble! If your jelly is too firm to wobble, it may simply be too cold. Jellies become very firm on chilling and may need to be brought back to room temperature. Gelatin-set dishes do not freeze well and separate when thawed.

fruit jellies

Fruit jellies can be made with a variety of fruits. But some fruits just don't work well in jellies — pineapple, papaya, kiwi fruit and figs all contain enzymes that prevent the jelly setting. Fruit juices and purées can both be set, though juices give clearer, more sparkling jellies.

Cut the fruit into whatever size pieces you think would look best in the jelly. Your spoon should be able to slide through the jelly and cut through the fruit easily, so pieces of fruit that are too big will make it harder to cut and eat if you are making a terrine.

Make up a quantity of jelly using the method that follows. To dissolve powdered gelatin, sprinkle it in an even layer over the surface of a little cold water (about 2 tablespoons) in a small heatproof bowl and leave it to become spongy. For it to dissolve properly, it is important that the gelatin lies on top of the water and not underneath. Put a large saucepan filled with about 4 cm (1½ inches) water on to boil. When it boils, remove from the heat and carefully lower the gelatin bowl into the water (the water should come halfway up the side of the bowl). Stir until the gelatin dissolves, then leave to cool slightly. For leaf gelatin, soak in a large bowl of cold water until floppy, then remove and squeeze out any excess water. It can then be stirred straight into a hot liquid or melted like powdered gelatin. Gelatin sets at 20°C (68°F) so, if you are incorporating melted gelatin into a liquid or purée, make sure the liquid is not too cold or the gelatin will form lumps or strings. Leave the jelly to cool.

Rinse out the mould you are using and shake out the excess water. Make sure the mould is not too big for the jelly or it will be difficult to turn out. Pour a small layer of jelly into the mould and refrigerate until set — this gives a nice shiny surface when the jelly is turned out and ensures the fruit doesn't stick out of the top. Carefully place the fruit in the mould and pour the rest of the jelly over it. Give the mould a sharp tap on the work surface to dislodge any air bubbles, cover and refrigerate until set.

To turn out the jelly, use a wet finger to pull it away from the mould all the way around. Invert onto a plate and give the whole thing a firm shake to break the airlock — you should hear a squelching noise. If this fails, wrap a warm cloth around the mould for a few seconds and try again. If the jelly seems to have melted too much, refrigerate it again until it sets. If you are turning the jelly out onto a plate, remember that unless you wet the plate first, the jelly will stick and you won't be able to move it.

You can, of course, eat jelly out of the dish it is made in. Jellies also look lovely set in wine or champagne glasses.

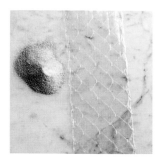

gelatin

Before the invention of commercial, unflavoured gelatin in 1889, using gelatin was rather a palaver. Beef or veal bones, or calves' feet, had to be boiled and the resulting liquid strained and clarified before use. Despite its ease of use now, gelatin still holds a certain mystique, unless it comes in the form of a packet of jelly. It is, however, very easy to use. Six sheets of gelatin is the same as 3 teaspoons of powder or a 10 g (¼ oz) sachet, all of which will set 500 ml (17 fl oz/2 cups) of liquid. If you have a disaster with your jelly and it either sets too solid, has chewy strings through it, or tastes bland, chop it up with a wet knife and fold whipped cream through it—the addition of a liqueur will cover any strong gelatin taste.

striped fruit jelly

❋ ❋ ❋

Preparation time: 35 minutes + chilling time
Cooking time: 30 minutes
Serves 6–8

200 g (7 oz) caster (superfine) sugar
finely grated zest and juice of 2 limes
6 teaspoons powdered gelatin
125 ml (4 fl oz/½ cup) thick (double/heavy) cream
1 tablespoon caster (superfine) sugar, extra
125 g (4½ oz/½ cup) plain yoghurt
415 g (14¾ oz) tin pitted cherries, drained and syrup reserved

1 Stir the sugar with 1¼ cups (310 ml/ 10¾ fl oz) water in a saucepan over low heat until the sugar dissolves. Bring slowly to the boil. Simmer for 15 minutes or until reduced to 200 ml (7 fl oz). Tip half into a jug and reserve. Return the pan to the heat, add the lime zest and juice to the remaining syrup and cook very gently for 5 minutes. Strain into a bowl. Discard the zest. Put 2 tablespoons water in a small heatproof bowl, sprinkle 2 teaspoons gelatin over the surface in an even layer and leave to go spongy. Put a large pan filled with about 4 cm (1½ inches) water on to boil. When it boils, remove from the heat and carefully lower the gelatin bowl into the water (it should come halfway up the side of the bowl), then stir until dissolved. Cool slightly, then add to the lime syrup. Rinse a 750 ml (26 fl oz/3 cup) mould. Pour in the lime syrup and chill until just set. Don't leave too long or the next layer won't stick.
2 Place 2 tablespoons water in a small heatproof bowl, sprinkle on 2 teaspoons gelatin and leave to go spongy. Put cream and extra sugar in a small saucepan and heat slowly, stirring until sugar dissolves. Add to the gelatin mixture and stir until dissolved. Whisk in the yoghurt. Cover and cool in the refrigerator (don't leave it too long or it will set). Pour carefully onto the lime layer, then refrigerate until just set.

3 Place 2 tablespoons of the cherry liquid in a small heatproof bowl, sprinkle on 2 teaspoons gelatin, leave to go spongy, then add to the remaining sugar syrup, which should still be warm. Add to this another 150 ml (5 fl oz) cherry juice, stir to dissolve, cover and cool.

4 When the yoghurt layer sets, spoon in the cherries and pour the cherry juice over them. Refrigerate until set. To unmould, gently pull the jelly away from the sides of the mould with wet fingers and invert onto a plate, shaking to loosen.

orange jellies

Preparation time: **10 minutes + 4 hours chilling time**
Cooking time: **5 minutes**
Serves **6**

750 ml (26 fl oz/3 cups) orange juice
6 teaspoons powdered gelatin
1 tablespoon Grand Marnier (optional)
orange segments, to serve

1 Pour 125 ml (4 fl oz/½ cup) of the juice into a small heatproof bowl, sprinkle the gelatin in an even layer over the surface and leave to go spongy. Put a large saucepan with about 4 cm (1½ inches) water on to boil. When it boils, remove from the heat and lower the gelatin bowl into the water (it should come halfway up the side of the bowl). Stir until dissolved. Cool slightly. Stir into the rest of the juice.

2 Strain the liquid and stir in the liqueur, if desired. Wet six 125 ml (4 fl oz/½ cup) moulds and place on a tray. Fill with the jelly mixture and refrigerate for 4 hours, or until set. Top with orange segments

blackberry jelly

Preparation time: **10 minutes + 4 hours chilling time**
Cooking time: **20 minutes**
Serves **6–8**

orange jellies

300 g (10½ oz) fresh blackberries or frozen, thawed
185 g (6 oz/¾ cup) caster (superfine) sugar
60 ml (2 fl oz/¼ cup) vodka (optional)
3 tablespoons powdered gelatin

1 Place the blackberries with any residual juice, sugar, vodka (if desired) and 1 litre (35 fl oz/4 cups) water in a saucepan. Stir over low heat until the sugar dissolves. Cover and bring to the boil, reduce the heat and simmer for 15 minutes. Uncover and cool for 10 minutes.

2 Place the fruit in a muslin-lined (cheesecloth-lined) sieve and strain into a bowl without pushing any fruit through. Put a little of the juice in a small pan, sprinkle the gelatin in an even layer over the surface, leave to go spongy, then stir over low heat until dissolved. Do not boil. Combine with the remaining juice.

3 Wet a 1.25 litre (44 fl oz/5 cup) jelly mould and pour in the jelly mixture. Refrigerate for 4 hours, or until set.

champagne berry terrine

✳ ✳

Preparation time: 15 minutes + 1 hour
cooling and chilling time
Cooking time: 5 minutes
Serves 4–6

75 g (2½ oz) caster (superfine) sugar
finely grated zest of 1 orange
3 teaspoons powdered gelatin
 or 6 sheets gelatin
625 ml (21½ fl oz/2½ cups) pink Champagne

300 g (10½ oz) mixed berries, fresh or frozen
fresh mixed berries, extra, to serve
cream or ice cream, to serve (optional)

1 Put the sugar and zest in a saucepan with 330 ml (11 fl oz/1⅓ cups) water. Bring to the boil, stirring over low heat until the sugar dissolves. Remove from the heat and leave for 1 hour.

2 Strain the zest out of the syrup. Put 60 ml (2 fl oz/¼ cup) syrup in a small heatproof bowl, sprinkle the gelatin in an even layer over the top and leave to go spongy. Put a large pan filled with about 4 cm (1½ inches) water on to boil. When it boils, remove from the heat and carefully lower the gelatin bowl into the water (it should come halfway up the side of the bowl), then stir until dissolved. (If you want to use sheets of gelatin, follow steps 1 and 2, below left.) Cool slightly, add to the rest of the syrup and mix. Add the Champagne, then pour a little of the jelly into the base of a 1.25 litre (44 fl oz/5 cup) loaf tin and refrigerate until just set. Don't leave too long or the next layer won't stick.

3 Arrange the fruit in the tin, pour in a little more jelly up to the top of the fruit and set in the refrigerator. Add remaining jelly and refrigerate until set completely.

Remove the gelatin when floppy and squeeze out any excess water.

Add the gelatin to the hot sugar syrup and stir until thoroughly dissolved.

Spread the fruit across the top of the set layer of jelly. Pour in more jelly, up to the top of the fruit.

4 To serve, unmould by wiping the tin with a cloth dipped in hot water and inverting the terrine onto a plate. Bring the terrine to room temperature — it should not be stiff and should sag very slightly. Serve with berries and cream or ice cream.

red wine jelly with frosted fruits

✷ ✷

Preparation time: 20 minutes + 3 hours
    chilling time
Cooking time: 5 minutes
Serves 4

600 ml (21 fl oz/2½ cups) quality red wine
finely grated zest of 1 lemon
finely grated zest and juice of 1 orange
2 cinnamon sticks
125 g (4½ oz/½ cup) caster (superfine) sugar
5 teaspoons powdered gelatin
1 egg white
caster (superfine) sugar, for frosting
200 g (7 oz) mixed seedless grapes or
    blackcurrants and redcurrants

1 Combine the wine, zests, cinnamon and sugar in a small saucepan. Heat gently until sugar dissolves. Put the orange juice in a small heatproof bowl, sprinkle the gelatin in an even layer over the surface and leave it to go spongy. Put a large pan filled with about 4 cm (1½ inches) water on to boil. When it boils, remove from the heat and carefully lower the gelatin bowl into the water (which should come halfway up the side of the bowl), then stir until dissolved. Cool slightly.

2 Stir the gelatin into the wine mixture. Pour through a muslin-lined (cheesecloth-lined) strainer into a wetted 1.5 litre (52 fl oz/6 cup) mould. Refrigerate for 3 hours or until set.

3 Whisk the egg white lightly in a bowl. Put the sugar in another bowl. Dip the fruit first into the egg, then into the sugar, shaking off excess. Leave to dry on non-stick paper. Turn out the jelly, cut into squares and serve with the frosted fruit.

grapes

The world's largest fruit crop, grapes are available in many varieties. These include Muscat, both white and black, Flame, a seedless red grape, Sultana, the most widely available variety, and Waltham Cross, with large gold-green oval berries. Grapes should be fully ripe before being picked as they do not sweeten with age. They should not be stored damp as they may go mouldy. They are best refrigerated and should be eaten shortly after purchase.

pancakes

There is something rather special about pouring the batter into the sizzling pan, tilting and tipping, then flipping it high into the air to reveal the crispy, golden underside. The best thing about pancakes is that they're fun — fun to make, fun to toss and fun to eat. Whether it's with a squeeze of fresh lemon and sprinkling of sugar, or drizzled with a rich liqueur sauce, pancakes are a universal treat and we've included all our favourites from the extended family, from delicate lacy crêpes suzette to chunky chocolate waffles, creamy ricotta cheese-filled blintzes and even crunchy golden-fried fruit fritters.

crepes with sugar, lemon and cream

✻ ✻

Preparation time: 10 minutes + 30 minutes
    standing time
Cooking time: 20 minutes
Makes about 14 crepes

125 g (4½ oz/1 cup) plain (all-purpose) flour
1 egg
310 ml (10 ¾ fl oz/1¼ cups) milk

30 g (1 oz) unsalted butter, melted
sugar, lemon juice and thick (double/heavy)
    cream, to serve

1 Sift the flour and a pinch of salt into a large bowl and make a well in the centre. Gradually whisk in the combined egg, milk and melted butter until the batter is smooth. Transfer to a jug for easy pouring, cover and set aside for 30 minutes.
2 Heat a small crepe or non-stick frying pan and brush lightly with melted butter. Pour a little batter into the pan, swirling to thinly cover the base, and pour any excess back into the jug. If the batter is too thick, add 2–3 teaspoons milk. Cook for about 20 seconds, or until the edges just begin to curl, then toss or turn over and lightly brown the other side. Transfer to a plate and cover with a tea towel (dish towel) while cooking the rest, greasing the pan when necessary. Stack the crepes between baking paper.
3 Sprinkle the crepes with sugar and lemon juice and fold into quarters. Put two or three on each plate and top with cream.

Using a wire whisk, mix batter until it is free of lumps.

Cook the first side of the crepe until the edges just begin to curl.

crêpes suzette

✻ ✻

Preparation time: 10 minutes + 30 minutes
    standing time
Cooking time: 45 minutes
Serves 4–6

125 g (4½ oz) unsalted butter
125 g (4½ oz/½ cup) caster (superfine)
    sugar
grated zest of 1 orange
185 ml (6 fl oz/¾ cup) orange juice
80 ml (2½ fl oz/⅓ cup) orange liqueur
2 tablespoons brandy
zest of 1 orange, cut into thin strips

CREPES
250 g (9 oz/2 cups) plain (all-purpose) flour
3 eggs, lightly beaten
200 ml (7 fl oz) milk
50 g (1¾ oz) unsalted butter, melted

1 To make the crepes, sift the flour into a large bowl and make a well in the centre. Gradually whisk in the beaten egg, drawing the flour in from the edges. As the mixture becomes thicker, add the milk combined with 250 ml (9 fl oz/1 cup) water and whisk until smooth. Stir in the melted butter. Transfer to a jug for easy pouring, cover and set aside for 30 minutes.
2 Heat a 20 cm (8 inch) crepe pan or non-stick frying pan and brush lightly with melted butter. Pour in a little batter, swirling to thinly cover the base, and pour any excess back into the jug. Cook until the

edges just begin to curl, then turn and brown the other side. Transfer to a plate and cover with a tea towel (dish towel) while cooking the rest, greasing the pan when necessary. Stack the crepes between baking paper.

3 Put the butter, sugar, orange zest, juice and liqueur in a large frying pan and simmer for 2 minutes. Add the crepes one at a time to the pan, adding each one flat and then folding into quarters and pushing to one side.

4 Pour the brandy over the crepes and with care, ignite the crepes, either with a gas flame or a match. (Keep a lid large enough to cover the pan beside you in case you need to smother the flame.) Serve on warmed plates with the orange zest scattered over the top.

pancakes with lemon syrup pears

❋ ❋

Preparation time: 40 minutes + 30 minutes standing time
Cooking time: 1 hour 10 minutes
Serves 6

125 g (4½ oz/1 cup) plain (all-purpose) flour
85 g (3 oz/⅔ cup) self-raising flour
2 tablespoons caster (superfine) sugar
3 eggs, lightly beaten
375 ml (13 fl oz/1½ cups) milk
60 g (2¼ oz) unsalted butter, melted

LEMON SYRUP PEARS
5 firm ripe pears, such as beurre bosc
1 lemon
185 g (6½ oz/¾ cup) caster (superfine) sugar
2 tablespoons honey
125 ml (4 fl oz/½ cup) lemon juice
250 g (9 oz/1 cup) sour cream

1 Sift flours into a large bowl, add the sugar, make a well in the centre and whisk in the combined eggs, milk and butter until smooth. Transfer to a jug for easy pouring, cover and set aside for 30 minutes.

2 To make the lemon syrup pears, peel, halve and core the pears, then cut into wedges. Peel the lemon and cut the zest into thin strips. Combine the sugar, honey and 375 ml (13 fl oz/1½ cups) water in a pan, stirring over low heat until the sugar dissolves. Add the lemon juice, bring to the boil, reduce the heat and simmer for 8 minutes. Skim any froth, add the pears and simmer for another 5 minutes, or until just tender. Remove from the heat, stir in the lemon zest and leave to cool slightly.

3 Pour 60 ml (2 fl oz/¼ cup) pancake batter into a lightly greased 20 cm (8 inch) non-stick frying pan and cook over medium heat for 2 minutes each side. Transfer to a plate and cover with a tea towel (dish towel) while cooking the rest, greasing the pan when necessary. Stack the pancakes between baking paper. Strain 125 ml (4 fl oz/½ cup) of the lemon syrup and mix with the sour cream to make a sauce. Drain the pears to serve. Decorate with strips of zest.

NOTE: Poached pears can be left in the syrup, covered in the refrigerator, for up to two days. Reheat to serve.

hints and tips

crepe pans The classic French pôele or crepe pan is the best pan for the job. It is available in several sizes and is inexpensive to buy. You will not need to wash it after use—just wipe it clean with a damp cloth. Non-stick pans also work well but tend not to brown the crepes as well. Season your pan by heating vegetable oil and coarse salt until smoking, and then wiping it out.

making crepes Whisk the liquid into the flour, rather than beating it in with a spoon. If you do this, the batter will amalgamate more quickly with less lumps. Beating out lumps with a spoon will develop the gluten in the flour and result in a tough batter.

Prepare crepe batter in advance and allow to stand before cooking. This makes the batter lighter by letting the starch in the flour expand and the gluten relax.

The first crepe is often a disaster so don't despair, just throw it away. Adjust the batter if it is too thick by adding a little water until you have the right consistency. Be careful as it is much easier to thin batter than thicken it.

coconut pancakes with palm sugar syrup

✳ ✳

Preparation time: 40 minutes + 30 minutes standing time
Cooking time: 45 minutes
Serves 6

125 g (4½ oz/1 cup) plain (all-purpose) flour
1 egg
250 ml (9 fl oz/1 cup) coconut cream
mango and pineapple slices, to serve

SHREDDED COCONUT FILLING
185 g (6½ oz) palm sugar (jaggery), roughly chopped
120 g (4¼ oz/2 cups) shredded coconut
125 ml (4 fl oz/½ cup) coconut cream

1 To make the shredded coconut filling, stir the sugar with 375 ml (13 fl oz/1½ cups) water in a small heavy-based saucepan over low heat until the sugar dissolves, then simmer for 15 minutes to make a syrup. Place the coconut in a bowl with 170 ml (5½ fl oz/⅔ cup) of the syrup and the coconut cream and stir to combine. Return the pan with the remaining palm sugar syrup to the heat and simmer for 15 minutes, or until reduced to a thick, sticky syrup.
2 Mix the flour, egg, coconut cream and 125 ml (4 fl oz/½ cup) water until smooth. Transfer to a jug for easy pouring, cover and set aside for 30 minutes.
3 Heat a small crepe or non-stick frying pan and brush lightly with melted butter. Pour a little batter into the pan, swirling, to thinly cover the base, then pour off any excess. Cook for about 20 seconds, or until the edges just begin to curl, then turn over and cook the other side. Transfer to a plate and cover with a tea towel (dish towel) while cooking the rest, greasing the pan when necessary. Stack the pancakes between baking paper.
4 Place 1 tablespoon of shredded coconut filling in the centre of each pancake. Roll

each pancake up firmly, folding in the ends to form a parcel. Serve with mango and pineapple slices and drizzle with the remaining palm sugar syrup.

ricotta crepes with orange sauce

✳ ✳

Preparation time: 40 minutes + 30 minutes
  standing time
Cooking time: 30 minutes
Serves 4

85 g (3 oz/⅔ cup) plain (all-purpose) flour
pinch of salt
1 egg, lightly beaten
350 ml (12 fl oz/1⅓ cups) milk
30 g (1 oz) sultanas (golden raisins)
250 ml (9 fl oz/1 cup) orange juice
200 g (7 oz) ricotta cheese
1 teaspoon finely grated orange zest
¼ teaspoon natural vanilla extract
poached orange segments, to serve

ORANGE SAUCE
50 g (1¾ oz) unsalted butter
60 g (2¼ oz/¼ cup) caster (superfine) sugar

1 Sift the flour and salt into a bowl. Make a well and gradually whisk in the combined egg and milk until the batter is smooth. Transfer to a jug for easy pouring, cover and set aside for 30 minutes.
2 Heat a small crepe or non-stick frying pan and brush lightly with melted butter. Pour a little batter into the pan, swirling to make a 16 cm (6¼ inch) round. Pour any excess back into the jug. Cook over medium heat for 1–2 minutes, or until the underside is golden. Turn and cook the other side for 30 seconds, or until the edges just begin to curl. Transfer to a plate while cooking the rest, greasing the pan when necessary. Stack the crepes between baking paper. Preheat the oven to 160°C (315°F/Gas 2–3).
3 Meanwhile, put the sultanas in a bowl, cover with orange juice and soak

for 15 minutes. Drain, reserving the juice. Mix together the ricotta, zest, vanilla and sultanas. Place a large tablespoon of mixture at the edge of each crepe, fold in half and then half again. Put the filled crepes in an ovenproof dish and bake for 10 minutes.
4 To make the orange sauce, melt the butter and sugar in a small pan over low heat. Add the reserved juice and stir over low heat until the sugar dissolves.

Bring to the boil, reduce the heat and simmer for 10 minutes to thicken. Cool for 3–4 minutes, then pour over the filled crepes. Serve immediately with poached orange segments.

NOTE: Crepes can be cooked in advance and frozen. Defrost, fill and heat close to serving time.

deep-fried fruit with golden nut sauce

✳ ✳

Preparation time: 55 minutes + 2 hours
    chilling time
Cooking time: 30 minutes
Serves 6

215 g (7½ oz/1¾ cups) plain (all-purpose)
    flour, sifted
2½ teaspoons baking powder
2 tablespoons oil
2 tablespoons caster (superfine) sugar
2 eggs, separated
oil, for deep-frying
800 g (1 lb 12 oz) fresh fruit, such as pitted
    cherries, pineapple pieces, banana pieces,
    apple wedges and pear wedges
vanilla ice cream, to serve

GOLDEN NUT SAUCE
125 g (4½ oz) unsalted butter
230 g (8½ oz/1¼ cups) soft brown sugar
125 ml (4 fl oz/½ cup) thick
    (double/heavy) cream
2 teaspoons lemon juice
2 tablespoons chopped roasted macadamias

1 Sift the flour and baking powder into a large bowl and make a well in the centre. Add the oil, sugar, egg yolks and 250 ml (9 fl oz/1 cup) warm water. Whisk until smooth, cover and refrigerate for 2 hours. (You will add the egg white later.)
2 To make the golden nut sauce, melt the butter in a small saucepan over low heat. Add the sugar and stir until dissolved. Add the cream and lemon juice. Bring to the boil, stirring. Add the nuts. Keep warm.
3 Whisk the egg whites until stiff peaks form and fold into the batter. Heat the oil in a large heavy-based pan or deep-fryer to 180°C (350°F), or until a cube of bread browns in 15 seconds. Turn the heat down. Dip the fruit in the batter, shaking off any excess. Deep-fry in small batches, draining on paper towels. Serve immediately, with the golden nut sauce and ice cream.

macadamia nuts

Macadamia nuts, an Australian indigenous food, are grown commercially. Macadamia trees were also exported to Hawaii as shade trees and the nuts are known in America as Hawaiian nuts. They were part of the Aboriginal diet for thousands of years and have a very high protein content.

They are spherical, waxy, creamy-flavoured nuts within a very hard shell that has to be cracked with special equipment. Roasting them brings out the flavour. In Hawaii, macadamia nuts are used in everything from confectionery to biscuits, cakes and jams.

dates

Dates have been an important part of the diet of Arab, Middle Eastern and North African countries for thousands of years. They are always used to break the daily fast during Ramadan. Fresh dates are often frozen when they are imported. Their high sugar content makes them easy to freeze and defrost. They are best eaten at room temperature and do not usually need to be refrigerated. Semi-dried dates have a darker skin than fresh dates, and have a more concentrated sweetness, making them excellent in baked goods and desserts. Choose plump, soft dates when buying. There are many varieties and they are used in desserts such as baked puddings and fruit salads.

date pancakes with caramel sauce

Preparation time: 40 minutes
Cooking time: 30 minutes
Serves 4

185 g (6½ oz) pitted dates, chopped
1 teaspoon bicarbonate of soda (baking soda)
250 g (9 oz/2 cups) self-raising flour, sifted
95 g (3¼ oz/½ cup) soft brown sugar
250 g (9 oz/1 cup) sour cream
3 eggs, separated
vanilla ice cream, to serve

CARAMEL SAUCE
185 g (6½ oz/1 cup) soft brown sugar
250 ml (9 fl oz/1 cup) pouring (whipping) cream
200 g (7 oz) unsalted butter

1 Put the dates with 250 ml (9 fl oz/ 1 cup) water in a small saucepan. Bring to the boil. Remove from the heat, stir in the bicarbonate of soda and cool for 5 minutes. Purée in a food processor. Cool.
2 Mix the flour and sugar in a bowl. Stir in the date purée. Make a well in the centre.
3 Whisk the sour cream and egg yolks and pour into the well, stirring until the batter is just smooth. Set aside for 15 minutes. Beat the egg whites in a clean, dry bowl until soft peaks form. Stir a heaped tablespoon of egg white into the batter, then fold in the rest until just combined.
4 Heat a frying pan and brush lightly with melted butter or oil. Pour 60 ml (2 fl oz/¼ cup) batter into the pan. Cook for 2–3 minutes, or until bubbles form on the surface. Turn over and cook the other side. Transfer to a plate and cover with a tea towel (dish towel) while cooking the rest, greasing the pan when necessary. Stack the pancakes between baking paper.
5 To make the sauce, stir all ingredients in a pan, without boiling, until dissolved. Simmer gently for 3–4 minutes. Serve over the pancakes, with ice cream.

sugar

From the natural soft brown sugars with a lingering taste of sugar cane, to the pure white crystals that give us instant energy, sugars are the foundation of all desserts.

Sugar is produced from sugar cane, sugar beet, palm trees, maple trees and sorghum. Sugar is sucrose, a pure carbohydrate that adds sweetness to dishes, and is either white or brown, refined or unrefined. Sugar cane is harvested and crushed to extract its juice. The juice is purified and any excess water evaporated off to leave a type of molasses. This is 'seeded' with sugar crystals — the crystals are planted in the molasses to grow into bigger crystals. When they reach the required size, the crystals are extracted from the molasses. At this stage, they are golden brown and contain some molasses and impurities. Unrefined sugar is part-purified and contains some molasses. Refined sugar has all impurities removed and is separated from its molasses.

white sugar is bleached in the refining process. It is refined sugar that has been graded (granulated), which has no colour or flavour except for sweetness. It is used for caramel, in drinks and for cakes, puddings, biscuits and jams. Use it when a recipe requires 'sugar'.

caster (superfine) sugar is white sugar with very small crystals, which dissolves easily and has no colour and flavour other than sweetness. It is used in meringues and baking, and is often used instead of granulated sugar.

icing (confectioners') sugar is white sugar crushed to a fine powder. Pure icing sugar has no additives and dissolves easily. Icing sugar mixture contains starch to prevent lumps.

muscovado sugar (dark and light) has small crystals and a rich flavour. Light muscovado has a fudge-like taste; dark is richer. Molasses coats each crystal, making it a moist soft sugar.

raw sugar is a natural, golden sugar with a distinctive raw flavour. It can be used in the same way as white sugar.

raw (demerara) sugar has a rich caramel taste, is less refined than white sugars and contains a little molasses.

soft brown sugar has a caramel flavour and a light or dark-coloured fine grain.

dark brown sugar is a richer, moister sugar with a molasses flavour.

sugar cubes are granulated sugar compressed into cubes.

coffee sugar has large crunchy, golden crystals. Sprinkle on crumble as topping.

molasses sugar is almost black and has a strong flavour, which adds richness.

palm sugar (jaggery) is made from the boiled sap of palm trees. It has a fine texture and is usually sold in jars or set into solid lumps that must be grated or crushed before use. It has a fudgy flavour and is slightly less sweet than cane sugar.

golden syrup contains sucrose, glucose and fructose that is manufactured from the syrup left after white sugar is extracted.

treacle is produced in the same way as golden syrup but with its original colour and a strong flavour. It adds colour and rich flavour to puddings and cakes.

grating coconut

To make grated fresh coconut, gently prise the flesh away from the shell using a flat-bladed knife. Use a vegetable peeler to remove the tough skin and then grate the flesh or use the vegetable peeler to flake it. Roast in a slow oven for 10–15 minutes to dry out before using.

banana fritters in coconut batter

Preparation time: 15 minutes + 1 hour resting time
Cooking time: 20 minutes
Serves 6

100 g (3½ oz) glutinous rice flour
100 g (3½ oz) freshly grated coconut or 60 g (2¼ oz/⅔ cup) desiccated coconut
55 g (2 oz/¼ cup) sugar
1 tablespoon sesame seeds
60 ml (2 fl oz/¼ cup) coconut milk
6 sugar bananas

oil, for deep-frying
vanilla ice cream, to serve
sesame seeds, toasted, extra, to decorate

1 Combine the flour, coconut, sugar, sesame seeds, coconut milk and 60 ml (2 fl oz/¼ cup) water in a large bowl. Whisk to a smooth batter, adding more water if the batter is too thick. Set aside to rest for 1 hour.
2 Peel the bananas and cut in half lengthways (cut each portion in half again crossways if the bananas are large).
3 Fill a wok or large heavy-based saucepan one-third full of oil and heat to 180ºC (350ºF), or until a cube of bread dropped into the oil browns in

15 seconds. Dip each piece of banana into the batter then drop gently into the hot oil. Cook in batches for 4–6 minutes, or until golden brown all over. Remove with a slotted spoon and drain on crumpled paper towels. Serve hot with ice cream and a sprinkling of toasted sesame seeds.

crepe ribbons with zesty lemon sauce

✳ ✳

Preparation time: 15 minutes + 30 minutes standing time
Cooking time: 30–40 minutes
Serves 4–6

155 g (5½ oz/1¼ cups) plain (all-purpose) flour
3 eggs, beaten
500 ml/17 fl oz/2 cups) milk
20 g (¾ oz) unsalted butter, melted
oil, for shallow-frying
icing (confectioners') sugar, to dust
fruit and cream, to serve

ZESTY LEMON SAUCE
125 ml (4 fl oz/½ cup) lemon juice
1 tablespoon finely grated lemon zest
80 g (2¾ oz) unsalted butter
125 g (4½ oz/½ cup) caster (superfine) sugar

1 Sift the flour and a pinch of salt into a large bowl and make a well in the centre. Gradually whisk in the combined egg and milk until smooth. Stir in the melted butter. Transfer the batter to a jug for easy pouring, cover and set aside for 30 minutes.
2 Heat a small crepe or non-stick frying pan and brush lightly with melted butter. Pour a little batter into the pan, swirling to thinly cover the base, then pour any excess back into the jug. Cook gently for 20 seconds, or until the edges just begin to curl, then turn over and cook the other side. Transfer to a plate and cover with a tea towel (dish towel)

while cooking the rest, greasing the pan when necessary.
3 To make the zesty lemon sauce, combine the lemon juice, zest, butter and sugar in a small saucepan. Bring to the boil, reduce the heat and simmer until the liquid becomes syrupy. Keep warm until ready to serve.
4 Cut the cold crepes into ribbons about 2 cm (¾ inch) wide. Heat the oil in a large frying pan and cook the ribbons in batches until crisp. Drain on paper towels. Pile up the ribbons onto individual serving plates, pour the sauce over and dust with icing sugar. Serve with fruit and cream.

NOTE: Crepes and sauce can both be made in advance. Fry the ribbons just before serving.

coconut and banana pancakes

✳ ✳

Preparation time: 20 minutes
Cooking time: 30 minutes
Serves 4–6

40 g (1¼ oz/⅓ cup) plain (all-purpose) flour
2 tablespoons rice flour
60 g (2¼ oz/¼ cup) caster (superfine) sugar
25 g (1 oz/¼ cup) desiccated coconut
250 ml (9 fl oz/1 cup) coconut milk
1 egg, lightly beaten
4 large bananas
60 g (2¼ oz) unsalted butter

60 g (2¼ oz/⅓ cup) soft brown sugar
80 ml (2½ fl oz/⅓ cup) lime juice
1 tablespoon shredded toasted coconut, to serve
strips of lime zest, to serve

1 Sift the flours into a bowl. Add the sugar and coconut, mix through and make a well in the centre. Gradually whisk in the combined coconut milk and egg and mix until smooth.
2 Heat a small crepe or non-stick frying pan and brush lightly with melted butter. Pour 80 ml (2½ fl oz/⅓ cup) of the pancake mixture into the pan and cook over medium heat until the underside is golden. Turn the pancake over and cook the other side. Transfer to a plate and cover with a tea towel (dish towel) while cooking the rest, greasing the pan when necessary. Stack the pancakes between baking paper. Keep the pancakes warm while preparing the bananas.
3 Cut the bananas diagonally into thick slices. Heat the butter in the pan, add the bananas and toss until coated. Cook over medium heat until the bananas start to soften and brown. Sprinkle with the brown sugar and shake the pan gently until the sugar melts. Stir in the lime juice. Divide the bananas among the pancakes and fold over to enclose. Sprinkle with toasted coconut and strips of lime zest.

NOTE: These pancakes are quite delicate so it may be easier to turn them over if you slide each one out onto a plate and then invert it back into the frying pan.

bananas

Native to Southeast Asia, bananas are now grown in many other places that have a warm climate. There are many varieties but the most common are Cavendish and Lady Finger. Bananas can be purchased green and will slowly ripen. If you need to hurry up the ripening process, place the green bananas in a brown paper bag with a ripe banana or apple. For baking purposes a very ripe, or even an over-ripe banana, is very useful. An over-ripe banana adds an intense banana flavour to baked cakes, muffins and ice cream.

amaretti apple stack with caramel sauce

✸ ✸

Preparation time: 20 minutes + 30 minutes
 standing time
Cooking time: 1 hour
Serves 4–6

125 g (4½ oz/1 cup) plain (all-purpose) flour
2 eggs
250 ml (9 fl oz/1 cup) milk
30 g (1 oz) unsalted butter, melted
1 tablespoon Amaretto liqueur (optional)
125 g (4½ oz) amaretti biscuits
5 cooking apples, peeled and cored
185 g (6½ oz) unsalted butter
185 g (6½ oz/1 cup) soft brown sugar
175 g (6 oz/½ cup) golden syrup
125 ml (4 fl oz/½ cup) pouring
 (whipping) cream
185 g (6½ oz/ ¾ cup) light sour cream

1 Sift the flour into a large bowl and
make a well. Gradually whisk in the
combined eggs and milk until the batter is
smooth. Stir in the butter and Amaretto.
Transfer to a jug, cover and set aside for
30 minutes. Heat a small crepe or
non-stick frying pan and brush lightly
with melted butter. Pour a little batter into
the pan, swirling quickly, to thinly cover
the base, pouring any excess back into the
jug. Cook for 30 seconds, or until the
edges just begin to curl, then turn and
cook the other side until lightly browned.
Transfer to a plate and cover with a tea
towel (dish towel). Repeat with the
remaining batter to make 10 crepes,
greasing the pan when necessary. Stack
the crepes between baking paper.
2 Preheat the oven to 180ºC (350ºF/
Gas 4). Roughly chop the biscuits in a
food processor. Place on a baking tray and
bake for 5–8 minutes, stirring
occasionally, until crisp. Cut the apples
into very thin slices and mix in a bowl
with 60 g (2¼ oz) of the butter, melted,
and half the brown sugar. Spread evenly
onto a tray and place under a moderate

amaretti biscuits

Amaretti are small, macaroon-
type biscuits from Italy.
Amaretti di Saronno, the most
well known, are flavoured with
bitter almonds and often come
as two biscuits wrapped in
coloured paper, which is
twisted at the ends like a
giant sweet. Amaretti are
usually eaten with dessert
wine or coffee, or crushed and
added to desserts.

grill (broiler) for 5 minutes. Turn and grill (broil) until light brown and soft (you may need to do this in batches). Set aside.

3 Put a crepe on a large heatproof plate. Spread evenly with some apple, slightly mounded in the middle, and sprinkle with chopped biscuits. Continue to fill and layer until all the crepes are stacked. Cover with foil and heat in the oven for 10 minutes, or until warm.

4 Put the remaining brown sugar, golden syrup, cream and remaining butter in a small saucepan. Stir over low heat until the sugar dissolves, then simmer for 1 minute. Pour a little warm sauce over the stack, cut into wedges and serve with the sour cream.

waffles with hot chocolate sauce

✳

Preparation time: **20 minutes**
Cooking time: **25 minutes**
Serves **8**

250 g (9 oz/2 cups) self-raising flour
1 teaspoon bicarbonate of soda
   (baking soda)
2 teaspoons sugar
2 eggs, at room temperature
90 g (3¼ oz) unsalted butter, melted
435 ml (15¼ fl oz/1¾ cups) buttermilk
vanilla ice cream, to serve

HOT CHOCOLATE SAUCE
50 g (1¾ oz) unsalted butter
200 g (7 oz/1⅓ cups) chopped
   dark chocolate
125 ml (4 fl oz/½ cup) pouring
   (whipping) cream
1 tablespoon golden syrup

1 Sift the flour, bicarbonate of soda, sugar and a pinch of salt into a large bowl and make a well in the centre. Whisk the eggs, melted butter and the buttermilk in a jug and gradually pour into the well, whisking until the batter is just smooth. Set aside for 10 minutes. Preheat a waffle iron.

2 To make the chocolate sauce, put the butter, chopped chocolate, cream and golden syrup in a saucepan and stir over low heat until smooth. Remove from the heat and keep warm.

3 Grease the waffle iron. Pour 125 ml (4 fl oz/½ cup) batter into the centre and spread almost to the corners of the grid. Cook for 2 minutes, or until golden and crisp. Serve with the warm chocolate sauce and ice cream.

waffles

Waffles are pancakes made from batter, with deep indentations on both sides, formed by baking between hinged irons, which give the waffles a honeycomb effect. Belgian waffles are thicker and fluffier with deeper pockets in their surface. Waffle irons can either be electric or stovetop and, except on older models, usually have non-stick surfaces.

ricotta blintzes

Preparation time: 30 minutes + 30 minutes
  standing time
Cooking time: 30–40 minutes
Makes about 14

125 g (4½ oz/1 cup) plain (all-purpose) flour
2 eggs
310 ml (10¾ fl oz/1¼ cups) milk
30 g (1 oz) unsalted butter, melted

RICOTTA FILLING
60 g (2¼ oz) raisins
1 tablespoon Grand Marnier or
  Cointreau (optional)
375 g (13 oz) ricotta cheese
90 g (3¼ oz/⅓ cup) caster (superfine) sugar
1 tablespoon finely grated lemon zest
2 tablespoons lemon juice
20 g (1 oz) unsalted butter, melted
icing (confectioners') sugar, to dust

1 Sift the flour into a large bowl and make a well in the centre. Gradually whisk in the combined eggs and milk until the batter is smooth. Stir in the melted butter. Transfer to a jug, cover and set aside for 30 minutes.
2 Heat a crepe pan or small non-stick frying pan and brush lightly with melted butter. Pour enough batter into the pan, swirling quickly, to thinly cover the base. Pour any excess back into the jug. Cook for 30 seconds, or until golden brown and completely set on the top surface. Remove and cover with a tea towel (dish towel) while cooking the rest, greasing the pan when necessary. Stack the crepes between baking paper.

3 To make the ricotta filling, put the raisins in a bowl, mix with the liqueur, if desired, then set aside for 30 minutes. Beat the ricotta, sugar, zest and juice for 1–2 minutes, or until smooth. Stir in the raisins and liqueur.
4 Preheat the oven to 160°C (315°F/Gas 2–3). Place a heaped tablespoon of filling on the centre of each crepe, then fold into a flat parcel. Place the filled crepes, fold-side-down, in a greased ovenproof dish in a single layer. Brush each crepe lightly with the melted butter. Cover with foil and bake for about 10–15 minutes, or until hot. Serve dusted with icing sugar.

chocolate chip pancakes with hot fudge sauce

Preparation time: 50 minutes
Cooking time: 30 minutes
Serves 4–6

250 g (9 oz/2 cups) self-raising flour
2 tablespoons unsweetened cocoa powder
1 teaspoon bicarbonate of soda (baking soda)
55 g (2 oz/¼ cup) caster (superfine) sugar
130 g (4½ oz/¾ cup) dark chocolate chips
250 ml (9 fl oz/1 cup) milk
250 ml (9 fl oz/1 cup) pouring (whipping)
  cream
2 eggs, at room temperature, lightly beaten
30 g (1 oz) unsalted butter, melted
3 egg whites, at room temperature
icing (confectioners') sugar, to dust
whipped cream or ice cream, to serve

HOT FUDGE SAUCE
150 g (5½ oz/1 cup) chopped dark chocolate
30 g (1 oz) unsalted butter
2 tablespoons light corn syrup
95 g (3¼ oz/½ cup) soft brown sugar
125 ml (4 fl oz/½ cup) pouring (whipping)
  cream

1 Sift the flour, cocoa and bicarbonate of soda into a large bowl. Stir in the sugar and choc chips and make a well in the centre. Whisk together the milk, cream, 2 eggs and melted butter in a jug, then gradually pour into the well and whisk until just combined. Cover and set aside for 15 minutes.
2 Whisk the 3 egg whites in a clean dry bowl until soft peaks form. Use a large metal spoon to stir a heaped tablespoon of the beaten egg white into the batter to loosen it up, then lightly fold in the remaining egg white until just combined.
3 Heat a frying pan and brush lightly with melted butter or oil. Pour 60 ml (2 fl oz/¼ cup) batter into the pan and cook over medium heat until the underside is browned. Flip or turn the pancake over with a spatula and cook the other side. Transfer to a plate and cover with a tea towel (dish towel) while cooking the rest, greasing the pan when necessary. Stack the pancakes between baking paper.
4 To make the hot fudge sauce, put all the ingredients in a saucepan and stir over low heat until melted and smooth.
5 Dust the warm pancakes with icing sugar and serve with the cream or ice cream and drizzled with hot fudge sauce.

pancakes

Pancakes are thicker and more substantial than delicate crepes. Some are yeasted to help them rise, others have raising agents such as bicarbonate of soda (baking soda). Pancake batter should be left to rest, like crepe batter, to lighten it. Cook pancakes on a griddle or in a heavy-based pan. They need an even heat or they may burn before they are cooked through. When cooking pancakes, wait until a few bubbles break through the top surface before turning them over. If it is still too runny, when you flip it over the inside will leak out and spoil the even shape. Pancakes should be fluffy inside and eaten immediately. Unlike crepes, they do not benefit from keeping.

pastries

Perfect pastry is one of the hallmarks of a great cook. Pastry making has a reputation as elusive, moody, even downright difficult, but once you've mastered a few commonsense rules you'll probably find it all rather easy. Whether it is puff, shortcrust, choux or filo, beautiful pastry with a light buttery touch can raise any dish to sublime heights, so it is not surprising that almost every country in the world has its own traditional recipe — pecan pie, apple pie, cherry strudel, treacle tart, pithivier ... A chapter on pastries really is a mouthwatering journey of culinary exploration.

puff pastry

Puff pastry is made by layering dough with butter and folding to create hundreds of layers. When cooked, the butter melts and the dough produces steam, forcing the layers apart and making the pastry rise to great heights.

For perfect puff pastry that rises evenly, the edges must be cut cleanly with a sharp knife or cutter, not torn. Egg glazes give shine but apply them carefully — any drips down the side may glue the layers together and stop them rising evenly. The pastry should be chilled for at least 30 minutes before baking to relax it.

Always bake puff pastry at a very high temperature. It should rise evenly so, if your oven has areas of uneven heat, turn the pastry around when it has set. If you have an oven with a bottom element, cook your pastry on the bottom shelf. When puff pastry is cooked, the top and base should be browned and crisp, and the layers should be visible. Puff pastry is not always perfect — it may fall over or not rise to quite the heights you had imagined — but provided you don't burn it and it is well cooked it will still be delicious.

making puff pastry

We've given a range of fat quantities — if you've never made puff pastry before, you'll find it easier to use the lesser amount. This recipe makes about 500 g (1 lb 2 oz) pastry. You will need 200–250 g (7–9 oz) unsalted butter, 250 g (9 oz/2 cups) plain (all-purpose) flour, ½ teaspoon salt and 170 ml (5½ fl oz/⅔ cup) chilled water.

1 Melt 30 g (1 oz) butter in a saucepan. Sift the flour and salt onto a work surface and make a well in the centre. Add the butter and water to the centre and blend with your fingertips, gradually drawing in the flour. You should end up with a crumb mixture. If it seems a little dry, add extra drops of water before bringing it all together to form a dough.

2 Cut the dough with a pastry scraper, using a downward cutting action, then turn the dough and repeat in the opposite direction.

The dough should now come together to form a soft ball. Score a cross in the top, wrap and refrigerate for 15–20 minutes.

3 Soften the remaining butter by pounding it between 2 sheets of baking paper with a rolling pin. Then, still between the sheets of baking paper, roll it into a 10 cm (4 inch) square. The butter must be the same consistency as the dough or they will not roll out the same amount and the layers will not be even. If the butter is too soft, it will squeeze out of the sides; too hard and it will break through the dough and disturb the layers.

4 Put the pastry on a well-floured surface. Roll it out to form a cross, leaving the centre slightly thicker than the arms. Place the butter in the centre of the cross and fold over each of the arms to make a parcel. Turn the dough so that it looks like a book with the hinge side to the left. Tap and roll out the dough to form a 15 x 45 cm (6 x 18 inch) rectangle. Make this as neat as possible, squaring off the corners, otherwise the layers will not be even.

5 Fold the dough like a letter, the top third down and the bottom third up, to form another square, brushing off any excess flour between the layers. Turn the dough 90 degrees to bring the hinge side to your left and press the seam sides down with the rolling pin to seal them. Re-roll and fold as before to complete two turns and mark the dough by gently pressing into the corner with your fingertip for each turn — this will remind you where you're up to. Wrap the dough and chill again.

6 Re-roll and fold twice more and then chill, and then again to complete six turns. If it is a very hot day, you may need to chill between each turn. The pastry should now be an even yellow and is ready to use. If it looks a little streaky, roll and fold once more. Refrigerate until required.

lemon brûlée tarts

☀ ☀

Preparation time: 40 minutes + 2 hours
    chilling time
Cooking time: 35 minutes
Serves 4

310 ml (10¾ fl oz/1¼ cups) pouring
    (whipping) cream
2 teaspoons finely grated lemon zest
4 egg yolks
2 tablespoons caster (superfine) sugar
2 teaspoons cornflour (cornstarch)
2 tablespoons lemon juice

410 g (14½ oz) block puff pastry or
    2 sheets ready-rolled
80 g (2¾ oz/⅓ cup) sugar

1 Heat the cream in a saucepan with the lemon zest until almost boiling. Allow to cool slightly. Whisk the egg yolks, sugar, cornflour and lemon juice in a bowl until thick and pale.

2 Add the cream gradually, whisking constantly. Strain into a clean saucepan and stir over low heat until thickened slightly—the mixture should coat the back of a wooden spoon. Pour into a heatproof bowl, cover with plastic wrap and refrigerate for 2 hours or overnight.

3 Preheat the oven to 210°C (415°F/ Gas 6–7). Lightly grease four 12 cm (4½ inch) shallow loose-based flan (tart) tins. If using block pastry, roll it to 25 x 48 cm (10 x 19 inches) on a lightly floured surface, then cut four rounds, large enough to fit the base and side of the tins. If using sheets, cut two rounds of pastry from each sheet to line the tins. Line each tin with pastry, trim the edges and prick the bases lightly with a fork. Line with baking paper and spread a layer of baking beads or uncooked rice evenly over the paper. Bake for 15 minutes, remove the paper and beads and bake for another 5 minutes, or until lightly golden. Leave to cool.

4 Spoon the lemon custard into each pastry shell, smooth the top, leaving a little room for the sugar layer. Cover the edges of the pastry with foil and sprinkle the sugar generously over the surface of the custard in an even layer. Cook under a preheated high grill (broiler) until the sugar just begins to colour. Put the tarts close to the grill so they brown quickly, but watch carefully that they do not burn. Serve immediately.

individual pithiviers

✳ ✳

Preparation time: 40 minutes
Cooking time: 25 minutes
Serves 8

60 g (2¼ oz) unsalted butter
60 g (2¼ oz/¼ cup) sugar
1 egg
95 g (3¼ oz/⅔ cup) ground almonds
1 tablespoon plain (all-purpose) flour
2 teaspoons finely grated orange zest
1 tablespoon Cointreau
375 g (13 oz) block puff pastry
1 egg, lightly beaten
thick (double/heavy) cream, to serve

1 Preheat the oven to 210°C (415°F/ Gas 6–7). Grease two baking trays and line with baking paper. Use electric beaters to beat the butter and sugar until light and creamy. Add the egg and beat until well combined. Stir in the ground almonds, flour, orange zest and Cointreau. Cover and refrigerate.
2 Cut the block of puff pastry in half. On a lightly floured surface, roll one half out to a large enough rectangle to cut out eight 10 cm (4 inch) rounds. Carefully transfer to baking trays. Use a smaller round cutter to mark a 7 cm (2¾ inch) impression in the middle of each circle. Divide the nut cream among the pastry circles, spreading evenly inside the marked impression. Brush the edges with beaten egg.
3 Roll out the remaining puff pastry. Use the cutter to cut out eight more 10 cm (4 inch) circles and place over the top of the filling, pressing the edges to seal. Brush the tops with beaten egg, being careful not to let any drip down the side, as this will prevent the pastry rising. Use the tip of a small knife to score a spiral pattern on the top of each pithivier. Bake for 20–25 minutes, or until puffed and golden. Serve with a drizzle of cream.

NOTE: You can use 4 sheets ready-rolled puff pastry instead of the block, if desired.

pithivier

Pithivier is named after the French town, Pithiviers, in the Loire Valley, where the pastry is traditionally served on Twelfth Night and is known as Galette des Rois. This delicious dessert consists of two circles of puff pastry enclosing a frangipan filling. The top is decorated with a rosette pattern and the edges are usually scalloped. The Galette des Rois version usually contains a bean that brings good luck to the person who finds it in their slice.

Use the tip of a small knife to score a spiral pattern on the top of each pithivier.

puff pastry

Commercially made puff pastry can be bought in different forms. Blocks of puff pastry are available frozen or fresh and sheets are available frozen flat or as a roll, sometimes fresh. You do not need to roll out sheets of puff but they benefit from having their edges trimmed. Commercial puff pastries use vegetable or canola (rapeseed) oil or butter as their fat. If you are using a pastry with vegetable fat as its base, you can add a buttery flavour by brushing the pastry with melted butter and chilling it before glazing.

jalousie

☀ ☀

Preparation time: 40 minutes
Cooking time: 45 minutes
Serves 4–6

30 g (1 oz) unsalted butter
50 g (1¾ oz/¼ cup) soft brown sugar
500 g (1 lb 2 oz) apples, peeled, cored and cubed
1 teaspoon finely grated lemon zest
1 tablespoon lemon juice
¼ teaspoon freshly grated nutmeg
¼ teaspoon ground cinnamon
30 g (1 oz/¼ cup) sultanas (golden raisins)
375 g (13 oz) block puff pastry, thawed
1 egg, lightly beaten, to glaze

1 Preheat the oven to 220°C (425°F/ Gas 7). Lightly grease a baking tray and line with baking paper.
2 Melt the butter and sugar in a frying pan. Add the apple, zest and juice. Cook over medium heat for 10 minutes, stirring occasionally, until the apples are cooked and the mixture is thick and syrupy. Stir in the nutmeg, cinnamon and sultanas. Cool.
3 Cut the block of puff pastry in half. On a lightly floured surface, roll out one half of the pastry to an 18 x 24 cm (7 x 9½ inch) rectangle. Spread the fruit mixture onto the pastry, leaving a 2.5 cm (1 inch) border. Brush the edges with the egg.
4 Roll the second half of the pastry on a lightly floured surface to a 18 x 25 cm (7 x 10 inch) rectangle. Use a sharp knife to cut slashes in the pastry across its width, leaving a 2 cm (¾ inch) border around

the edge. The slashes should open slightly and look like a venetian blind (jalousie in French). Place over the fruit and press the edges together. Trim any extra pastry. Knock up the puff pastry (brush the sides upwards) with a knife to ensure rising during cooking. Glaze the top with egg. Bake for 25–30 minutes, or until golden.

mille-feuille

Preparation time: 30 minutes
Cooking time: 1 hour 30 minutes
Makes 6

600 g (1 lb 5 oz) block puff pastry
625 ml (21½ fl oz/2½ cups) thick
   (double/heavy) cream
500 g (1 lb 2 oz) small strawberries, halved
70 g (2½ oz) blueberries (optional)
icing (confectioners') sugar, to dust

1   Preheat the oven to 220°C (425°F/ Gas 7). Line a baking tray with baking paper. Cut the block of puff pastry into three. On a lightly floured surface, roll out each portion to a 25 cm (10 inch) square. Place one sheet of puff pastry on the tray, prick all over and top with another piece of baking paper and another baking tray and bake for 15 minutes. Flip the trays over together and bake on the other side for 10–15 minutes, or until golden brown. Allow to cool and repeat with the remaining pastry.
2   Trim the edges of each pastry sheet and cut each one into six rectangles. Whisk the cream to firm peaks. Place six of the pastry pieces on serving plates and spread with half the cream. Carefully arrange half the strawberries and blueberries over the cream, pressing them well down. Top each one with another pastry sheet and repeat with the cream, strawberries and blueberries. Top with a final layer of pastry and dust with icing sugar.

NOTE: You can use 3 sheets ready-rolled puff pastry instead of the block, if desired.

apple galettes

Preparation time: 45 minutes + 1 hour
   chilling time
Cooking time: 30 minutes
Serves 8

8 apples, peeled, cored and thinly sliced
175 g (6 oz/¾ cup) caster (superfine) sugar
125 g (4½ oz) unsalted butter, chopped

PUFF PASTRY
250 g (9 oz/2 cups) plain (all-purpose) flour
250 g (9 oz) unsalted butter, chopped
125 ml (4 fl oz/½ cup) chilled water

1   To make the puff pastry, put the flour and butter in a bowl and cut the butter into the flour with two knives until it resembles large crumbs. Gradually add the chilled water, stirring with a knife and pressing together, until a rough dough forms. Turn onto a lightly floured board and roll into a rectangle. (The dough will be crumbly and hard to manage at this point.) Fold the pastry into thirds — turn it so the hinge is on your left and roll into a large rectangle. Always turn the pastry the same way so the hinge is on the left. Wrap in plastic wrap and refrigerate for 30 minutes. Complete two more turns and folds before refrigerating the pastry for another 30 minutes. Repeat the process so that you have completed six folds and turns. Wrap in plastic wrap and refrigerate before use.
2   Preheat the oven to 190°C (375°F/ Gas 5) and grease two baking trays. Roll the pastry out on a lightly floured surface until 3 mm (⅛ inch) thick. Cut into eight 10 cm (4 inch) rounds and place on the trays. Arrange the apple in a spiral on the pastry. Sprinkle well with sugar and dot with butter. Bake for 20–30 minutes, until the pastry is crisp and golden. Serve warm.

mille-feuille

banana tart

✻ ✻

Preparation time: 60 minutes
Cooking time: 35 minutes
Serves **6**

zest and juice of 2 oranges
80 g (2¾ oz/⅓ cup) soft brown sugar
¼ teaspoon cardamom seeds
1 tablespoon dark rum
3–4 ripe bananas

FLAKY PASTRY
220 g (7¾ oz/1¾ cups) plain
    (all-purpose) flour
60 g (2¼ oz) unsalted butter, chilled
    and cubed
150 ml (5 fl oz) chilled water
100 g (3½ oz) unsalted butter, extra,
    chilled and cubed

1 To make the pastry, sift the flour into
a bowl with a pinch of salt. Use your
fingertips to rub in the butter until the
mixture resembles fine breadcrumbs.
Add enough of the chilled water, mixing
with a flat-bladed knife and using a
cutting action, to make a dough-like
consistency. Turn onto a lightly floured
work surface and knead until just smooth.
2 Roll into a rectangle 10 x 30 cm
(4 x 12 inches), dot one-third of the extra
butter all over the top two-thirds of the
pastry, leaving a little room around the
edge. Fold the bottom third of the pastry
up and the top third down and press the
edges down to seal. Now turn the pastry
to your left, so the hinge is on your right,
and roll and fold as before. Refrigerate for
20 minutes, then with the hinge to your
right, roll it out again, cover the top two-
thirds of the pastry with another third of
the cubed, extra butter and roll and fold.
Repeat, using the rest of the butter, then
roll and fold once more without adding
any butter.
3 Roll the pastry out on a lightly floured
work surface into a rectangle 25 x 30 cm
(10 x 12 inches), cut a 2 cm (¾ inch)
strip off each side and use this to make a
frame on the pastry by brushing the edges

Roll the dough into a rectangle and
dot the top two-thirds with cubes
of chilled butter.

Fold the bottom third of the pastry
up over the butter and then the top
third down.

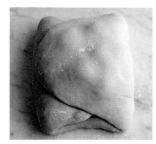
Turn the pastry so the hinge is to
the right. Press the edges down to
seal, then roll and fold as before.

of the pastry with water and sticking the strips onto it. Trim off any excess and put the tart base on a baking tray lined with baking paper, cover with plastic wrap and refrigerate until required.

4 Combine the orange zest, juice, brown sugar and cardamom seeds in a small saucepan, bring to the boil, simmer for 5 minutes, then remove from the heat and add the rum. Set aside to cool. Preheat the oven to 220°C (425°F/Gas 7).

5 Slice the bananas in half lengthways, arrange on the tart in a single layer, cut side up, and brush with a little syrup. Bake on the top shelf of the oven for 20–30 minutes, making sure the pastry does not overbrown. Brush with remaining syrup and serve.

feuilletté with cherries jubilee

✹ ✹

Preparation time: **35 minutes**
Cooking time: **25 minutes**
Serves **4**

375 g (13 oz) block puff pastry, thawed
1 egg, lightly beaten
20 g (¾ oz) unsalted butter
20 g (¾ oz) sugar
500 g (1 lb 2 oz) cherries, pitted
300 ml (10½ fl oz) thick
    (double/heavy) cream
125 ml (4 fl oz/½ cup) brandy or Kirsch
icing (confectioners') sugar, to dust

1 To make the feuilletés, roll the pastry out on a floured work surface to 3 mm (⅛ inch) and cut out four rectangles of 10 x 12 cm (4 x 4½ inches) each. Put them on a baking tray and brush with the beaten egg, being careful not to let any drip down the sides of the pastry. Refrigerate for 30 minutes. Preheat the oven to 220°C (425°F/Gas 7).

2 Melt the butter and sugar together in a saucepan and add the cherries. Cook over high heat for about 1 minute, then reduce the heat and simmer for about 3 minutes,

or until the cherries are tender. Reduce heat to low and keep the cherries warm.

3 Bake the feuilletés on the top shelf of the oven for 15 minutes until golden and puffed, then cut them in half horizontally and gently pull any doughy bits out of the centre. Turn the oven off and put the feuilletés back in the oven and allow to dry out for a couple of minutes.

4 When you are ready to serve, whisk the cream until stiff peaks form. Place a warm feuilleté base on each serving plate. Heat the brandy or Kirsch in a small saucepan and set it alight, then pour it over the

cherries (keep a saucepan lid nearby in case the flames get too high). Spoon some cherries into each feuilleté and top with a little cream. Put the lids on and dust with icing sugar to serve.

help with your pastry

To make sure you get a well-cooked base on pastry, put a baking tray on the shelf of the oven when you preheat the oven and put the baking tray with the pastry on it straight on top of this.

shortcrust pastry

The secret to good pastry is to work quickly and lightly, with cool ingredients, in a cool room and, preferably, not on a hot day. A cold marble slab is the ideal work surface.

If you don't have a marble slab, rest a tray of chilled water on the work surface for a while before you start. Use real unsalted butter for pastry, not margarine or softened butter blends. Unsweetened pastry works well with sweet fillings, giving a good contrast of flavours. Add two tablespoons of caster (superfine) sugar to the flour for a sweet pastry. Some recipes contain egg yolks to enrich the pastry and give good colour.

shortcrust pastry

To make enough to line a 23 cm (9 inch) tin, use 185 g (6½ oz/1½ cups) plain (all-purpose) flour, 100 g (3½ oz) cubed, chilled unsalted butter, and 2–4 tablespoons chilled water.

1 Sift the flour into a large bowl and add the butter. Use just your fingertips to rub the butter into the flour until the mixture resembles fine breadcrumbs.

2 Make a well in the centre, then add 2 tablespoons water and mix with a flat-bladed knife. Use a cutting rather than a stirring action and turn the bowl with your free hand. The mixture will come together in small beads of dough. To test if you need more water, pinch a little dough between your fingers. If it doesn't hold together, add a little more water. If the pastry is too dry, it will fall apart when you roll it; too wet and it will be sticky and shrink when baked.

3 Gently gather the dough together with your hand and lift out onto a sheet of baking paper or a floured work surface.

4 Press, don't knead, the dough together into a ball. Handle gently, keeping your actions light and to a minimum.

5 Press the dough into a flat disc, wrap and refrigerate for 20 minutes. Roll out between two sheets of baking paper, or on a lightly floured surface. Roll from the centre outwards, rotating the dough, rather than rolling backwards and forwards.

6 If you used baking paper to roll out the pastry, remove the top sheet, carefully invert the pastry over the tin (centre the pastry, as it can't be moved once in place), and peel away the paper. If you rolled out on a lightly floured surface, roll the pastry back over the rolling pin so it is hanging, and ease it into the tin.

7 Once the pastry is in the tin, lift up the sides so they don't break over the edges of the tin. Use a small ball of excess dough to help ease and press the pastry into the side of the tin. Allow the excess to hang over the side and, if using a flan tin, roll the rolling pin over the top of the tin to cut off excess pastry. If using a glass or ceramic pie dish, use a small sharp knife to do this.

8 Dough is bound to shrink a little, so let it sit a little above the sides of the tin. If you rolled off the excess pastry with a rolling pin, it might have 'bunched' down the sides. Gently press the sides of the pastry with your thumbs to flatten and lift it. Refrigerate in the tin for 15 minutes. Preheat the oven.

blind baking

If pastry is to have a moist filling, it will probably require partial blind baking to prevent the base becoming soggy. If it is not cooked again after filling, it will need to be fully blind baked. This means baking the pastry without the filling, but with some weight to prevent it rising. Line the shell with crumpled baking paper. Pour in some baking beads, dried beans or uncooked rice (these can be used again). Bake the pastry for the given time, then lift out the filled paper. Return the pastry to the oven. When cooked, it should look dry with no greasy patches. Small pastry shells can just be pricked with a fork to prevent them rising or bubbling, but only do this if specified, as the filling may run through.

Cool pastry completely before filling. Cooked filling should also be cooled before adding, to prevent soggy pastry.

Arrange all the fruit over the custard, pressing in slightly.

Heat the jam for glazing until liquid, then sieve to remove any lumps. Gently brush over the fruit.

fruit tart

✹ ✹

Preparation time: 60 minutes
Cooking time: 40 minutes
Serves 6

SHORTCRUST PASTRY

150 g (5½ oz/1¼ cups) plain
   (all-purpose) flour
2 tablespoons caster (superfine) sugar
90 g (3¼ oz) unsalted butter, chilled
   and cubed
1 egg yolk
1 tablespoon chilled water

FILLING

250 ml (9 fl oz/1 cup) milk
3 egg yolks
55 g (2 oz/¼ cup) caster (superfine) sugar
2 tablespoons plain (all-purpose) flour
1 teaspoon natural vanilla extract
strawberries, kiwi fruit and blueberries,
   to decorate
apricot jam, to glaze

1 To make the pastry, sift the flour into a bowl and stir in sugar. Use your fingertips to rub in the butter until the mixture resembles fine breadcrumbs. Make a well in the centre and add the egg yolk and

water. Mix to a dough with a flat-bladed knife, using a cutting action. Turn out onto a lightly floured work surface and gather into a ball. Press together gently until smooth, then roll out to fit a 10 x 34 cm (4 x 13½ inch) loose-based fluted flan (tart) tin. Line the tin with pastry and trim away any excess. Cover with plastic wrap and refrigerate for 20 minutes. Preheat the oven to 190°C (375°F/Gas 5).
2 Line the pastry-lined tin with baking paper and spread a layer of baking beads or uncooked rice evenly over the paper. Bake for 15 minutes, remove the paper and beads and bake for another

20 minutes, or until cooked on the base and golden brown around the edge. Set aside to cool completely.

3 To make the filling, put the milk into a small saucepan and bring to the boil. Set aside while quickly whisking the egg yolks and sugar together in a bowl, until light and creamy. Whisk in the flour. Pour the hot milk slowly onto the egg mixture, whisking constantly. Wash out the pan, return the milk mixture to the pan and bring to the boil over medium heat, stirring with a wire whisk. Boil for 2 minutes, stirring occasionally. Transfer to a bowl, stir in the vanilla, and leave to cool, stirring frequently to avoid a skin forming. When cooled to room temperature, cover the surface with plastic wrap and refrigerate until cold.

4 Hull and halve the strawberries and peel and slice the kiwi fruit. Spoon the cold custard into the cold pastry shell, then arrange all the fruit over the custard, pressing in slightly. Heat the jam in the microwave or in a small saucepan until liquid, sieve to remove any lumps, then, using a pastry brush, glaze the fruit with the jam. Serve the tart on the same day, at room temperature. If it is to be left for a while on a hot day, refrigerate it.

NOTE: If you don't have a rectangular tin, this tart may be made in a 23 cm (9 inch) round flan tin. You can use different fruits to top the tart, according to taste and season.

lemon almond tart

✳ ✳

Preparation time: **60 minutes**
Cooking time: **1 hour**
Serves **6–8**

LEMON PASTRY
250 g (9 oz/2 cups) plain (all-purpose) flour, sifted
55 g (2 oz/¼ cup) caster (superfine) sugar
125 g (4½ oz) unsalted butter, softened
1 teaspoon finely grated lemon zest
2 egg yolks

FILLING
350 g (12 oz) ricotta cheese, sieved
80 g (2¾ oz/⅓ cup) caster (superfine) sugar
3 eggs, well beaten
1 tablespoon finely grated lemon zest
80 g (2¾ oz/½ cup) blanched almonds, finely chopped
30 g (1 oz/⅓ cup) flaked almonds

1 Combine the flour, sugar and a pinch of salt in a large bowl. Make a well in the centre and add the butter, lemon zest and egg yolks. Work the flour into the centre with the fingertips of one hand until a smooth dough forms (add a little more flour if necessary). Wrap in plastic wrap, flatten slightly, then refrigerate for 20 minutes.

2 To make the filling, beat the ricotta and sugar together using electric beaters.

Add the eggs gradually, beating well after each addition. Add the lemon zest, beating briefly to combine, and then stir in the chopped almonds.

3 Preheat the oven to 180°C (350°F/ Gas 4). Brush a 20 cm (8 inch) fluted loose-based flan (tart) tin with melted butter. Roll out the pastry on a lightly floured work surface large enough to line the tin. Line the tin with the pastry, trimming away the excess. Pour in the filling and smooth the top. Sprinkle with the flaked almonds and bake for 55–60 minutes, or until lightly golden and set.

4 Allow to cool. Serve chilled or at room temperature.

pastry tips

To stop a pastry base becoming soggy when it has a wet filling, sprinkle a tablespoon of dried breadcrumbs or semolina into the base before adding the filling. Alternatively, brush the base with egg white and rebake it for a few minutes, or brush it with a glaze such as apricot jam.

If the pastry base splits when you cook it, plug any gaps with raw pastry and rebake it for 5 minutes, then brush it with egg white and rebake it for a couple of minutes.

Tart cases which are not going to hold runny fillings can be pricked all over with a fork to help them cook evenly and also to get rid of air bubbles.

Smaller tart cases which are fiddly to line with paper and rice or baking beads can be lined with another tart mould while baking. They will need to be dried out for a minute or two when the mould has been taken out.

Wet fillings in covered pies will steam so it is important to make holes in the pastry lid.

butterscotch tart

Preparation time: 30 minutes + 40 minutes chilling time
Cooking time: 1 hour
Serves 6–8

SHORTCRUST PASTRY
250 g (9 oz/2 cups) plain (all-purpose) flour
125 g (4½ oz) unsalted butter, chilled and cubed
2 tablespoons caster (superfine) sugar
1 egg yolk
1 tablespoon chilled water

BUTTERSCOTCH FILLING
185 g (6½ oz/1 cup) soft brown sugar
40 g (1½ oz/⅓ cup) plain (all-purpose) flour
250 ml (9 fl oz/1 cup) milk
50 g (1¾ oz) unsalted butter
1 teaspoon natural vanilla extract
1 egg yolk

MERINGUE
2 egg whites
2 tablespoons caster (superfine) sugar

1 Preheat the oven to 180°C (350°F/Gas 4). Grease a deep 22 cm (8½ inch) flan (tart) tin. Sift the flour into a large bowl. Use your fingertips to rub in the butter until the mixture resembles fine breadcrumbs. Stir in the sugar, egg yolk and chilled water. Mix to a soft dough with a flat-bladed knife, using a cutting action, then gather into a ball. Wrap and refrigerate for 20 minutes.
2 Roll the pastry between two sheets of baking paper, large enough to cover the base and side of the tin. Trim the edge and prick the pastry evenly with a fork. Refrigerate for 20 minutes. Line the pastry with baking paper and spread baking beads or uncooked rice over the paper. Bake for 35 minutes, then remove the paper and beads.
3 To make the filling, place the sugar and flour in a small saucepan. Make a well in the centre and gradually whisk in the milk to form a smooth paste. Add the butter and stir with a whisk over low heat for

8 minutes, or until the mixture boils and thickens. Remove from the heat, add the vanilla extract and egg yolk and whisk until smooth. Spread into the pastry case and smooth the surface.

4 To make the meringue, whisk the egg whites until firm peaks form. Add the sugar gradually, whisking until thick and glossy and all the sugar has dissolved. Spoon over the filling and swirl into peaks with a fork or flat-bladed knife. Bake for 5–10 minutes, or until the meringue is golden. Serve warm or cold.

NOTE: This tart may be made in a 23 cm (9 inch) round flan tin. You can use different fruits to top the tart.

date and mascarpone tart

✹ ✹

Preparation time: 1 hour
Cooking time: 45 minutes
Serves 6–8

COCONUT PASTRY
90 g (3¼ oz/½ cup) rice flour
60 g (2¼ oz/½ cup) plain (all-purpose) flour
2 tablespoons icing (confectioners') sugar
100 g (3½ oz) unsalted butter, chilled and cubed
25 g (1 oz/¼ cup) desiccated coconut
100 g (3½ oz) marzipan, grated

FILLING
8 fresh dates (about 200 g/7 oz), stoned and quartered lengthways
2 eggs
2 teaspoons custard powder or instant vanilla pudding mix
125 g (4½ oz) mascarpone cheese
2 tablespoons caster (superfine) sugar
80 ml (2½ fl oz/⅓ cup) pouring (whipping) cream
2 tablespoons flaked almonds

1 Preheat oven to 180°C (350°F/Gas 4). Grease a shallow, 10 x 34 cm (4 x 13½ inch) fluted loose-based flan (tart) tin.

2 To make the pastry, sift the flours and icing sugar into a large bowl. Use your fingertips to rub in the butter until the mixture resembles fine breadcrumbs. Stir in the coconut and marzipan, then press the mixture together gently. Turn out onto a lightly floured work surface and gather together into a disc. Flatten slightly, wrap in plastic wrap and refrigerate for 15 minutes.

3 Roll out the pastry between two sheets of baking paper until large enough to line the tin. Ease pastry into the tin and trim the edge. Refrigerate for 5–10 minutes.

Line the pastry-lined tin with baking paper and spread a layer of baking beads or uncooked rice evenly over the paper. Place the tin on a baking tray and bake for 10 minutes. Remove the paper and beads and bake for another 5 minutes, or until just golden, then allow to cool.

4 Arrange date quarters over the pastry. Whisk together the eggs, custard powder, mascarpone, sugar and cream until smooth. Pour the mixture over the dates, then sprinkle with flaked almonds. Bake for 25–30 minutes, or until golden and just set, then allow to cool slightly. Serve warm.

banoffie pie

then arrange half the bananas over the pastry and pour over the caramel. Smooth the surface. Refrigerate for 30 minutes.
4 Drop spoonfuls of cream over the caramel and arrange the remaining banana on top. Drizzle with the chocolate.

custard tart

✹ ✹

Preparation time: 20 minutes + 30 minutes
    chilling time
Cooking time: 1 hour
Serves 8

185 g (6½ oz/1½ cups) plain
    (all-purpose) flour
30 g (1 oz/¼ cup) custard powder
125 g (4½ oz) unsalted butter,
    chilled and cubed
1½ tablespoons caster (superfine) sugar
1 egg yolk

CUSTARD
4 eggs, lightly beaten
2 teaspoons natural vanilla extract
125 g (4½ oz/½ cup) caster (superfine) sugar
375 ml (13 fl oz/1½ cups) milk
¼ teaspoon ground nutmeg

1 To make the pastry, sift the flour and custard powder into a bowl. Use your fingertips to rub in the butter until the mixture resembles breadcrumbs. Stir in the sugar, then use a flat-bladed knife to mix in the yolk and 1–2 tablespoons water, to form a soft dough. Wrap in plastic wrap and refrigerate for 30 minutes.
2 Preheat the oven to 190°C (375°F/Gas 5). Lightly grease a pie plate, about 20 cm (8 inch) diameter. Roll the pastry out between two sheets of baking paper and line the base and side of the plate. Trim the edge with a sharp knife. Make a decorative edge if you wish. Line with crumpled baking paper, fill with baking beads or rice and bake for 10 minutes. Remove the paper and beads and bake for 5 minutes, or until the base is dry (cover the edges with foil if overbrowning). Cool. Reduce the oven to 180°C (350°F/Gas 4).

banoffie pie

✹ ✹

Preparation time: 35 minutes + 1 hour
    5 minutes chilling time
Cooking time: 30 minutes
Serves 8

WALNUT PASTRY
150 g (5½ oz/1¼ cups) plain
    (all-purpose) flour
2 tablespoons icing (confectioners') sugar
85 g (3 oz/¾ cup) ground walnuts
80 g (2¾ oz) unsalted butter,
    chilled and cubed
2–3 tablespoons chilled water

FILLING
400 g (14 oz) tin condensed milk
30 g (1 oz) unsalted butter
1 tablespoon golden syrup or dark corn syrup
4 bananas, sliced
375 ml (13 fl oz/1½ cups) pouring
    (whipping) cream, whipped
50 g (1¾ oz) dark chocolate, melted

1 To make the pastry, sift the flour and icing sugar into a large bowl and add the walnuts. Use your fingertips to rub in the butter until the mixture resembles fine breadcrumbs. Mix in the chilled water with a flat-bladed knife, using a cutting action, until the mixture forms a firm dough. Add more water if the dough is too dry. Turn onto a lightly floured work surface and gather together into a ball. Wrap and refrigerate for 15 minutes. Roll out to fit a 23 cm (9 inch) flan (tart) tin. Refrigerate for 20 minutes.
2 Preheat the oven to 180°C (350°F/Gas 4). Line the pastry base with baking paper and spread baking beads or uncooked rice over the paper. Bake for 15 minutes, remove the paper and beads and bake for another 10 minutes, or until lightly golden. Set aside to cool completely.
3 To make the filling, put the condensed milk, butter and golden syrup in a small saucepan. Stir over medium heat for 5 minutes, until it boils and thickens and turns a light caramel colour. Cool slightly,

3 To make the custard, mix together the eggs, vanilla and sugar. Bring the milk to the boil, remove from the heat and gradually pour onto the egg mixture. Place the pie plate on a baking tray, strain the egg mixture into the pastry case and sprinkle with ground nutmeg. Bake for 40 minutes, or until just set in the centre. Allow to cool and serve cut into wedges.

lattice mincemeat tarts

Preparation time: 40 minutes
Cooking time: 1 hour 10 minutes
Serves 6

1 egg, lightly beaten, to glaze
icing (confectioners') sugar, to dust
cream, to serve

PASTRY
60 g (2¼ oz/½ cup) self-raising flour
185 g (6½ oz/1½ cups) plain
    (all-purpose) flour
125 g (4½ oz) unsalted butter,
    chilled and cubed
2 tablespoons caster (superfine) sugar
2–3 tablespoons chilled water

MINCEMEAT
35 g (1¼ oz/¼ cup) currants
40 g (1½ oz/⅓ cup) sultanas
    (golden raisins)
2 tablespoons mixed peel (mixed candied
    citrus peel)
30 g (1 oz/¼ cup) slivered almonds
50 g (1¾ oz/¼ cup) soft brown sugar
¼ teaspoon freshly grated nutmeg
¼ teaspoon ground cinnamon
1 apple, cored and grated
1 teaspoon finely grated orange zest
1 teaspoon finely grated lemon zest
100 g (3½ oz) pitted fresh cherries
100 g (3½ oz) white grapes, halved
1 tablespoon whisky

1 Preheat the oven to 200°C (400°F/ Gas 6). Brush six 8 cm (3¼ inch) fluted loose-based, 3 cm (1¼ inch) deep flan (tart) tins with oil or melted butter.
2 To make the pastry, sift the flours into a bowl. Use your fingertips to rub in the butter until the mixture resembles fine breadcrumbs. Stir in the sugar and mix in the chilled water with a flat-bladed knife, using a cutting action. Turn onto a lightly floured work surface and gather together. Wrap in plastic wrap and refrigerate for 15 minutes.
3 Set aside one-quarter of the dough. Divide the remaining dough into six. Roll each portion out and line the base and side of the tins. Refrigerate for 10 minutes. Line the pastry cases with crumpled baking paper and fill with baking beads or uncooked rice. Bake for 10 minutes, remove the paper and beads and bake for another 10 minutes. Cool. Reduce the oven to 180°C (350°F/Gas 4).

4 Mix together all the mincemeat ingredients. Divide the mixture evenly among the pastry cases.
5 Roll out the remaining pastry on a lightly floured surface to 3 mm (⅛ inch) thick. Use a lattice pastry cutter (see Note) to run it along the length of the pastry. Gently pull the lattice open. Use a 10 cm (4 inch) cutter to cut out six rounds. Brush the tart edges with beaten egg, place the pastry lattice rounds on top and press gently to seal. Brush with beaten egg and bake for 45 minutes, or until golden brown. Leave in the tin for 5 minutes, then carefully remove and cool on a rack. Dust with icing sugar and serve with cream.

NOTE: Special lattice cutters are available from speciality kitchenware stores, or simply cut strips instead.

pumpkin pie

✿ ✿

Preparation time: 40 minutes
Cooking time: 1 hour 10 minutes
Serves 8

FILLING

500 g (1 lb 2 oz) seeded and peeled pumpkin
(winter squash), chopped into small chunks
2 eggs, lightly beaten
140 g (5 oz/¾ cup) soft brown sugar
80 ml (2½ fl oz/⅓ cup) pouring
(whipping) cream
1 tablespoon sweet sherry
1 teaspoon ground cinnamon
½ teaspoon freshly grated nutmeg
½ teaspoon ground ginger
vanilla ice cream or whipped cream, to serve

PASTRY

150 g (5½ oz/1¼ cups) plain
(all-purpose) flour
100 g (3½ oz) unsalted butter, chilled
and cubed
2 teaspoons caster (superfine) sugar
80 ml (2½ fl oz/⅓ cup) chilled water
1 egg yolk, lightly beaten with 1 tablespoon
milk, to glaze

1 Lightly grease a 23 cm (9 inch) round pie dish. Steam or boil the pumpkin for 10 minutes, or until just tender. Drain the pumpkin thoroughly, then mash and set aside to cool.
2 To make the pastry, sift the flour into a large bowl. Use your fingertips to rub in the butter until the mixture resembles fine breadcrumbs. Stir in the sugar. Make a

well in the centre, add almost all the water and mix with a flat-bladed knife, using a cutting action, until the mixture comes together in beads. Add the remaining water if the dough is too dry.
3 Gather the dough together and roll out between two sheets of baking paper until large enough to cover the base and side of the pie dish. Line the dish with pastry, trim away the excess and crimp the edges. Roll out the pastry trimmings to 2 mm (1⁄16 inch) thick. Use a sharp knife to cut out leaf shapes of different sizes and score vein markings onto the leaves. Refrigerate the pastry-lined dish and the leaf shapes for about 20 minutes.
4 Preheat the oven to 180°C (350°F/ Gas 4). Line the pastry-lined dish with baking paper. Spread baking beads or

pumpkin

The pumpkin probably originated in Europe. Recipes date back to the Renaissance and the cuisine of Northern Italy uses pumpkin with almonds and orange in Crosta di Zucca. English recipes for pumpkin pie appear in the 17th and 18th centuries, but seemed to go out of fashion after that.

uncooked rice over the paper. Bake for 10 minutes, remove the paper and beads and bake for another 10 minutes, or until lightly golden. Meanwhile, place the leaves on a baking tray lined with baking paper, brush with the combined egg yolk and milk and bake for 10–15 minutes, or until lightly golden. Set aside to cool.

5 To make the filling, whisk the eggs and brown sugar in a large bowl. Add the cooled pumpkin, cream, sherry, cinnamon, nutmeg and ginger and stir to combine thoroughly. Pour the filling into the pastry shell, smooth the surface with the back of a spoon, then bake for 40 minutes, or until set. If the pastry edges begin to brown too much during cooking, cover the edges with foil. Allow the pie to cool to room temperature, then decorate the top with the leaves. Serve with ice cream or cream.

anzac apple tart

Preparation time: 40 minutes + 30 minutes
    chilling time
Cooking time: 50 minutes
Serves 6

vanilla ice cream, to serve

SHORTCRUST PASTRY
125 g (4½ oz/1 cup) plain (all-purpose) flour
75 g (2½ oz) unsalted butter, chilled
    and cubed
1 egg yolk, lightly beaten
1 tablespoon chilled water

FILLING
125 g (4½ oz/1¼ cups) rolled oats
60 g (2¼ oz/¼ cup) caster (superfine) sugar
60 g (2¼ oz/½ cup) plain (all-purpose) flour
100 g (3½ oz) unsalted butter
2 tablespoons golden syrup
410 g (14½ oz) tinned pie apple

1 Preheat the oven to 180°C (350°F/ Gas 4). Sift the flour into a large bowl and use your fingertips to rub in the butter until the mixture resembles breadcrumbs. Add the egg yolk and almost all the water

and mix to a firm dough, adding more water if necessary. Turn onto a lightly floured surface and gather together into a ball. Flatten slightly, Wrap in plastic wrap and refrigerate for at least 30 minutes.

2 Roll out the pastry between two sheets of baking paper until it is large enough to fit the base and side of a 20 cm (8 inch) round flan tin. Line the pastry-lined tin with a sheet of crumpled baking paper and spread a layer of baking beads or rice evenly over the paper. Bake for 10 minutes, then remove the paper and beads. Bake the pastry for another

5 minutes, or until lightly golden. Set aside to cool.

3 To make the filling, combine the oats, sugar and sifted flour in a large bowl and make a well in the centre. Combine the butter and golden syrup in a small saucepan. Stir over low heat until the butter melts, then add to the dry ingredients. Stir until well combined.

4 Spread the pie apple into the pastry shell. Spoon the oat mixture on top and smooth. Bake for 30 minutes, or until golden brown. Leave in the tin for 15 minutes. Serve with ice cream.

lemon meringue pie

Preparation time: 1 hour + cooling time
Cooking time: 40 minutes
Serves 6

185 g (6½ oz/1½ cups) plain
    (all-purpose) flour
2 tablespoons icing (confectioners') sugar

125 g (4½ oz) unsalted butter,
    chilled and cubed
60 ml (2 fl oz/¼ cup) chilled water

FILLING AND TOPPING
30 g (1 oz/¼ cup) cornflour (cornstarch)
30 g (1 oz/¼ cup) plain (all-purpose) flour
230 g (8 oz/1 cup) caster (superfine) sugar
185 ml (6 fl oz/¾ cup) lemon juice
3 teaspoons finely grated lemon zest

40 g (1½ oz) unsalted butter, cubed
6 eggs, at room temperature, separated
350 g (12 oz/1½ cups) caster
    (superfine) sugar, extra
½ teaspoon cornflour (cornstarch), extra

1 Sift the flour and icing sugar into a large bowl. Use your fingertips to rub in the butter until the mixture resembles fine breadcrumbs. Add almost all the water and mix with a flat-bladed knife, using a cutting action, until the mixture forms a firm dough. Add more liquid if the dough is too dry. Turn onto a lightly floured surface and gather together into a ball. Roll between two sheets of baking paper until large enough to fit a 23 cm (9 inch) pie dish. Line the pie dish with the pastry, trim the edge and refrigerate for 20 minutes. Preheat the oven to 180°C (350°F/Gas 4).
2 Line the pastry with a sheet of baking paper and spread a layer of baking beads or uncooked rice evenly over the paper. Bake for 10 minutes, then remove the paper and beads. Bake for a further 10 minutes, or until the pastry is lightly golden. Leave to cool.
3 To make the filling, put the flours and sugar in a saucepan. Whisk in the lemon juice, zest and 375 ml (13 fl oz/1½ cups) water. Whisk continually over medium heat until the mixture boils and thickens. Reduce the heat and cook for 1 minute, then whisk in the butter and egg yolks, one yolk at a time. Transfer to a bowl, cover the surface with plastic wrap and allow to cool completely. Preheat the oven to 220°C (425°F/Gas 7).
4 To make the topping, whisk the egg whites in a small dry bowl using electric beaters, until soft peaks form. Add the extra sugar gradually, whisking constantly until the meringue is thick and glossy. Whisk in the extra cornflour. Pour the cold filling into the cold pastry shell. Spread with meringue to cover, forming peaks. Bake for 5–10 minutes, or until lightly browned. Serve warm or cold.

lime chiffon pie

✺ ✺

Preparation time: **50 minutes**
Cooking time: **1 hour**
Serves **12**

110 g (3¾ oz/½ cup) sugar
finely shredded zest of 4 limes

ALMOND PASTRY
150 g (5½ oz/1¼ cups) plain
　(all-purpose) flour
90 g (3¼ oz) ground almonds
90 g (3¼ oz) unsalted butter,
　chilled and cubed
1–2 tablespoons chilled water

FILLING
6 egg yolks
115 g (4 oz/½ cup) caster
　(superfine) sugar
100 g (3½ oz) unsalted butter,
　melted
80 ml (2½ fl oz/⅓ cup) lime juice
2 teaspoons finely grated lime zest
2 teaspoons powdered gelatin
125 ml (4 fl oz/½ cup) pouring
　(whipping) cream, whipped

1 Sift the flour into a large bowl and add the almonds. Use your fingertips to rub in the butter until the mixture resembles fine breadcrumbs. Add almost all the chilled water and mix with a flat-bladed knife, using a cutting action, until the mixture forms a firm dough. Add more water if necessary. Turn onto a lightly floured surface and gather together into a ball. Roll the pastry out to fit a 23 cm (9 inch) fluted flan (tart) tin. Line the tin, trim the edges and refrigerate for 20 minutes.
2 Preheat the oven to 180°C (350°F/ Gas 4). Line the pastry-lined tin with a sheet of baking paper and spread a layer of baking beads or uncooked rice evenly over the paper. Bake for 20 minutes, then remove the paper and beads and bake for another 20 minutes, or until lightly golden. Allow to cool completely.
3 To make the filling, put the egg yolks, sugar, butter, lime juice and zest in a heatproof bowl. Whisk to combine thoroughly and dissolve the sugar. Stand the bowl over a saucepan of simmering water, making sure the base of the bowl does not touch the water, and stir constantly for 15 minutes, or until the mixture thickens. Remove from the heat and cool slightly. Put 1 tablespoon water in a small heatproof bowl, sprinkle the gelatin in an even layer over the surface and leave to go spongy. Do not stir. Bring a small saucepan filled with about 4 cm (1½ inches) water to the boil, remove from the heat and place the bowl into the pan. The water should come halfway up the side of the bowl. Stir the gelatin until clear and dissolved. Cool slightly, add to the lime curd and stir to combine. Cool to room temperature, stirring occasionally.
4 Fold the cream through the lime curd and pour into the pastry case. Refrigerate for 2–3 hours, until set. Leave the pie for 15 minutes at room temperature to serve.
5 To prepare the shredded lime zest, combine the sugar with 1 tablespoon water in a small saucepan. Stir over low heat until the sugar dissolves. Bring to the boil, add the zest and simmer for 3 minutes. Drain the zest on a wire rack, then use to decorate the lime chiffon pie to serve.

tarte tatin

✳ ✳

Preparation time: 30 minutes + 30 minutes
   chilling time
Cooking time: 55 minutes
Serves 6

210 g (7½ oz/1⅔ cups) plain
   (all-purpose) flour
125 g (4½ oz) unsalted butter,
   chilled and cubed
2 tablespoons caster (superfine) sugar
1 egg, lightly beaten

2 drops natural vanilla extract
8 granny smith apples
110 g (3¾ oz/½ cup) sugar
40 g (1½ oz) unsalted butter, extra,
   cubed
vanilla ice cream, to serve

1 Sift the flour into a bowl. Use your
fingertips to rub in the butter until the
mixture resembles fine breadcrumbs. Stir
in the sugar, then make a well in the
centre. Add the egg and vanilla and mix
with a flat-bladed knife, using a cutting
action, until the mixture comes together

in beads. Gather the dough together, then
turn out onto a lightly floured work
surface and shape into a disc. Wrap in
plastic wrap and refrigerate for at least
30 minutes, to firm.

2 Peel and core the apples and cut each
into eight wedges. Put the sugar and
1 tablespoon water in a heavy-based
25 cm (10 inch) frying pan that has a
metal or removable handle, so that it can
safely be placed in the oven. Stir over low
heat until the sugar dissolves. Increase the
heat to medium and cook, without
stirring, until it becomes golden. Remove

Stir the butter and sugar until the
sugar dissolves, then cook until
golden brown.

from the heat. Add the extra butter and stir to incorporate.

3 Place the apple wedges in neat circles to cover the base of the frying pan. Return the pan to low heat and cook for 10–12 minutes, or until the apple is tender and caramelised. Remove from the heat and leave to cool for 10 minutes.

4 Preheat the oven to 220°C (425°F/ Gas 7). Roll the pastry out on a lightly floured surface to a 27 cm (10¾ inch) circle. Working quickly, place the pastry over the apple to cover it completely, tucking the pastry down firmly at the edges. Bake for 30–35 minutes, or until the pastry is cooked. Leave for 15 minutes before turning out onto a plate. Serve warm or cold with ice cream.

NOTE: High-sided tatin tins are available from speciality kitchenware shops.

orange macadamia tarts

✹ ✹

Preparation time: **55 minutes**
Cooking time: **45 minutes**
Serves **6**

icing (confectioners') sugar, to dust
vanilla ice cream, to serve

SHORTCRUST PASTRY
185 g (6½ oz/1½ cups) plain
    (all-purpose) flour
100 g (3½ oz) unsalted butter,
    chilled and cubed
3–4 tablespoons chilled water

FILLING
240 g (8½ oz/1½ cups) macadamia nuts
45 g (1½ oz/¼ cup) soft brown sugar
2 tablespoons light corn syrup
20 g (¾ oz) unsalted butter, melted
1 egg, lightly beaten
2 teaspoons finely grated orange zest

1 Preheat the oven to 180°C (350°F/ Gas 4). Sift the flour into a bowl. Add the

butter and use your fingertips to rub it in until the mixture resembles breadcrumbs. Add almost all the water and mix in with a flat-bladed knife until the mixture comes together, adding more water if necessary. Turn onto a lightly floured surface and gather together into a ball. Divide into six equal portions, roll out and line six 8 cm (3 inch) fluted flan tins, then refrigerate for 15 minutes. Cut sheets of baking paper to fit the pastry-lined tins, crumple the paper, put in the tins, then spread baking beads or rice evenly over the paper. Put the tins on a baking tray and bake for 15 minutes. Remove the

beads and paper. Bake for another 10 minutes, or until the pastry is lightly golden. Cool completely.

2 Spread the macadamia nuts in a single layer on a baking tray. Bake for about 8 minutes, until lightly golden. Set aside to cool.

3 Divide the macadamia nuts evenly among the pastry shells. Use a whisk to whisk together the brown sugar, light corn syrup, butter, egg, orange zest and a pinch of salt. Pour the mixture over the nuts and bake for 20 minutes, or until set and lightly browned. Dust with icing sugar and serve warm with ice cream.

prune and almond tart

✳ ✳

Preparation time: 1 hour + 1 hour soaking
  + 2 hours chilling time
Cooking time: 50 minutes
Serves 6–8

375 g (13 oz) pitted prunes
170 ml (5½ fl oz/⅔ cup) brandy
105 g (3½ oz/⅓ cup) redcurrant
  jelly

ALMOND PASTRY
185 g (6½ oz/1½ cups) plain
  (all-purpose) flour

125 g (4½ oz) unsalted butter, chilled
  and cubed
60 g (2¼ oz/⅓ cup) ground almonds
60 g (2¼ oz/¼ cup) caster
  (superfine) sugar
1 egg yolk
2–3 tablespoons chilled water
50 g (1¾ oz) marzipan, grated

CUSTARD CREAM
30 g (1 oz/¼ cup) custard powder
420 ml (14½ fl oz/1⅔ cups) milk
1 tablespoon caster (superfine)
  sugar
125 g (4½ oz/½ cup) sour cream
2 teaspoons natural vanilla extract

1 Put the prunes in a saucepan with the brandy, leave to soak for 1 hour, then simmer over very low heat for 10 minutes, or until the prunes are tender but not mushy. Remove the prunes with a slotted spoon. Leave to cool. Add the redcurrant jelly to the pan and stir over low heat until dissolved. Cover and set aside.

2 To make the almond pastry, sift the flour into a large bowl. Use your fingertips to rub in the butter until the mixture resembles breadcrumbs. Stir in the almonds and sugar using a flat-bladed knife. Add the egg yolk and water, and stir until the dough just comes together. Turn out onto a lightly floured surface and gather together into a ball. Flatten slightly, wrap in plastic wrap and refrigerate for 15 minutes. Preheat the oven to 180°C (350°F/Gas 4) and heat a baking tray.

3 Roll out the chilled pastry between two sheets of baking paper until large enough to line the base and side of a lightly greased 23 cm (9 inch) loose-bottomed flan tin. Ease the pastry into the tin and trim the edge. Refrigerate for 15 minutes. Line the pastry with a sheet of crumpled baking paper and spread an even layer of baking beads or rice over the paper. Bake on the heated baking tray for 15 minutes.

4 Remove the paper and beads and bake the pastry for another 5 minutes. Reduce the heat to 160°C (315°F/Gas 2–3). Sprinkle marzipan over the pastry base, then bake for another 5–10 minutes, or until golden. Leave in the tin to cool.

5 To make the custard cream, mix the custard powder with a little milk until smooth. Transfer to a saucepan and add the remaining milk and sugar. Stir over medium heat for 5 minutes, or until it boils and thickens. Stir in the sour cream and vanilla, remove from the heat and cover surface with plastic wrap. Cool slightly.

6 Spread the custard cream, while it is still warm, evenly over the pastry case. Cut the prunes in half lengthways and arrange over the custard. Warm the redcurrant mixture and carefully spoon over the tart to cover it completely. Refrigerate for at least 2 hours to allow the custard to firm then serve.

raspberry shortcake

Preparation time: 30 minutes + 30 minutes chilling time
Cooking time: 35 minutes
Serves 6–8

pouring (whipping) cream, to serve

PASTRY
125 g (4½ oz/1 cup) plain (all-purpose) flour
40 g (1½ oz/⅓ cup) icing (confectioners') sugar
90 g (3¼ oz) unsalted butter, chilled and cubed
1 egg yolk
½ teaspoon natural vanilla extract
½–1 tablespoon chilled water

TOPPING
750 g (1 lb 10 oz/6 cups) fresh raspberries
30 g (1 oz/¼ cup) icing (confectioners') sugar
110 g (3¾ oz/⅓ cup) redcurrant jelly

1 To make the pastry, sift the flour and icing (confectioners') sugar into a large bowl. Use your fingertips to rub in the butter until the mixture resembles fine breadcrumbs. Add the egg yolk, vanilla and enough of the chilled water to make the ingredients come together, then mix to a dough with a flat-bladed knife, using a cutting action. Turn out onto a lightly floured work surface and gather together into a ball. Flatten slightly, wrap in plastic wrap and refrigerate for 30 minutes.
2 Preheat the oven to 180°C (350°F/ Gas 4). Roll out the pastry to fit a fluted 10 x 34 cm (4 x 13½ inch) loose-based flan (tart) tin and trim the edge. Prick all over with a fork and refrigerate for 20 minutes. Line the pastry with baking paper and spread a layer of baking beads or uncooked rice evenly over the paper. Bake for 15–20 minutes, or until golden. Remove the paper and beads and bake for another 15 minutes. Cool on a wire rack.
3 To make the topping, set aside 500 g (1 lb 2 oz/4 cups) of the best raspberries

and mash the rest with the icing sugar. Spread the mashed raspberries over the shortcake just before serving.
4 Cover with the whole raspberries. Heat the redcurrant jelly in a small saucepan until melted and smooth. Use a soft pastry brush to coat the raspberries heavily with warm glaze. Cut into slices and serve with cream.

NOTE: Strawberry shortcake is a classic American dish. It is usually made as a round of shortcake which is split, then filled or topped with fresh strawberries.

raspberries

Like the strawberry, the raspberry is a member of the rose family, hence the beautiful fragrant flavour and aroma. Originally from Europe, they are now grown world-wide in cooler climates. They have a short season, only lasting from summer to early autumn. They are highly perishable and will only last a couple of days, so take care when buying them. Check both the top and bottom of the punnet for signs of mould or juices leaching out. Raspberries should be refrigerated if not being used immediately and should never be washed.

beauty tips

Traditionally, only savoury pies were decorated, to distinguish them at a glance from sweet pies. Today we are unlikely to bake more than one pie in a day, so confusion shouldn't be a problem.

Pies are usually double crusted (with a pastry base and top) or just crusted on the top, whereas tarts are generally open with no pastry on top. Pies or tarts that are made in pie dishes with a lip can all be decorated around the edge.

decorative crust edges

Fork pressed — press a lightly floured fork around the edge of the pie crust.

Fluted — press the pastry edge between your thumbs at a slight angle, to create a ripple effect.

Crimped — press the pastry between thumb and forefinger, while indenting with the other forefinger.

Scalloped — mark or cut out semi-circles with a spoon.

Checkerboard — make small cuts in the pastry edge. Turn every other square inwards.

Leaves — cut out leaf shapes with a cutter or template and place over the lip of the pie, fixing with water or egg glaze.

Plait — cut three long strips and plait them to the length of the circumference of the tart. Brush the pastry edge with a little water and press gently into place.

Rope — twist two long sausages of pastry together and attach to the edge with water.

Feathering — lift the pastry off the lip so it stands upright and snip diagonally into the edge of the pie. Push one point inwards and one outwards.

decorative tops

When decorating with pastry trimmings, don't make the shapes too thick or they won't cook through. Re-roll the leftover pastry to an even thickness and cut out shapes with small cutters. If you want to make a shape you don't have a cutter for, draw it on a piece of stiff card and cut out to make a template. The shapes can indicate the pie filling, such as cherries or apples, or be whimsical, such as hearts or stars. Attach the shapes to the pastry top with the glaze (lightly beaten egg, egg white or egg yolk, or milk) or just with water, then glaze the shapes as well.

You can place pastry shapes onto an open tart or around the edge. If the filling is quite liquid, cook the shapes separately and arrange on the middle of the tart after it is baked.

If your tart cooks for a long time, check that the edges are not over-browning and cover with pieces of foil if necessary.

lattice top

A lattice makes a very impressive top for a pie, and is actually quite easy to make. On a sheet of baking paper, roll the pastry out to a square or rectangle a little larger than the pie (just as you would to cover normally). Use a fluted pastry wheel, or a small, sharp knife, to cut strips of pastry about 1.5 cm (⅝ inch) wide. Use a ruler to make perfect straight lines. Lay half the strips on another sheet of baking paper, all in the same direction, and about 1 cm (½ inch) apart. Fold every second strip of pastry back away from you (all the way back to start with). Lay a strip of pastry horizontally across the unfolded strips, then fold the other strips back into place. Fold the lower strips back this time, and lay another strip of pastry across. Repeat with all the strips, alternating the vertical strips. If the pastry is very soft, refrigerate it until firm. Invert the lattice onto the pie and peel the paper away. Press the edges to seal, and trim off the excess pastry. Alternatively, make life easy for yourself and buy a special lattice-cutter, then simply roll out your pastry and roll over it once with your cutter, gently open the lattice out and lift it onto your pie and then trim the edges.

tarte au citron

❋ ❋

Preparation time: 30 minutes + 30 minutes
  chilling time
Cooking time: 1 hour
Serves 6–8

3 eggs
2 egg yolks
175 g (6 oz/¾ cup) caster (superfine) sugar
125 ml (4 fl oz/½ cup) pouring
  (whipping) cream
185 ml (6 fl oz/¾ cup) lemon juice
1½ tablespoons finely grated lemon zest
2 small lemons
140 g (5 oz/⅔ cup) sugar
pouring (whipping) cream (optional), to
  serve

PASTRY
125 g (4½ oz/1 cup) plain (all-purpose) flour
80 g (2¾ oz) unsalted butter, softened
1 egg yolk
2 tablespoons icing (confectioners')
  sugar, sifted

1 To make the pastry, sift the flour and a
pinch of salt into a large bowl. Make a
well in the centre and add the butter, egg
yolk and icing sugar. Work together the
butter, yolk and sugar with your
fingertips, then slowly incorporate the
flour. Bring together into a ball — you
may need to add a few drops of cold
water. Flatten the ball slightly, wrap in
plastic wrap and refrigerate for
20 minutes.
2 Preheat the oven to 200°C (400°F/
Gas 6). Lightly grease a shallow, 21 cm
(8¼ inches) loose-based flan (tart) tin.
3 Roll out the pastry between two sheets
of baking paper until it is 3 mm (⅛ inch)
thick and gently place it in the tin. Trim
the edge. Refrigerate for 10 minutes. Line
the pastry with baking paper, fill with
baking beads or uncooked rice and bake
for 10 minutes. Remove the paper and
beads and bake for another 6–8 minutes,
or until the pastry looks dry all over.
Allow to cool. Reduce the oven to 150°C
(300°F/Gas 2).

4 Whisk the eggs, egg yolks and sugar
together, add the cream and lemon juice
and mix well. Strain and then add the
lemon zest. Place the flan tin on a baking
tray on the middle shelf of the oven and
carefully pour in the filling right up to the
top. Bake for 40 minutes, or until it
is just set — it should wobble in the
middle when the tin is firmly tapped. Cool
the tart before removing from the tin.
5 Meanwhile, wash and scrub the lemons
well. Cut into 2 mm (1⁄16 inch) thick slices.

Combine the sugar and 200 ml (7 fl oz)
water in a small frying pan and stir over
low heat until the sugar dissolves. Add the
lemon slices and simmer over low heat for
40 minutes, or until the peel is very tender
and the pith looks translucent. Remove
from the syrup and drain on baking paper.
If serving the tart immediately, cover the
surface with the lemon slices. If not, keep
the slices covered and decorate the tart
when ready to serve. Serve warm or chilled
with cream, if desired.

apple tart

☀ ☀

Preparation time: **50 minutes**
Cooking time: **1 hour 15 minutes**
Serves **6–8**

2 cooking apples
3 tablespoons sugar
1 egg
80 ml (2½ fl oz/⅓ cup) pouring
    (whipping) cream
1 tablespoon Calvados or Kirsch
vanilla ice cream, to serve

PASTRY
185 g (6½ oz/1½ cups) plain
    (all-purpose) flour
100 g (3¾ oz) unsalted butter,
    chilled and cubed
2–3 tablespoons chilled water

1 To make the pastry, sift the flour into a bowl. Use your fingertips to rub the butter into the flour until the mixture resembles breadcrumbs. Make a well in the centre and add almost all the water. Use a knife to mix to a dough, adding more water if necessary. Gather together and turn out onto a sheet of baking paper. Press together gently until smooth, wrap and chill for 15 minutes. Roll out to fit a 23 cm (9 inch) loose-bottomed, fluted flan (tart) tin. Line the tin with the pastry, trimming any excess. Refrigerate for 20 minutes. Preheat the oven to 190°C (375°F/Gas 5).
2 Line the pastry with a sheet of crumpled baking paper and fill with baking beads or rice. Bake for 10 minutes, remove the paper and beads and bake for 15 minutes, until cooked on the base and golden around the edge. Cool.
3 Peel, core and thinly slice the apples. Arrange in the pastry shell with the slices overlapping, sprinkle with 2 tablespoons sugar and bake for 15 minutes. Meanwhile, whisk together the egg, remaining sugar and cream. Stir in the liqueur, then pour over the apples. Bake for 35 minutes, or until the cream mixture is set and is puffed and golden (it will sink as it cools). Serve hot or at room temperature with ice cream.

apples

Apples were possibly the first fruit to be cultivated by humans. The original apple was probably a wild type of crab apple. Apples have long been significant in mythology and are related to the acquisition of knowledge. There are many metaphors using apples, the 'apple of someone's eye' dates back to King Alfred, and in cockney rhyming slang 'apples and pears' means stairs. There are thousands of varieties of apple but those widely available tend to be the types that travel and keep well. Apples should feel heavy and be firm with no wrinkles, bruises or broken flesh. Store in plastic bags in the refrigerator to keep the flesh crisp.

pecans

Native to North America, pecans are grown across America, as well as in Australia and South Africa. Pecans look like long versions of walnuts but have a smooth, very hard, brown-red shell. The trees can grow to 50 metres and the nuts have to be harvested by shaking the trees, sometimes with mechanical tree shakers. The nuts are usually sold shelled—the hard shells have to be cracked carefully to extract the nuts intact. Pecan pie is a popular dessert that appears on tables around the world but always seems American.

pecan pie

✹ ✹

Preparation time: 40 minutes
Cooking time: 1 hour 15 minutes
Serves 6

vanilla ice cream, to serve

SHORTCRUST PASTRY
185 g (6½ oz/1½ cups) plain (all-purpose) flour
125 g (4½ oz) unsalted butter, chilled and cubed
2–3 tablespoons chilled water

FILLING
200 g (7 oz/2 cups) pecans
3 eggs, lightly beaten
50 g (1¾ oz) unsalted butter, melted and cooled
140 g (5 oz/¾ cup) soft brown sugar
170 ml (5½ fl oz/⅔ cup) light corn syrup
1 teaspoon natural vanilla extract

1 Preheat the oven to 180°C (350°F/Gas 4). Sift the flour into a large bowl. Use your fingertips to rub in the butter until the mixture resembles fine breadcrumbs. Add almost all the water and mix with a flat-bladed knife, using a cutting action, until the mixture comes together in beads. Add more water if the dough is too dry. Turn out onto a lightly floured work surface and gather together into a ball.

2 Roll out the pastry to a 35 cm (14 inch) round. Line a 23 cm (9 inch) round flan (tart) tin with pastry, trim the edges and refrigerate for 20 minutes. Pile the pastry trimmings together, roll out on baking paper to a rectangle about 2 mm (1/16 inch) thick, then refrigerate with the pastry case.

3 Line the pastry-lined tin with a sheet of baking paper and spread a layer of baking beads or uncooked rice evenly over the paper. Bake for 15 minutes, remove the paper and beads and bake for another 15 minutes, or until lightly golden. Cool completely.

4 To make the filling, spread the pecans over the pastry base. Whisk together the eggs, butter, sugar, corn syrup, vanilla extract and a pinch of salt until well combined, then pour over the nuts.

5 Use a fluted pastry wheel or small sharp knife to cut narrow strips from half of the pastry trimmings. Cut out small stars with a biscuit (cookie) cutter from the remaining trimmings. Arrange decoratively over the filling. Bake the pie for 45 minutes, or until firm. Allow to cool completely and serve at room temperature with ice cream.

cherry pie

✹ ✹

Preparation time: 45 minutes
Cooking time: 40 minutes
Serves 6–8

150 g (5½ oz/1¼ cups) plain
     (all-purpose) flour
30 g (1 oz/¼ cup) icing (confectioners')
     sugar
100 g (3½ oz) unsalted butter,
     chilled and cubed
60 g (2¼ oz) ground almonds
60 ml (2 fl oz/¼ cup) chilled water
2 x 700 g (1 lb 9 oz) jars pitted morello
     cherries, drained
1 egg, lightly beaten, to glaze
caster (superfine) sugar, to sprinkle
vanilla ice cream, to serve

1 To make the pastry, sift the flour and icing sugar into a bowl. Use your fingertips to rub in the butter until the mixture resembles fine breadcrumbs. Stir in the ground almonds, then add almost all the water. Mix with a flat-bladed knife, using a cutting action, until the mixture forms a dough. Add the remaining water if the dough is too dry. Turn the dough onto a lightly floured work surface and gather together into a ball. Roll out on a sheet of baking paper into a circle about 26 cm (10½ inches) in diameter. Flatten slightly,

almonds

Almonds are the seeds of a tree related to apricot and peach trees. Almonds are native to the Middle East and have a tough, oval, pale brown outer shell that is pointed at one end. In Europe, almonds are also picked when the shell is still covered by a velvety green outer coating. The inner shell has a dark brown skin, which can be removed by blanching. Almonds are available whole in shells, shelled with their skins on, blanched, flaked, chopped and ground. Ground almonds are the basis of many biscuits and cakes, as well as being used in pastries and desserts.

wrap in plastic wrap and refrigerate for 20 minutes. Spread the cherries into a 23 cm (9 inch) round pie dish.

2 Preheat the oven to 200°C (400°F/ Gas 6). Line the pie dish with the pastry and trim the edge. Roll out the remaining scraps of pastry and use a small, sharp knife to cut out decorations. Brush the pastry top all over with beaten egg and arrange the decorations on top. Brush these with egg as well, and then sprinkle lightly with sugar. Place the pie dish on a baking tray (the cherry juice may overflow). Bake for 35–40 minutes, or until the pastry is golden brown and cooked through. Serve warm with ice cream.

rhubarb

Originating in northern Asia, rhubarb was first documented in China in about 2700 BC. It was used as a medicine for the next few centuries and was believed to be a purgative. It was grown in monastery gardens and by herbalists but was not eaten as a food until around 1800. Rhubarb became common in the British diet as it was easily grown in gardens. It is used in pies, crumbles, fools and, of course, rhubarb and custard. Only the stalks are eaten as the leaves contain oxalic acid and are poisonous in quantity. Forced rhubarb, grown in hothouses in the off season, has a redder, more tender stem than that available in season, which has a greener, thicker stem sometimes requiring peeling. Buy stalks that are still crisp and have not wilted. Redder stems give a sweeter flavour.

farmhouse rhubarb pie

Preparation time: 55 minutes
Cooking time: 50 minutes
Serves 6

250 g (9 oz/1 cup) sugar
750 g (1 lb 10 oz) rhubarb, chopped
2 large apples, peeled, cored and chopped
2 teaspoons finely grated lemon zest
3 pieces preserved ginger, thinly sliced
2 teaspoons sugar
sprinkle of ground cinnamon
icing (confectioners') sugar, to dust

SHORTCRUST PASTRY
185 g (6½ oz/1½ cups) plain (all-purpose) flour, sifted
2 tablespoons icing (confectioners') sugar
125 g (4½ oz) unsalted butter, chilled and cubed
1 egg yolk

1 Sift the flour into a large bowl and add the icing sugar. Use your fingertips to rub in the butter until the mixture resembles breadcrumbs. Add the egg yolk and 1 tablespoon water and mix with a knife until the dough comes together. Turn onto a lightly floured surface, gather into a ball and flatten slightly. Wrap in plastic wrap and refrigerate for 15 minutes. Preheat oven to 190°C (375°F/Gas 5). Roll the pastry out to a rough 35 cm (14 inch) circle and line a greased 20 cm (8 inch) pie plate, leaving the extra pastry to hang over the edge. Refrigerate.
2 Heat the sugar and 125 ml (4 fl oz/ ½ cup) water in a saucepan for 4–5 minutes or until syrupy. Add rhubarb, apple, lemon zest and ginger, then cover and simmer for 5 minutes, until the rhubarb is cooked but still holds its shape.
3 Drain off the liquid and cool the rhubarb mixture. Spoon into the pastry base and sprinkle with sugar and cinnamon. Fold the overhanging pastry over the fruit and bake for 40 minutes, until golden. Dust with icing sugar.

lemons

Historians seem unable to agree on where the lemon originated. However, it has been documented by the Greeks and Romans, in China and in the Indus Valley. Lemons have had all kinds of properties attributed to them — the Romans believed they were an antidote to poisons, and French ladies in the time of Louis XIV used to suck on them to keep their lips looking red. Lemons remained expensive for a long time, but luckily the prices dropped by the time the British Admiralty began to issue sailors with lemon juice to prevent scurvy in 1795 — the connection between scurvy and the lack of vitamin C had been made in the late 16th century. Lemons are used in sweet and savoury dishes. They are usually juiced and/or zested and used for flavouring in lemon pies, tarts, puddings, ice creams and sorbets.

real lemon pie

 ❉ ❉

Preparation time: 30 minutes + overnight
    standing time
Cooking time: 50–55 minutes
Serves 8–10

4 thin-skinned lemons, washed well
450 g (1 lb/2 cups) caster (superfine) sugar
220 g (7¾ oz/1¾ cups) plain
    (all-purpose) flour
150 g (5½ oz) unsalted butter, chilled
    and cubed
2 tablespoons caster (superfine) sugar,
    extra
1–2 tablespoons chilled water
4 eggs
milk, to glaze

1 Slice two lemons very thinly and remove the seeds. Peel the other lemons, removing all the pith, and slice the flesh very thinly. Remove the seeds. Put all the lemons in a bowl with the sugar and stir until all the slices are coated. Cover and leave overnight.

2 Preheat the oven to 180°C (350°F/ Gas 4). Sift the flour and a pinch of salt into a bowl. Use your fingertips to rub in the butter until the mixture resembles fine breadcrumbs. Stir in the extra sugar. Gradually add the chilled water and mix with a flat-bladed knife, using a cutting action until the mixture comes together in beads. Gather the dough together, divide in half and, on a lightly floured surface, roll each portion into a 25 cm (10 inch) circle. Lightly grease a 23 cm (9 inch) pie dish and line with pastry. Cover and refrigerate the other circle.

3 Beat the eggs and add to the lemon slices, mixing gently but thoroughly. Spoon into the pastry shell and cover with the pastry circle, crimping the edges to seal. Decorate the top with shapes made from pastry scraps, brush with milk and bake for 50–55 minutes, or until golden brown.

1 To make the pastry, sift the flours into a large bowl. Use your fingertips to rub in the butter until the mixture resembles fine breadcrumbs. Stir in the sugar, then add the egg and almost all the milk. Mix with a flat-bladed knife, using a cutting action, until the mixture comes together in beads. Add more milk if the dough is too dry. Turn out onto a lightly floured surface and gather together into a ball. Divide into two portions and roll each portion out on a sheet of baking paper, making sure one is the right size to fit the top of a 750 ml (26 fl oz/3 cup) pie dish. Wrap in plastic wrap and refrigerate for 30 minutes.

2 To make the berry filling, mix the cornflour, sugar, orange zest and juice in a saucepan. Add half the berries to the pan and stir over low heat for 5 minutes, or until the mixture boils and thickens. Remove from the heat and set aside to cool. Add the remaining berries to the pan, pour into the pie dish and smooth the surface with the back of a spoon.

3 Preheat the oven to 180°C (350°F/ Gas 4). Place the pie top over the fruit and trim the edges. Make sure you do not stretch the pastry or it may shrink during baking and fall back into the dish. Use heart-shaped pastry cutters of various sizes to cut out enough hearts from the remaining pastry sheet to cover the pie top. Arrange them on top of the pie, moistening each one with a little water to make it stick.

4 Brush all over the surface with the egg glaze. Bake for 35–40 minutes, or until the pastry is crisp and golden brown. Dust with icing (confectioners') sugar and serve the pie warm or cold.

NOTE: Use just one variety of berry or a combination if you prefer. If you want to make the pie when the berries are out of season, use frozen berries. Defrost the berries thoroughly, reserving the juice. Add the berries and juice to the filling and omit the orange juice. You can also use tinned berries if you drain them well first.

berry pie

Preparation time: 30 minutes + 30 minutes chilling time
Cooking time: 45 minutes
Serves 4–6

1 egg yolk, mixed with 1 teaspoon water, to glaze
icing (confectioners') sugar, to dust

PASTRY
125 g (4½ oz/1 cup) self-raising (self-rising) flour
125 g (4½ oz/1 cup) plain (all-purpose) flour
125 g (4½ oz) unsalted butter, chilled and cubed
2 tablespoons caster (superfine) sugar
1 egg, lightly beaten
60–80 ml (2–2½ fl oz/¼–⅓ cup) milk

BERRY FILLING
2 tablespoons cornflour (cornstarch)
2–4 tablespoons caster (superfine) sugar, to taste
1 teaspoon finely grated orange zest
1 tablespoon orange juice
600 g (1 lb 5 oz) fresh berries (such as boysenberries, blackberries, loganberries, mulberries, raspberries or youngberries)

treacle tart

Preparation time: 20 minutes + 40 minutes
   chilling time
Cooking time: 35 minutes
Serves 4–6

icing (confectioners') sugar, to dust
vanilla ice cream or cream, to serve

SHORTCRUST PASTRY
150 g (5½ oz/1¼ cups) plain
   (all-purpose) flour
90 g (3¼ oz) unsalted butter,
   chilled and cubed
2–3 tablespoons chilled water
1 egg, lightly beaten, to glaze

FILLING
350 g (12 oz/1 cup) light treacle
   or golden syrup
25 g (1 oz) unsalted butter
½ teaspoon ground ginger
140 g (5 oz/1¾ cups) fresh white
   breadcrumbs

1   To make the pastry, sift the flour into a large bowl. Use your fingertips to rub in the butter until the mixture resembles fine breadcrumbs. Add almost all the chilled water and mix to a firm dough, with a flat-bladed knife, using a cutting action. Add more water if the dough is too dry. Turn onto a lightly floured work surface and gather into a ball. Wrap in plastic wrap and refrigerate for 20 minutes.

2   Brush a 20 cm (8 inch) diameter flan (tart) tin with melted butter. Roll out the pastry large enough to fit the base and side of the tin, allowing a 4 cm (1½ inch) overhang. Ease the pastry into the tin and trim by running a rolling pin firmly across the top of the tin. Re-roll the trimmed pastry to a rectangle 10 x 20 cm (4 x 8 inches). Use a sharp knife or fluted pastry wheel to cut into long 1 cm (½ inch) strips. Cover the pastry-lined tin and strips with plastic wrap and refrigerate for 20 minutes. Preheat the oven to 180°C (350°F/ Gas 4).

3   To make the filling, combine golden syrup, butter and ginger in a small saucepan and stir over low heat until the butter melts. Stir in the breadcrumbs until combined. Pour the mixture into the pastry case. Lay half the pastry strips over the tart, starting at the centre and working outwards. Lay the remaining strips over the tart to form a lattice pattern. Brush the lattice with beaten egg. Bake for 30 minutes, or until the pastry is lightly golden. Serve warm or at room temperature. Dust the top with icing sugar and serve with ice cream or cream.

profiteroles

Preparation time: **30 minutes**
Cooking time: **1 hour**
Serves **10**

CHOUX PASTRY

50 g (1¾ oz) unsalted butter
90 g (3¼ oz/¾ cup) plain (all-purpose)
　flour, sifted twice
3 eggs, lightly beaten

FILLING

375 ml (13 fl oz/1½ cups) milk
4 egg yolks
80 g (2¾ oz/⅓ cup) caster (superfine)
　sugar
30 g (1 oz/¼ cup) plain (all-purpose) flour
1 teaspoon natural vanilla extract

TOPPING

110 g (3¾ oz) good-quality dark chocolate
2 teaspoons vegetable oil

1 Preheat the oven to 210°C (415°F/
Gas 6–7). Lightly grease two baking trays.
2 To make the pastry, put the butter in a
large heavy-based saucepan with 185 ml
(6 fl oz/¾ cup) water and stir over
medium heat until the mixture comes
to the boil. Remove from the heat and
quickly beat in the flour with a wooden
spoon. Return to the heat and continue
beating until the mixture comes together,
forms a ball and leaves the side of the
pan. Allow to cool slightly.
3 Transfer to a bowl and beat to release
any remaining heat. Gradually add the
beaten egg, about 3 teaspoons at a time,
beating well after each addition, until all
the egg has been added and the mixture
is thick and glossy — a wooden spoon
should stand upright in it. If it is too
runny, the egg has been added too quickly.
If this happens, beat for several more
minutes, or until thickened.
4 Sprinkle the baking trays with
water — this creates steam, helping the
puffs to rise. Spoon heaped teaspoons
of the mixture onto the baking trays,
leaving room for spreading. Bake for

20–30 minutes, or until browned and
hollow sounding, then remove and make
a small hole in the base of each puff with
a skewer. Return to the oven for 5 minutes
to dry out. Cool on a wire rack.
5 To make the filling, put the milk in a
small saucepan and bring to the boil. Set
aside while quickly whisking the yolks and
sugar in a bowl until combined. Whisk the
flour into the egg mixture. Pour the hot
milk slowly onto the egg and flour mixture,
whisking constantly. Wash out the pan,
return the milk mixture to the pan and
bring to the boil, stirring with a wooden
spoon until the mixture comes to the boil
and thickens. Boil for 2 minutes, stirring
often. Transfer to a heatproof bowl and

stir in the vanilla extract. Lay plastic wrap
directly over the surface to prevent a skin
forming, then refrigerate until cold.
6 Pipe the filling into the profiteroles
through the hole in the base, using a
piping (icing) bag with a small nozzle.
7 For the topping, chop the chocolate
and put it in a heatproof bowl with the
oil. Bring a saucepan of water to the boil
and remove from the heat. Sit the bowl
over the saucepan, making sure the base
of the bowl does not touch the water.
Allow to stand, stirring occasionally,
until the chocolate has melted. Stir
until smooth, then dip the top of each
profiterole in the chocolate. Allow to set
completely before serving.

Remove the boiling butter mixture
from the heat and quickly beat in
the flour.

Return the pan to the heat and
continue beating until the mixture
comes together and leaves the
side of the pan.

Gradually add the beaten egg,
about 3 teaspoons at a time,
beating well until all the egg is used
and the mixture is thick and glossy.

paris brest

✳ ✳

Preparation time: **50 minutes + cooling time**
Cooking time: **1 hour 15 minutes**
Serves 6–8

CHOUX PASTRY
50 g (1¾ oz) unsalted butter
90 g (3¼ oz/¾ cup) plain (all-purpose)
   flour, sifted
3 eggs, lightly beaten

FILLING
3 egg yolks
55 g (2 oz/¼ cup) caster
   (superfine) sugar
2 tablespoons plain (all-purpose) flour
250 ml (9 fl oz/1 cup) milk
1 teaspoon natural vanilla extract
250 ml (9 fl oz/1 cup) pouring (whipping)
   cream, whipped
200 g (7 oz) raspberries or 250 g (9 oz)
   strawberries, halved, or a mixture
   of both

TOPPING
125 g (4½ oz) dark chocolate, chopped
30 g (1 oz) unsalted butter
1 tablespoon pouring (whipping) cream

1 Preheat the oven to 210°C (415°F/ Gas 6–7). Brush a large baking tray with melted butter or oil. Mark a 23 cm (9 inch) circle on a piece of baking paper, turn the paper over and place on the baking tray.
2 To make the pastry, stir the butter with 185 ml (6 fl oz/¾ cup) water in a saucepan over low heat until the butter melts and the mixture boils. Remove from the heat, add the flour all at once and use a wooden spoon to beat until smooth. Return to the heat and beat until the mixture thickens and comes away from the side of the pan. Remove from the heat and cool slightly. Transfer to a large bowl. Use electric beaters to add the eggs gradually, beating until stiff and glossy. Place heaped tablespoons of mixture touching each other, using the marked circle as a guide. Bake for 25–30 minutes,

or until browned and hollow sounding when the base is tapped. Turn off the oven and leave the pastry to dry in the oven.
3 To make the filling, whisk the egg yolks, sugar and flour in a bowl until pale. Heat the milk in a saucepan until almost boiling. Gradually add to the egg mixture, stirring constantly. Return to the pan and stir constantly over medium heat until the mixture boils and thickens. Cook for another 2 minutes, stirring constantly. Remove from the heat and stir in the vanilla extract. Transfer to a bowl, cover the surface with plastic wrap to prevent a skin forming and refirgerate until cooled.
4 To make the topping, combine all the ingredients in a heatproof bowl. Stand the bowl over a saucepan of simmering water

and stir until the chocolate melts and the mixture is smooth. Cool slightly.
5 To assemble, cut the pastry ring in half horizontally using a serrated knife. Remove any excess dough that remains in the centre. Fold the whipped cream through the custard and spoon into the base of the pastry. Top with the fruit. Replace the remaining pastry half on top. Use a flat-bladed knife to spread the chocolate mixture over the top of the pastry.

NOTE: The pastry ring may be made up to 4 hours in advance. Store in an airtight container. The custard may be made up to 4 hours in advance — refrigerate until required. Assemble close to serving time.

strudel pastry

Traditional strudel dough uses flour with a high gluten content, which makes the pastry strong and less tearable. It is rolled as thinly as possible before being layered with breadcrumbs and wrapped around the filling. Filo is an easier option that gives a similar result. Strudel is an Austrian speciality although it appears in the cuisine of many countries and the name means, literally, whirlpool.

cherry cheese strudel

Preparation time: **25 minutes**
Cooking time: **45 minutes**
Serves **8–10**

500 g (1 lb 2 oz) ricotta cheese
2 teaspoons finely grated lemon or
    orange zest
55 g (2 oz/¼ cup) sugar
40 g (1½ oz/½ cup) fresh white breadcrumbs
2 tablespoons ground almonds
2 eggs
415 g (14¾ oz) tin pitted black cherries
2 teaspoons cornflour (cornstarch)
8 sheets filo pastry
60 g (2¼ oz) unsalted butter, melted
2 tablespoons dry breadcrumbs
icing (confectioners') sugar, to dust

1 Preheat the oven to 180°C (350°F/ Gas 4). Lightly grease a baking tray.
2 Combine the ricotta, zest, sugar, fresh breadcrumbs and almonds in a bowl.

Add the eggs and mix well. Drain the cherries, reserving half the juice. Blend the cornflour with the reserved cherry juice in a saucepan. Stir over medium heat until the mixture boils and thickens, then cool slightly.
3 Layer the pastry sheets, brushing between each sheet with melted butter and sprinkling with a few dry breadcrumbs. Form a large square by placing the second sheet halfway down the first sheet. Alternate layers, brushing with melted butter and sprinkling with breadcrumbs.
4 Put the ricotta mixture along one long edge of the pastry. Shape into a log and top with cherries and cooled syrup. Roll the pastry around the ricotta filling, folding in the edges as you roll. Finish with a pastry edge underneath. Place on the prepared tray and bake for 35–40 minutes, or until the pastry is golden. Dust with icing sugar. Serve cold, cut into slices.

custard rolls

✹ ✹

Preparation time: 35 minutes
Cooking time: 20 minutes
Makes 18 rolls

375 ml (13 fl oz/1½ cups) milk
115 g (4 oz/½ cup) caster (superfine) sugar
60 g (2¼ oz/½ cup) semolina
1 teaspoon finely grated lemon zest
1 egg, lightly beaten
12 sheets filo pastry
125 g (4½ oz) unsalted butter, melted
2 tablespoons icing (confectioners') sugar
½ teaspoon ground cinnamon

1 Put the milk, sugar, semolina and lemon zest in a saucepan and stir until it comes to the boil. Reduce the heat and simmer for 3 minutes.

2 Remove from the heat and gradually whisk in the egg. Pour the custard into a bowl, cover the surface with plastic wrap and set aside to cool. Preheat the oven to 180°C (350°F/Gas 4). Lightly brush two baking trays with melted butter.
3 Work with two sheets of pastry at a time. Cover the rest with a tea towel (dish towel). Brush one with melted butter, then top with another. Cut lengthways into three. Brush the edges with melted butter.
4 Spoon about 1 tablespoon of the custard 5 cm (2 inches) in from the short edge of each pastry strip. Roll the pastry over the filling, fold the ends in, then roll up. Repeat with the remaining pastry and custard. Arrange on the trays 2 cm (¾ inch) apart. Brush with the remaining butter. Bake for 12–15 minutes, or until crisp and golden. Cool on a wire rack. Dust with combined icing sugar and cinnamon.

chocolate shortbread

✹ ✹

Preparation time: 25 minutes
Cooking time: 10 minutes
Serves 6

185 g (6½ oz/1½ cups) plain
    (all-purpose) flour
40 g (1½ oz/⅓ cup) unsweetened
    cocoa powder
90 g (3¼ oz/¾ cup) icing
    (confectioners') sugar
225 g (8 oz) unsalted butter,
    chilled and cubed
2 egg yolks
1 teaspoon natural vanilla extract
250 ml (9 fl oz/1 cup) pouring (whipping)
    cream, whipped
250 g (9 oz) strawberries, quartered

BERRY SAUCE
250 g (9 oz) fresh strawberries,
    or frozen, thawed
1 tablespoon caster (superfine) sugar

1 Preheat the oven to 210°C (415°F/Gas 6–7). Line two baking trays with baking paper. Sift the flour, cocoa and icing sugar into a large bowl. Use your fingertips to rub in the butter until the mixture resembles breadcrumbs. Add the egg yolks and vanilla and mix with a knife until the mixture comes together. Turn onto a lightly floured surface and gather into a ball.
2 Roll the pastry between two layers of baking paper to 5 mm (¼ inch) thick. Use a 7 cm (2¾ inch) fluted round cutter to cut 18 rounds from the pastry. Place on the trays and bake for 8 minutes, or until cooked. Transfer to a wire rack to cool.
3 Place a shortbread on a plate, top with a little cream and some strawberries. Top with a second shortbread, cream and strawberries, then a third shortbread. Repeat to make another five stacks. For the sauce, process the strawberries and sugar until smooth and stir in 1–2 tablespoons water, until pourable. Serve with the shortbreads.

custard rolls

sicilian cannoli

Preparation time: 30 minutes + 30 minutes
   chilling time
Cooking time: 5 minutes
Makes 12

300 g (10½ oz) plain (all-purpose)
   flour
1 tablespoon caster (superfine) sugar
1 teaspoon ground cinnamon
40 g (1½ oz) unsalted butter
60 ml (2 fl oz/¼ cup) Marsala
vegetable oil, for deep-frying
icing (confectioners') sugar, to dust

FILLING
500 g (1 lb 2 oz) ricotta cheese
1 teaspoon orange flower water
100 g (3½ oz) cedro, diced (see Note)
60 g (2¼ oz) dark chocolate, coarsely
   grated or chopped
1 tablespoon finely grated orange zest
60 g (2¼ oz/½ cup) icing
   (confectioners') sugar

1 To make the filling, combine all the ingredients in a bowl and mix. Add 2 tablespoons water and mix well. Cover with plastic wrap and refrigerate.

2 Combine the flour, sugar and cinnamon in a bowl, rub in the butter and add the Marsala. Mix until the dough comes together in a loose clump, then knead on a lightly floured surface for 4–5 minutes, or until smooth. Wrap in plastic wrap and refrigerate for at least 30 minutes.

3 Cut the dough in half and roll each portion on a lightly floured surface into a thin sheet about 5 mm (¼ inch) thick. Cut each dough half into six 9 cm (3½ inch) squares. Place a cannoli tube (see Note) diagonally across the middle of each square. Fold the sides over the tube, moistening the overlap with water, then press together.

4 Heat the oil in a large deep frying pan to 180°C (350°F), or until a cube of bread dropped into the oil browns in 15 seconds. Drop one or two tubes at a time into the hot oil. Fry gently until golden brown and crisp. Remove from the oil, gently remove the moulds and drain on crumpled paper towels. When they are cool, fill a piping (icing) bag with the ricotta mixture and fill the shells. Dust with icing sugar and serve.

NOTE: Cedro, also known as citron, is a citrus fruit with a very thick, knobbly skin. The skin is used to make candied peel. Cannoli tubes are available at kitchenware shops. You can also use 2 cm (¾ inch) diameter wooden dowels cut into 12 cm (4½ inch) lengths.

baklava

Preparation time: 30 minutes + 2 hours
   cooling time
Cooking time: 1 hour 15 minutes
Makes 18 pieces

540 g (1 lb 3 oz/2⅓ cups) caster
   (superfine) sugar
1½ teaspoons finely grated lemon zest
90 g (3¼ oz/¼ cup) honey
60 ml (2 fl oz/¼ cup) lemon juice
2 tablespoons orange flower water
200 g (7 oz) walnuts, finely chopped
200 g (7 oz) pistachio nuts, finely chopped
200 g (7 oz) almonds, finely chopped
2 tablespoons caster (superfine) sugar, extra
2 teaspoons ground cinnamon
200 g (7 oz) unsalted butter, melted
375 g (13 oz) filo pastry

1 Put the sugar, lemon zest and 375 ml (13 fl oz/1½ cups) water in a saucepan and stir over high heat until the sugar dissolves, then boil for 5 minutes. Reduce the heat to low and simmer for 5 minutes, or until the syrup thickens slightly and just coats the back of a spoon. Add the honey, lemon juice and orange water and cook for 2 minutes. Remove from the heat and leave to cool completely.

2 Preheat the oven to 170°C (325°F/ Gas 3). Combine the nuts, extra sugar and cinnamon in a bowl. Brush the base and sides of a 27 x 30 cm (10¾ x 12 inch) ovenproof dish or tin with the melted

sicilian cannoli

butter. Cover the base with a single layer of filo pastry, brush lightly with the butter, folding in any overhanging edges. Continue layering the filo, brushing each new layer with butter and folding in the edges until 10 sheets have been used. Keep the unused filo under a damp tea towel (dish towel).

3 Sprinkle half the nut mixture over the pastry and pat down evenly. Repeat the layering and buttering of five more filo sheets, sprinkle with the remaining nuts, then continue to layer and butter the remaining sheets, including the top layer. Press down with your hands so the pastry and nuts stick to each other. Use a large sharp knife to cut into diamond shapes, ensuring you cut through to the bottom layer. Pour any remaining butter evenly over the top and smooth with your hands. Bake for 30 minutes, then reduce the temperature to 150°C (300°F/Gas 2) and cook for another 30 minutes.

4 Immediately cut through the diamond markings, then strain the syrup evenly over the top. Cool for 2 hours then lift the diamonds onto a serving platter.

NOTE: To achieve the right texture, it is important for the baklava to be piping hot and the syrup cold when pouring the syrup over.

pear dumplings

Preparation time: 40 minutes + cooling time
Cooking time: 40 minutes
Serves 4

250 g (8 oz/1 cup) caster (superfine) sugar
2 cinnamon sticks
2 cloves
4 pears
250 g (9 oz/2 cups) plain (all-purpose) flour
150 g (5 oz) unsalted butter, chilled and cubed
85 g (3 oz/⅔ cup) icing (confectioners') sugar
80 ml (2½ fl oz/⅓ cup) lemon juice

1 egg, lightly beaten
vanilla ice cream, to serve

1 Stir the sugar with 1.5 litres (52 fl oz/6 cups) water in a large saucepan over low heat until the sugar dissolves. Add the cinnamon and cloves and bring to the boil.
2 Peel the pears, leaving the stems intact. Add to the pan, cover and simmer for about 10 minutes, until just tender when tested with the point of a sharp knife. Remove the pears, drain and cool. Remove the pear cores using a corer — leave the stem attached.
3 Sift the flour into a large bowl and rub in the butter until it resembles fine breadcrumbs. Stir in the icing sugar. Add almost all the juice and mix with a flat-bladed knife until the mixture comes together, adding more juice if necessary. Turn onto a lightly floured surface and

gather into a ball. Wrap in plastic wrap and refrigerate for 20 minutes.
4 Preheat the oven to 180°C (350°F/Gas 4). Line a baking tray with baking paper. Divide the dough into four equal portions and roll one portion out to a 23 cm (9 inches) diameter circle. Place a pear in the centre of the pastry, cut the pastry into a wide cross and set cut-out sections aside. Carefully fold one section of pastry at a time up the side of the pear, trimming and pressing the edges together to neatly cover. Repeat with the remaining pears and pastry.
5 Cut leaf shapes from the leftover pastry. Brush the pears all over with egg and attach the leaves, then brush the leaves with egg. Put the pears on the tray and bake for 30 minutes, or until golden brown. Serve warm with ice cream.

baked desserts

Baked desserts are the stuff of childhood dreams ... reminiscences
of chilly afternoons and the hot rush of spicy-sweet air when the oven
door is opened. The majority of the recipes in this chapter are real
old-fashioned favourites — crumbles and cobblers, betties and
puddings. Comfort food to warm and nurture, these desserts are often
an irresistible combination of autumn fruits and buttery doughs. But
that's not to say this is strictly a cold-weather chapter ... the truly
dedicated can enjoy their baked desserts all year round.

slump

✹ ✹

Preparation time: **30 minutes**
Cooking time: **30 minutes**
Serves **6**

500 g (1 lb 2 oz) fresh cherries, pitted
caster (superfine) sugar, to taste
185 g (6½ oz/1½ cups) self-raising flour
1 teaspoon baking powder
50 g (1¾ oz) unsalted butter,
    chilled and cubed
55 g (2 oz/¼ cup) raw (demerara) sugar
150 ml (5 fl oz) pouring (whipping) cream
lightly whipped cream, to serve

1 Cook the cherries in 60 ml (2 fl oz/
¼ cup) water in a large saucepan over
moderate heat for 5 minutes, or until they
begin to soften. Add the sugar. Place in a
1 litre (35 fl oz/4 cup) ovenproof dish to
cool. Preheat oven to 200°C (400°F/Gas 6).
2 Sift the flour, baking powder and a
little salt into a large bowl, add the
butter and demerara sugar and rub in,
using your fingertips, to form fine crumbs.
Pour in the cream and stir well to mix
everything together.
3 Cover the cooled cherries with blobs of
the scone topping, leaving small gaps
between the blobs. Bake for 25 minutes,
or until the topping is puffed and golden.
Serve with cream.

plum cobbler

✹ ✹

Preparation time: **15 minutes**
Cooking time: **45 minutes**
Serves **6–8**

750 g (1 lb 10 oz) blood plums,
    or other plums
60 g (2¼ oz/¼ cup) caster (superfine)
    sugar

TOPPING
125 g (4½ oz/1 cup) self-raising flour
60 g (2¼ oz/½ cup) plain (all-purpose) flour
60 g (2¼ oz/¼ cup) caster (superfine) sugar

plum cobbler

125 g (4 ½ oz) unsalted butter, chopped
1 egg
125 ml (4 fl oz/½ cup) milk
icing (confectioners') sugar, to dust

1 Preheat the oven to 180°C (350°F/
Gas 4). Lightly grease a 2 litre (70 fl oz/
8 cup) ovenproof dish. Cut the plums into
quarters, discarding the stones.
2 Put the plums in a pan with the sugar
and 1 tablespoon water. Stir over low
heat for 5 minutes, or until the sugar
dissolves and the fruit softens slightly.

Spread the plum mixture in the
prepared dish.
3 Sift the flours into a bowl, add the
sugar and stir. Rub in the butter, using
your fingertips, until the mixture is fine
and crumbly. Combine the egg and milk
and whisk until smooth. Add to the flour
mixture and stir until just combined. Place
large spoonfuls of mixture on top of the
plums.
4 Bake for 30–40 minutes, or until the
top is golden and cooked through. Dust
with icing sugar to serve.

rice pudding with lemon thyme and strawberries

✳ ✳

Preparation time: 20 minutes + standing time
Cooking time: 1 hour 15 minutes
Serves 6–8

500 g (1 lb 2 oz) strawberries
2 tablespoons balsamic vinegar
90 g (3¼ oz/⅓ cup) caster (superfine) sugar
150 g (5½ oz/¾ cup) long-grain white rice
750 ml (26 fl oz/3 cups) milk
6 x 3 cm (1¼ inch) sprigs lemon thyme
90 g (3¼ oz/⅓ cup) sugar
3 egg yolks
1 egg

1 Hull the strawberries and cut in half. Put in a bowl with the vinegar. Sprinkle the sugar over the top and stir to combine. Leave to absorb the flavours while making the rice, turning occasionally.
2 Preheat the oven to 160°C (315°F/ Gas 2–3). Brush a 1.5 litre (52 fl oz/6 cup) ovenproof dish with oil or melted butter.
3 Rinse the rice well and put in a medium pan with 375 ml (13 fl oz/1½ cups) water. Bring to the boil, cover and cook over low heat for 8–10 minutes. Remove from the heat and leave the pan with the lid on for 5 minutes, until the liquid is absorbed and the rice is soft.
4 Heat the milk with the lemon thyme and sugar in a small pan. When bubbles form at the edge, remove from the heat and set aside for 10 minutes so that it absorbs flavour from the lemon thyme. Strain. Beat the egg yolks and egg in a large bowl, add the rice and gradually stir in the warm milk. Pour into the prepared dish. Place the dish in a baking dish and carefully pour in enough warm water to come halfway up the side of the pudding dish. Bake for 50–60 minutes, or until the pudding is just set (timing may vary according to the dish used). Remove from the oven and stand for 10 minutes. Serve warm or cold with the strawberries.

rice pudding

Short-grain rice is traditionally used for rice pudding, as the starch in the grains breaks down to thicken the pudding and give it a creamy quality. Short-grain rice is also much more absorbent. Long-grain rice can also be used but, as it does not contain the same amount of starch or have the same kind of absorbency, it needs a creamy mixture added to it to give the same effect. As a rule, rice grains absorb up to four or five times their own volume in liquid when cooked slowly in the oven or on the stovetop. Baked rice puddings do not require quite as much work as they do not need to be stirred as they cook. Asian rice puddings use glutinous black or white rice to give either creamy, silky puddings, or sticky puddings that can be cut into pieces.

self-saucing chocolate pudding

Preparation time: 25 minutes
Cooking time: 40 minutes
Serves 4–6

125 g (4½ oz/1 cup) self-raising flour
40 g (1½ oz/⅓ cup) unsweetened
   cocoa powder
310 g (11 oz/1¼ cups) caster
   (superfine) sugar
125 ml (4 fl oz/½ cup) milk
1 egg
60 g (2¼ oz) unsalted butter,
   melted

1 teaspoon natural vanilla extract
600 ml (21 fl oz) boiling water

ORANGE CREAM
310 ml (10¾ fl oz/1¼ cups) pouring
   (whipping) cream
1 teaspoon finely grated orange zest
1 tablespoon icing (confectioners') sugar
1 tablespoon Grand Marnier

1 Preheat the oven to 180°C (350°F/
Gas 4) and grease a 2 litre (70 fl oz/
8 cup) ovenproof dish. Sift the flour and
2 tablespoons of the cocoa into a large
bowl. Stir in 125 g (4½ oz/½ cup) of the
sugar and make a well in the centre.
2 Pour in the combined milk, egg, butter
and vanilla. Stir until smooth, but do not
overbeat. Pour into the dish. Dissolve the
remaining cocoa and sugar in the boiling
water. Pour gently over the back of a
spoon over the pudding mixture.
3 Bake the pudding for 40 minutes, or
until cooked when tested with a skewer.
4 To make the orange cream, beat the
cream, orange zest, icing sugar and Grand
Marnier until soft peaks form.
5 Serve the pudding immediately with
the orange cream.

eve's pudding

Preparation time: 25 minutes
Cooking time: 55 minutes
Serves 4–6

500 g (1 lb 2 oz) cooking apples
2 tablespoons sugar
125 g (4½ oz) unsalted butter
125 g (4½ oz/½ cup) caster (superfine) sugar
2 eggs
1 teaspoon natural vanilla extract
125 ml (4 fl oz/½ cup) milk
185 g (6½ oz/1½ cups) self-raising flour

1 Preheat the oven to 180°C (350°F/
Gas 4). Grease a deep, 1.5 litre (52 fl oz/
6 cup) ovenproof dish with oil or
melted butter.
2 Peel, core and thickly slice the
apples. Place the apple slices, sugar and
1 tablespoon water in a saucepan. Cover
and cook over medium heat for
12 minutes, or until the apples are soft
but still hold their shape. Use a slotted
spoon to transfer the apples to the base
of the prepared dish. Allow to cool.
3 Use electric beaters to beat the butter
and sugar until light and creamy. Add the
eggs, one at a time, beating well after
each addition. Use a large metal spoon to
fold in the combined vanilla and milk
alternately with the sifted flour.
4 Spoon the mixture over the apples
and smooth the surface. Bake for 40–45
minutes, or until the pudding is cooked
when tested with a skewer and a sauce
has formed underneath.

self-saucing chocolate pudding

lemon delicious

✹ ✹

Preparation time: 20 minutes
Cooking time: 40 minutes
Serves 4

60 g (2¼ oz) unsalted butter
185 g (6½ oz/¾ cup) caster
    (superfine) sugar
3 eggs, separated
1 teaspoon finely grated lemon zest
40 g (1½ oz/⅓ cup) self-raising flour, sifted
60 ml (2 fl oz/¼ cup) lemon juice
185 ml (6 fl oz/¾ cup) milk
icing (confectioners') sugar (optional),
    to dust

1 Preheat the oven to 180°C (350°F/
Gas 4). Brush a 1 litre (35 fl oz/4 cups)
ovenproof dish with butter or oil.
2 Use electric beaters to beat the butter,
sugar, egg yolks and lemon zest in a small
bowl until the mixture is light and creamy.
Transfer to a medium bowl.
3 Add the flour and stir with a wooden
spoon until just combined. Add the lemon
juice and milk and stir to combine.
4 Place the egg whites in a small, dry
bowl. Use electric beaters to whisk until
firm peaks form. Fold in the pudding
mixture with a metal spoon until just
combined.
5 Spoon into the ovenproof dish and
place the dish in a deep baking dish.
Pour in boiling water to come one-third
of the way up the side of the pudding
dish. Bake for 40 minutes or until a
cake-like topping forms over a sauce. Dust
with icing sugar, if desired. Spoon some
sauce on each serving.

lemon delicious

lemon tips

When buying lemons, select fruit that
are heavy for their size and feel firm.
Thinner-skinned lemons such as Lisbon
and Meyer are juicier than thick-
skinned ones such as Eureka. Lisbon
and Eureka have more acidity and are
tarter than Meyer lemons.

The juice of one lemon is usually
about three tablespoons. Lemons at
room temperature, or those warmed in
the microwave for a few seconds, juice
more easily than cold ones.

To grate zest easily, cover the fine
side of a grater with a piece of baking

paper and grate through the paper. Pull
the paper off the grater and scrape off
the zest.

The essential oils contained in
lemon zest give a perfume rather than
flavour. The flavour comes mainly from
the juice.

Discard any lemons that have soft
patches or look as if they are about to
go mouldy. Lemons will go mouldy
more quickly if stored with other fruit,
so store separately.

apple betty

for 10–15 minutes, until the apples are soft. Beat to a rough purée.

2 Preheat the oven to 180°C (350°F/Gas 4). Melt the remaining butter in a frying pan over low heat. Add the breadcrumbs and the remaining brown sugar. Toss together until all the crumbs are coated, and continue tossing while you fry the crumbs until golden brown.

3 Spread one-third of the crumbs in a 1 litre (35 fl oz/4 cup) ovenproof dish and top with half the apple purée in an even layer. Repeat with another one-third of the crumbs and the remaining apple, then finish with a layer of crumbs. Bake for 20 minutes, until crisp and golden on top.

apple crumble

Preparation time: **20 minutes**
Cooking time: **45 minutes**
Serves **4–6**

8 cooking apples (about 1.4 kg/3 lb 2 oz)
2 tablespoons caster (superfine) sugar
125 g (4½ oz/1 cup) plain (all-purpose) flour
95 g (3¼ oz/½ cup) soft brown sugar
¾ teaspoon ground cinnamon
100 g (3½ oz) butter, chopped
vanilla ice cream, to serve

1 Preheat the oven to 180°C (350°F/Gas 4). Peel and core the apples and cut each one into eight wedges. Place in a saucepan with 60 ml (2 fl oz/¼ cup) water, bring to a simmer, then reduce the heat to low and cover. Cook for about 15 minutes, or until the apples are just soft. Remove from the heat, drain and then stir in the sugar. Spoon the apple into a 1.5 litre (52 fl oz/6 cup) ovenproof dish.
2 Place the flour in a bowl and stir in the brown sugar and cinnamon. Add the butter and rub with your fingertips until the mixture resembles coarse breadcrumbs. Sprinkle evenly over the top of the apple mixture to cover completely. Bake for 25–30 minutes, or until crisp and golden brown. Serve immediately with ice cream.

apple betty

Preparation time: **15 minutes**
Cooking time: **50 minutes**
Serves **4–6**

5 cooking apples, peeled, cored and chopped
100 g (3½ oz) unsalted butter

95 g (3¼ oz/½ cup) soft brown sugar, plus 1 tablespoon extra
finely grated zest of 1 lemon
¼ teaspoon ground cinnamon
pinch of freshly grated nutmeg
240 g (8½ oz/3 cups) fresh breadcrumbs

1 Cook the apples with 1 tablespoon of the butter, 1 tablespoon brown sugar and the lemon zest, cinnamon and nutmeg,

rhubarb crumble

Preparation time: 15 minutes
Cooking time: 25 minutes
Serves 4–6

1 kg (2 lb 4 oz) rhubarb
140 g (5 oz/⅔ cup) sugar
100 g (3½ oz) unsalted butter
90 g (3¼ oz/¾ cup) plain (all-purpose) flour
75 g (2¾ oz/⅓ cup) raw (demerara) sugar
10 amaretti biscuits (cookies), crushed

CRUNCHY MAPLE CREAM
200 ml (7 fl oz) thick (double/heavy) cream
2 tablespoons pure maple syrup
   or golden syrup
3 amaretti biscuits (cookies), extra, crushed

1 Preheat the oven to 200°C (400°F/
Gas 6). Trim the rhubarb, cut into short
lengths and put in a saucepan with the
sugar. Stir over low heat until the sugar
dissolves, then cover and simmer for 8–10
minutes, or until the rhubarb is soft but
still holding its shape. Spoon into a deep
1.5 litre (52 fl oz/6 cup) ovenproof dish.
2 Rub the butter into the flour until the
mixture resembles fine breadcrumbs, then
stir in the demerara sugar and amaretti.
3 Sprinkle the crumble over the stewed
rhubarb and bake for 15 minutes, or until
the topping is golden brown.
4 To make the crunchy maple cream,
place the cream in a bowl then carefully
swirl the maple syrup and the crushed
amaretti through. Do not overmix —
there should be rich veins of the crunchy
syrup through the cream. Serve with
the crumble.

NOTE: Taste the rhubarb before putting
in the ovenproof dish, as you may need to
add a little more sugar.

maple syrup

The sap of North American (Canadian) maple trees is collected and concentrated for use as a sweetener. Traditionally used by natives such as the Algonquins, European colonists soon began to include it in their diet. Maple syrup is mostly sucrose and water, with a unique caramel or toffee flavour. Different grades of syrup range in colour from a light golden shade to a strongly flavoured dark amber.

bread and butter pudding

✳

Preparation time: 20 minutes + 30 minutes
    soaking and 1 hour chilling time
Cooking time: 40 minutes
Serves 4

60 g (2¼ oz) mixed raisins and sultanas
    (golden raisins)
2 tablespoons brandy or dark rum

30 g (1 oz) unsalted butter
4 thick slices quality white bread or brioche
3 eggs
3 tablespoons caster (superfine) sugar
750 ml (26 fl oz/3 cups) milk
60 ml (2 fl oz/¼ cup) pouring
    (whipping) cream
¼ teaspoon natural natural vanilla extract
¼ teaspoon ground cinnamon
1 tablespoon raw (demerara) sugar

1 Soak the raisins and sultanas in the
brandy or rum for about 30 minutes.

2 Butter the bread or brioche and cut
each into eight triangles. Arrange the
bread in a 1 litre (35 fl oz/4 cup)
ovenproof dish.
3 Mix the eggs with the sugar. Add the
milk, cream, vanilla and cinnamon and
mix well. Drain the raisins and sultanas
and add any liquid to the custard.
4 Scatter the soaked raisins and sultanas
over the bread and pour the custard over
the top. Cover with plastic wrap and
refrigerate for 1 hour.
5 Preheat the oven to 180°C (350°F/
Gas 4). Remove the pudding from the
refrigerator and sprinkle with the
demerara sugar. Bake for 35–40 minutes,
or until the custard is set and the top
crunchy and golden.

NOTE: It is very important that you use
good-quality bread for this recipe.
Ordinary sliced white bread will tend to
go a bit claggy when it soaks up the milk.

caramel bread pudding

✳ ✳

Preparation time: 60 minutes + overnight
    chilling time
Cooking time: 1 hour
Serves 6–8

160 g (5¾ oz/⅔ cup) caster (superfine) sugar
500 g (1 lb 2 oz) brioche or panettone
125 g (4½ oz/½ cup) caster (superfine)
    sugar, extra
500 ml (17 fl oz/2 cups) milk
2 wide strips lemon zest, white pith removed
3 eggs, lightly beaten
fresh fruit and cream, to serve

1 Lightly brush a 23 x 13 x 7 cm
(9 x 5 x 2¾ inch), 1.25 litre (44 fl oz/
5 cup) loaf tin with melted butter or oil.
2 Place the sugar with 2 tablespoons
water in a small saucepan over medium
heat and stir, without boiling, until the
sugar dissolves. Bring to the boil, reduce
the heat and simmer, without stirring, until

bread and butter pudding

bread and butter pudding

Bread and butter pudding can be made with all sorts of bread or cake leftovers. Croissants, Danish pastries, panettone, brioche and any kind of fruit loaf and buns make luscious bread and butter puddings. A sprinkling of demerara sugar or crushed sugar cubes will give a lovely crunchy topping. For a shiny top, glaze the hot pudding with apricot jam.

the syrup becomes a rich golden colour. Watch carefully towards the end of cooking to prevent burning. Pour immediately into the loaf tin and leave to cool.

3 Use a large serrated knife to cut the brioche or panettone into 2 cm (¾ inch) thick slices, removing the crusts. Trim into large pieces to fit the tin in three layers, filling any gaps with slices cut to size.

4 Stir the extra caster (superfine) sugar, milk and lemon zest in a saucepan over low heat until the sugar dissolves. Bring just to the boil, remove from the heat and transfer to a jug to allow the lemon flavour to be absorbed and the mixture to cool. Remove the lemon zest and whisk

in the beaten eggs. Pour the mixture gradually into the tin, allowing it to soak into the brioche after each addition. Set aside for 20 minutes. Preheat the oven to 180°C (350°F/Gas 4).

5 Place the loaf tin into a large baking dish and pour in enough hot water to come halfway up the sides of the tin. Bake the pudding for 50 minutes, until just set. Carefully remove the tin from the baking dish and set aside to cool. Refrigerate the pudding overnight.

6 Cut into slices and serve with fresh fruit and cream.

cointreau bread puddings
with orange cream

2 Whisk together the eggs, honey, milk, cream and reserved Cointreau. Slice the bread thickly. Remove the crusts. Put a slice in each ramekin, trimming to fit. Top each with another slice of bread. Pour the egg mixture over the top, giving it time to soak in.
3 Put ramekins in a baking dish and pour water into the dish to come halfway up the sides of the ramekins. Bake for 25–30 minutes, or until set. Leave for 5 minutes before turning out.
4 To make the orange cream, whip together the cream and icing sugar until peaks form. Fold in the Cointreau, zest and nutmeg. Serve with the puddings.

cabinet pudding

Preparation time: 40 minutes
Cooking time: 50 minutes
Serves 6

4 tablespoons sugar
100 g (3½ oz) mixed dried fruit
2 tablespoons dark rum or boiling water
150 g (5½ oz) sponge cake
500 ml (17 fl oz/2 cups) milk
4 eggs
1 teaspoon natural vanilla extract

1 Preheat the oven to 180°C (350°F/Gas 4). Grease six 185 ml (6 fl oz/¾ cup) dariole moulds. Sprinkle the base and side with 1 tablespoon of the sugar. Soak the fruit in the rum for 15–20 minutes.
2 Cut the sponge into 5 mm (¼ inch) cubes and combine with the fruit and rum mixture. Spoon evenly into the moulds. Warm the milk in a small saucepan, until bubbles appear around the edge. Whisk the eggs and remaining sugar together. Whisk in the milk and vanilla. Pour evenly into the moulds over the sponge mixture.
3 Place the moulds in a large baking dish, half filled with boiling water. Bake for 40–45 minutes, or until the custard is set. Remove from the water and leave for 2–3 minutes then turn out onto plates.

cointreau bread puddings with orange cream

Preparation time: 40 minutes + 2 hours soaking time
Cooking time: 30 minutes
Serves 4

60 g (2¼ oz) muscatels or sultanas (golden raisins)
80 ml (2½ fl oz/⅓ cup) Cointreau
5 eggs
115 g (4 oz/⅓ cup) honey
250 ml (9 fl oz/1 cup) milk

250 ml (9 fl oz/1 cup) pouring (whipping) cream
1 loaf crusty white bread

ORANGE CREAM
250 ml (9 fl oz/1 cup) pouring (whipping) cream
2 teaspoons icing (confectioners') sugar
2 teaspoons Cointreau
finely grated zest of 1 orange
sprinkle of freshly grated nutmeg

1 Soak the muscatels or sultanas in Cointreau for 2 hours, or overnight. Drain, reserving the liquid. Preheat the oven to 180°C (350°F/Gas 4). Grease four 250 ml (9 fl oz/1 cup) ramekins and divide the muscatels among the ramekins.

cherry clafoutis

Preparation time: **15 minutes**
Cooking time: **35 minutes**
Serves **6–8**

500 g (1 lb 2 oz) fresh cherries, pitted, or
   2 x 415 g (14¾ oz) tins pitted cherries
60 g (2¼ oz/½ cup) plain (all-purpose) flour
90 g (3¼ oz/⅓ cup) sugar
4 eggs, lightly beaten
250 ml (9 fl oz/1 cup) milk
25 g (1 oz) unsalted butter, melted
icing (confectioners') sugar, to dust

1 Preheat the oven to 180°C (350°F/
Gas 4). Brush a shallow ovenproof dish
or 23 cm (9 inch) pie plate with melted
butter.
2 Spread the cherries into the dish in a
single layer. If using tinned cherries, drain
them thoroughly in a sieve before
spreading in the plate. If they are still wet,
they will leak into the batter.
3 Sift the flour into a bowl, add the sugar
and make a well in the centre. Gradually
add the combined eggs, milk and butter,
whisking until smooth and free of lumps.
4 Pour the batter over the cherries
and bake for 30–35 minutes or until the
batter is risen and golden. Remove from
the oven and dust with icing sugar.
Serve immediately.

NOTE: Use a shallow ovenproof dish
or pie plate or the top will not turn
golden brown.

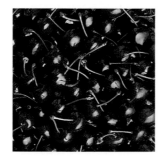

clafoutis

A clafoutis (pronounced 'clafootee') is a classic French batter pudding traditionally made with cherries. However, other berries such as blueberries, blackberries, raspberries or small strawberries can be used instead. A delicious version can also be made using slices of peach or pear.

hazelnut puddings

✳ ✳

Preparation time: 40 minutes
Cooking time: 30 minutes
Serves 8

30 g (1 oz) unsalted butter, melted
60 g (2¼ oz) ground hazelnuts
125 g (4½ oz) unsalted butter
125 g (4½ oz/½ cup) caster (superfine) sugar
3 eggs, lightly beaten
250 g (9 oz/2 cups) self-raising flour, sifted
60 g (2¼ oz) sultanas (golden raisins)

80 ml (2½ fl oz/⅓ cup) brandy
80 ml (2½ fl oz/⅓ cup) buttermilk
crème anglaise and white chocolate curls,
    to serve

CHOCOLATE CREAM SAUCE
250 ml (9 fl oz/1 cup) pouring (whipping)
    cream
30 g (1 oz) unsalted butter
200 g (7 oz) good-quality dark chocolate,
    chopped

1 Preheat the oven to 180°C (350°F/
Gas 4). Brush eight 125 ml (4 fl oz/
½ cup) ovenproof pudding moulds or
ramekins with the melted butter and
coat with the ground hazelnuts, shaking
off the excess.
2 Beat the butter and sugar until light
and creamy. Add the egg gradually,
beating well after each addition. Fold in
the flour, sultanas, brandy and buttermilk.
Divide among the ramekins, cover each
with a piece of greased foil with a pleat in
it, and secure with string.
3 Place the puddings in a large baking
dish and pour in enough water to come
three-quarters of the way up the sides of
the ramekins. Bake for 25 minutes, topping
up with more water if necessary. A skewer
inserted into the centre of the pudding will
come out clean when cooked.
4 To make the sauce, put the cream,
butter and chocolate in a small saucepan
and stir over low heat until melted and
smooth. Unmould the warm puddings
onto plates. If they are reluctant to
come out, run a knife around the edges
of the mould. Serve with chocolate cream
sauce, crème anglaise and chocolate curls
(page 208).

hazelnut puddings

apple charlotte

✳ ✳

Preparation time: 50 minutes
Cooking time: 40 minutes
Serves 8

1.25 kg (2 lb 12 oz) cooking apples,
    peeled, cored and sliced
125 g (4½ oz/½ cup) caster (superfine) sugar
finely grated zest of 1 lemon
1 cinnamon stick
30 g (1 oz) unsalted butter
1 loaf sliced white bread, crusts removed
a little softened unsalted butter

GARNISH
20 g (¾ oz) unsalted butter
3 tablespoons sugar
1 large apple, peeled, cored and sliced
200 ml (7 fl oz) orange juice

1 Cook the apples in a large saucepan with the sugar, lemon zest, cinnamon stick and butter over low heat, stirring occasionally, until the apples are tender and the mixture is thick.

2 Preheat the oven to 200°C (400°F/ Gas 6). Brush eight 125 ml (4 fl oz/½ cup) ramekins with melted butter, or a 1.25 litre (44 fl oz/5 cup) capacity charlotte tin or pudding basin (steamed pudding mould).

3 To make the mini charlottes, cut 16 rounds of bread, spread with butter and put a round in each ramekin, buttered-side-down. Cut the remaining bread into wide strips, butter and use to line the sides of the ramekins, either cutting to fit, or overlapping a little, with the buttered side against the ramekin. Spoon the apple into the ramekins, pressing down firmly. Put the remaining buttered rounds of bread on top, buttered-side-up. Press down and bake for 15 minutes, or until golden.

4 For the large charlotte, cut a round of bread to fit the base and wide strips to line the sides. Leave enough bread to cover the top. Butter the bread and line the mould, butter-side-out. Fill with the apple, cover with the remaining bread buttered-side-up and bake for 30–40 minutes. Cover if it starts to overbrown.

5 For the garnish, melt the butter, add the sugar and stir to dissolve. Add the apple and brown lightly. Add the orange juice, bring to the boil, reduce the heat and simmer until cooked. Remove the apple and reduce the syrup by two-thirds.

6 Cool the charlottes a little before turning out. Top the charlottes with the apple, pour syrup over and serve.

queen of puddings

Preparation time: **25 minutes**
Cooking time: **55 minutes**
Serves **6**

80 g (2¾ oz/1 cup) fresh white
   breadcrumbs
500 ml (17 fl oz/2 cups) milk, scalded
2 eggs, separated
90 g (3¼ oz/⅓ cup) sugar
3 tablespoons strawberry jam
150 g (5½ oz) strawberries, hulled
   and sliced

1 Preheat the oven to 180°C (350°F/ Gas 4). Place the breadcrumbs in a bowl with the hot milk and leave for 10 minutes. Beat the egg yolks with half the sugar and stir into the crumb mixture.

2 Spoon the custard into a greased ovenproof dish and bake for 45 minutes, or until firm. Reduce the oven to 160°C (315°F/Gas 2–3).

3 Combine the jam and strawberries and spread over the custard. Whisk the egg whites until stiff, then whisk in the remaining sugar to form a meringue. Swirl over the top. Bake for 8–10 minutes, or until the meringue is set and lightly browned. Serve warm.

brioche dough

Brioche dough, as used here, is a rich dough containing up to half its weight in butter, plus other enriching ingredients such as sugar and eggs. These ingredients all contribute to a softer, more tender texture, which makes the dough a little harder to handle. Lots of kneading and slow rising help this dough take on a smoothness. Yeast needs a little sugar to help it rise, but too much sugar will inhibit it and have the reverse effect. The sugar syrups for the savarin and babas are what give them their sweetness.

pineapple savarin

✿ ✿ ✿

Preparation time: 40 minutes + 55 minutes
 rising time
Cooking time: 40 minutes
Serves 6–8

2 teaspoons dried yeast
170 ml (5½ fl oz/⅔ cup) unsweetened
 pineapple juice, warmed
2 teaspoons caster (superfine) sugar
250 g (9 oz/2 cups) plain (all-purpose) flour
3 eggs, lightly beaten
90 g (3¼ oz) unsalted butter, softened
pineapple slices, to serve

RUM SYRUP
250 g (9 oz/1 cup) caster (superfine) sugar
375 ml (13 fl oz/1½ cups) unsweetened
 pineapple juice
5 cm (2 inch) piece lemon zest
125 ml (4 fl oz/½ cup) dark rum

1   Grease a 25 cm (10 inch) deep savarin ring. Dissolve the yeast in the pineapple juice, then stir in the sugar. Set aside for 5 minutes, or until frothy. Sift the flour and ¼ teaspoon salt into a large bowl. Add the yeast and eggs and beat with a cupped hand for 5 minutes. Add the butter and beat by hand for 5 minutes. Cover and set aside in a warm, draught-free place for

45 minutes, or until bubbly and well-risen. Press down on the dough to push the air out, and beat by hand for 1–2 minutes.
2   Ladle into the ring and cover loosely with plastic wrap. Set aside in a warm, draught-free place for 10 minutes. Preheat the oven to 190°C (375°F/Gas 5). Bake on a baking tray for 25 minutes, or until firm and golden (it may overflow in the centre).
3   Meanwhile, to make the rum syrup, stir the sugar, juice and zest in a small saucepan over low heat until the sugar dissolves. Bring to the boil and boil, without stirring, for 10–15 minutes or until slightly thickened. Remove the zest. Add the rum.

4 When the savarin is cooked, trim to a flat base with a knife. Turn out of the tin and stand on a rack over a tray. Prick all over with a toothpick. While the savarin is still hot, drizzle with rum syrup, pouring the excess back from where it is caught in the tray, until all the syrup is absorbed. Serve decorated with pineapple slices.

rum baba with figs

✳ ✳ ✳

Preparation time: 40 minutes + 55 minutes
  rising time
Cooking time: 30 minutes
Makes 10

185 g (6½ oz/1½ cups) plain
  (all-purpose) flour
2 teaspoons dried yeast
2 teaspoons sugar
80 ml (2½ fl oz/⅓ cup) lukewarm milk
80 g (2¾ oz) unsalted butter, cubed
3 eggs, lightly beaten
375 g (13 oz/1½ cups) caster
  (superfine) sugar
80 ml (2½ fl oz/⅓ cup) dark rum, plus
  2 tablespoons, extra
240 g (8½ oz/¾ cup) apricot jam
4–6 fresh figs, halved, to serve

1 Brush ten 125 ml (4 fl oz/½ cup) dariole or baba moulds lightly with oil. Place 1 tablespoon of the flour with the yeast, sugar, milk and ¼ teaspoon salt in a small bowl. Leave, covered with plastic wrap, in a warm, draught-free place for about 10 minutes, or until foamy.
2 Use your fingertips to rub the butter into the remaining flour in a large bowl, until the mixture has a fine crumbly texture. Add the yeast mixture and the eggs to the flour mixture. Beat with a cupped hand for 2 minutes, until smooth and glossy. Scrape the mixture down the side of the bowl. Leave, covered with plastic wrap, in a warm, draught-free place for 45 minutes, until well risen.
3 Preheat the oven to 210°C (415°F/ Gas 6–7). Use a wooden spoon or your hand to beat the mixture again for

2 minutes. Divide among the prepared tins. Set aside, covered with plastic wrap, for another 10 minutes, until well risen. Bake for 20 minutes, until golden brown.
4 Meanwhile, combine the sugar with 500 ml (17 fl oz/2 cups) water in a saucepan. Stir over low heat, without boiling, until the sugar dissolves. Bring to the boil, reduce the heat slightly and simmer, without stirring, for 15 minutes. Remove from the heat, cool slightly and add the rum.
5 Turn the babas out onto a wire rack placed over a tray. Prick all over with a toothpick. Brush the warm babas liberally with warm rum syrup until well soaked, then allow to drain. Pour the excess syrup from the baking tray into a jug, straining to remove any crumbs.

6 Heat the apricot jam in a small pan or in the microwave, then strain through a fine sieve. Add the extra rum, stir to combine and brush warm jam all over the babas, to glaze. Serve with warm babas with the reserved syrup and figs.

NOTE: Rum babas are best served on the day they are made. If you do not have dariole or baba moulds, use empty small baked bean tins. The 130 g (4½ oz) size is best. Wash and dry the tins thoroughly and prepare as directed.

  Baba is a yeasted, open-textured cake soaked in rum and sugar syrup. Babas sometimes include raisins in their dough.

semolina and tapioca

Semolina is a kind of wheat flour. The names derives from simila, a fine wheat flour in Latin, and semola, Italian for bran. Semolina is the coarse particles left when wheat is milled, then sifted. Semolina sprinkled in the base of a fruit tart soaks up any excess juice. Sago is made from the powdered starch made from the pith of various palm trees, including the sago palm. The name is from the Malay, sagu. It is a flavourless, easily digested starch, sometimes sold as 'seed tapioca'. Tapioca is starch from the cassava or manioc root. The moist starch is shaken in drops onto a hot plate, which makes it form 'pearls'. Tapioca and sago are interchangeable.

coconut tapioca

Combine 150 g (5½ oz/⅔ cup) small pearl tapioca and 875 ml (30 fl oz/3½ cups) coconut milk in a large heavy-based pan with a split vanilla bean. Stir over low heat until the tapioca pearls turn translucent, about 15 minutes. Keep stirring. Add 125 g (4 ¼ oz/½ cup) caster (superfine) sugar and stir until dissolved. Transfer the tapioca to a bowl, leave to cool, then refrigerate until cold. Serve in small dishes with a little coconut milk poured over, and sprinkled with chopped pistachio nuts.

semolina pudding

❋ ❋

Preparation time: 10 minutes
Cooking time: 30 minutes
Serves 6

90 g (3¼ oz/¾ cup) semolina
500 ml (17 fl oz/2 cups) milk
4 tablespoons sugar
40 g (1½ oz) unsalted butter
2 tablespoons ground almonds
¼ teaspoon natural natural vanilla extract
2 eggs, lightly beaten
50 g (1¾ oz) blanched almonds
    (optional), to serve

1 Preheat the oven to 180°C (350°F/ Gas 4). Combine the semolina, milk and 3 tablespoons of the sugar in a saucepan and bring to the boil. Reduce the heat and simmer for about 10 minutes, stirring continuously, until thick. When cooked, add the butter, ground almonds, vanilla and eggs. Mix until well combined.
2 Pour into six 125 ml (4 fl oz/½ cup) ramekins or moulds, sprinkle with the remaining sugar and bake for 15 minutes, or until golden brown. When baked, score the top with a hot metal skewer. (Heat the skewer over a gas flame or on an electric ring. When it is very hot, lay it across the

top of the pudding until it leaves a mark. Repeat to form a pattern.)

3 To serve, roast the blanched almonds, if using, until golden brown, chop finely and sprinkle over the top.

ricotta pots with raspberries

Preparation time: **20 minutes**
Cooking time: **25 minutes**
Serves **4**

4 eggs, separated
125 g (4½ oz/½ cup) caster (superfine) sugar
350 g (12 oz) ricotta cheese
35 g (1¼ oz) finely chopped pistachio nuts
1 teaspoon finely grated lemon zest
2 tablespoons lemon juice
1 tablespoon vanilla sugar (see Note)
200 g (7 oz) raspberries
icing (confectioners') sugar, to dust

1 Preheat the oven to 180°C (350°F/ Gas 4). Beat the egg yolks and sugar in a small bowl until thick and pale. Transfer to a large bowl and add the ricotta, pistachio nuts, lemon zest and juice and mix well.

2 In a separate bowl, whisk the egg whites to stiff peaks. Whisk in the vanilla sugar, then gently fold into the ricotta mixture, until just combined.

3 Lightly grease four 250 ml (9 fl oz/ 1 cup) ramekins. Divide the raspberries among the dishes and spoon the ricotta cheese mixture over the top. Place on a baking tray and bake for 20–25 minutes, or until puffed and lightly browned. Serve immediately, dusted with icing sugar.

NOTE: You can buy vanilla sugar or make your own. Split a whole vanilla bean in half lengthways and place in a jar of caster (superfine) sugar (about 1 kg/ 2 lb 4 oz). Leave for at least 4 days.

sticky & steamed

'What's for pudding?' The steamed pudding has become such a national institution in Britain that the word is now taken to refer to any dessert, from apple pie to lemon sorbet. Even the French call steamed puds 'le pouding' in acknowledgement of their country of origin. What is it that has made the steamed pudding one of the most beloved dishes since recipes were first written down? Why are they so adored that a special pudding is made every year and ritually eaten on Christmas Day? Just one sticky mouthful, with a pouring of hot sauce, and it's not too difficult to understand.

full steam ahead

Steamed puddings are one of the oldest, most traditional desserts. Whether dense and rich or light and cakey, they're usually served hot with a sauce.

Originally, pudding mixture was tied in a floured and buttered cloth and suspended from a wooden spoon in a saucepan of boiling water to cook. Now, it is more common to use a pudding basin (steamed pudding mould), available in ceramic, glass, steel and aluminium. Ceramic basins don't have a lid but are the best insulators and let the pudding cook through without overcooking the edges — the outside shouldn't be crusty when the centre is cooked.

to steam a pudding

First you will need a pudding basin with the right capacity. Measure this carefully by filling it with water from a measuring jug or cup. If your basin is too small, you might find your pudding expanding right out of it.

Next, you need a large saucepan with a tight-fitting lid. The pan should comfortably hold a trivet or upturned saucer with the basin on top, with space for the lid to fit properly. You can, of course, use a steamer to cook puddings, and collapsible metal vegetable steamers can have their handles unscrewed so that you can stand a basin on them. Mini puddings can be cooked in a bamboo steamer or bain marie in the oven.

Prepare the pudding basin by greasing it and placing a circle of baking paper in the bottom (the base may be very small but, if you don't do it, turning out your pudding can be a messy business). Next, make the foil and paper covering to go over the pudding while it cooks. Place a sheet of foil on the work surface, then a sheet of baking paper on top of it (a few dabs of oil on the foil will hold the paper in place). Grease the paper. Make a large pleat across the width of the foil and paper to allow for expansion as the pudding rises and pushes against it. Place the empty basin in the pan on top of its trivet and pour in cold

water to come halfway up the side of the basin. Remove the empty pudding basin from the pan and put the water on to boil.

Prepare the pudding mixture and spoon it into the basin, levelling off the top. Place the foil and paper across the top of the basin, foil-side-up, and smooth it down the side — do not press it onto the top of the pudding. If you are using a metal basin, just clip on the lid. If not, tie a double piece of string around the rim of the basin — ceramic basins have a rim under which the string will sit tightly. Tie the string tightly in a knot and then, using another double piece of string, tie a handle onto the string around the basin — this will enable you to lift the pudding in and out of the water easily. If you make steamed puddings often, you may want to buy a pudding cloth. Whatever you use, the covering should be fairly watertight as you need to keep the mixture dry.

Lower the pudding carefully into the boiling water and lower the heat to a fast simmer. Cover with the lid and cook as directed. If your lid fits well, you should not have to replenish the water too often, but you will need to keep an eye on the water level and top it up with boiling water (to keep the cooking temperature constant) when necessary.

When the cooking time is up, remove the basin from the pan and take off the foil and paper cover. If the pudding is a solid one, test it with a skewer (a fruit pudding, however, may leave the skewer sticky if you hit a piece of fruit) or press the top gently — it should be firm in the centre and well risen. Do not overcook the pudding — it should be moist with a light, even texture. If the pudding is not cooked, simply re-cover it and continue cooking until done. Leave to stand for 5 minutes, then invert carefully onto a plate.

If the pudding is reluctant to come out of the basin, carefully run a palette or flat-bladed knife around the edge.

spotted dick

This traditional suet pudding is usually made in the shape of a cylinder. It was also once known as spotted dog and plum bolster.

spotted dick

✳ ✳

Preparation time: 20 minutes
Cooking time: 1 hour 30 minutes
Serves 4

185 g (6½ oz/1¼ cups) plain
    (all-purpose) flour
1½ teaspoons baking powder
125 g (4½ oz/½ cup) sugar
1½ teaspoons ground ginger
160 g (5¾ oz/2 cups) fresh breadcrumbs
60 g (2¼ oz) sultanas (golden raisins)
110 g (3¾ oz) currants
125 g (4½ oz) suet, grated
2 teaspoons finely grated lemon zest
2 eggs, lightly beaten

170 ml (5½ fl oz/⅔ cup) milk
custard or pouring (whipping) cream,
    to serve

1   Sift the flour, baking powder, sugar and ginger into a large bowl. Add the breadcrumbs, sultanas, currants, suet and lemon zest. Mix with a wooden spoon.
2   Combine the egg and milk, add to the dry ingredients and mix well. Add a little more milk if necessary, then set aside for 5 minutes.
3   Lay a sheet of baking paper on a work surface and form the mixture into a roll shape about 20 cm (8 inches) long. Roll the pudding in the paper and fold up the ends — do not wrap it too tight as it has to expand as it cooks. Wrap the roll in a tea towel (dish towel), put it in the top of a bamboo or metal steamer over simmering water, cover and steam for 1 hour 30 minutes. Do not let the saucepan boil dry — replenish with boiling water as the pudding cooks. Unmould the pudding onto a plate and slice. Serve with custard or cream.

banana upside down cake

✳

Preparation time: 20 minutes
Cooking time: 45 minutes
Serves 8

50 g (1¾ oz) unsalted butter, melted
60 g (2¼ oz/⅓ cup) soft brown sugar
6 very ripe large bananas, halved
    lengthways
125 g (4½ oz) unsalted butter, extra,
    softened
230 g (8½ oz/1¼ cups) soft brown sugar,
    extra
2 eggs, lightly beaten
185 g (6½ oz/1¼ cups) self-raising flour
1 teaspoon baking powder
2 large bananas, extra, mashed

1   Preheat the oven to 180°C (350°F/ Gas 4). Grease and line a 20 cm (8 inch)

banana upside down cake

square cake tin. Pour the melted butter over the base of the tin and sprinkle with the sugar. Arrange the halved bananas, cut side down, over the brown sugar. Beat the butter and extra brown sugar using electric beaters until light and fluffy. Add the eggs gradually, beating well after each addition.
2 Sift the flour and baking powder into a bowl, then fold into the cake mixture with the mashed banana. Carefully spread into the tin. Bake for 45 minutes, or until a skewer inserted into the centre of the cake comes out clean. Turn out onto a wire rack while still warm. Serve warm or at room temperature.

sussex pond pudding

✳ ✳ ✳

Preparation time: **20 minutes**
Cooking time: **3–4 hours**
Serves **4–6**

340 g (11¾ oz/2¾ cups) self-raising flour
170 g (6 oz) suet or unsalted butter, frozen
150 ml (5 fl oz) milk
250 g (9 oz) unsalted butter, cubed
250 g (9 oz) raw (demerara) sugar
1 thin-skinned lemon

1 Grease a 1.5 litre (52 fl oz/6 cup) pudding basin (steamed pudding mould) and place in a saucepan on a trivet. Pour in enough water to come halfway up the side of the basin. Remove the basin and put the water on to boil. Place a sheet of foil on a work surface and put a sheet of baking paper on top. Grease the paper. Make a large pleat in the centre of the foil and paper.
2 Sift the flour into a large bowl, wrap one end of the frozen suet or butter in foil and grate into the flour. Mix into the flour, then mix in the milk and 150 ml (5 fl oz) water, using a flat-bladed knife. Bring together with your hand.
3 Keep one-quarter of the pastry aside for the lid and roll the rest into a 25 cm (10 inch) circle, leaving the middle thicker than the edges. Lift this into the basin and

Press the pastry upwards against the sides of the basin until it fits, leaving a little bit above the rim.

Add half the butter and sugar, then the lemon which has been pricked all over, followed by the remaining butter and sugar.

press upwards against the sides until it fits, leaving a little bit above the rim.
4 Put half the butter and sugar in the basin, prick the lemon all over with a skewer and add to the basin with the rest of the butter and sugar. Fold the edge of the pastry into the basin and brush with water. Roll out the remaining pastry to form a lid and press firmly onto the rim of the pastry. Place the foil and paper over the basin, foil-side-up. Cover if your basin

has a lid. If not, tie a double piece of string around the rim, knot tightly and, using another double piece of string, tie a handle onto the string to make it easier to remove when ready. Lower the basin into the water. Cover the pan with a lid and steam for 3–4 hours, topping up the water when necessary.
5 Invert the pudding onto a plate with a rim. When cut, juices will flow out to form the 'pond'.

Cut a square from a piece of calico or a tea towel (dish towel) and boil it in a pan of boiling water for 20 minutes.

Spread the cloth out and dust with a thick, even layer of sifted flour, leaving a border around the edge.

Bring the points of the cloth together, gathering in all the excess. Try to make the folds neat and even.

Tie the top as tightly as possible with a piece of unwaxed string, so that no water can get in.

christmas pudding

💥 💥 💥

Preparation time: 40 minutes
Cooking time: 8 hours
Serves 10–12

640 g (1 lb 7 oz/4 cups) mixed sultanas (golden raisins), currants and raisins
330 g (11¾ oz/1⅔ cups) mixed dried fruit, chopped
45 g (1½ oz/¼ cup) mixed peel (mixed candied citrus peel)
125 ml (4 fl oz/½ cup) brown ale
2 tablespoons dark rum or brandy
80 ml (2½ fl oz/⅓ cup) orange juice
80 ml (2½ fl oz/⅓ cup) lemon juice
1 teaspoon finely grated orange zest
1 teaspoon finely grated lemon zest
225 g (8 oz) suet, grated
245 g (8½ oz/1⅓ cups) soft brown sugar
3 eggs, lightly beaten
200 g (7 oz/2½ cups) fresh white breadcrumbs
90 g (3¼ oz/¾ cup) self-raising flour
1 teaspoon mixed (pumpkin pie) spice
¼ teaspoon freshly grated nutmeg
100 g (3½ oz/⅔ cup) blanched almonds, roughly chopped
thick (double/heavy) cream and brandy custard, to serve

1 Put the sultanas, currants, raisins, mixed dried fruit, mixed peel, brown ale, rum, orange and lemon juices and zests into a large bowl and stir together. Cover and leave overnight.
2 Add the suet, brown sugar, egg, breadcrumbs, flour, spices, almonds and a pinch of salt to the bowl and mix well. The mixture should fall from the spoon — if it is too stiff, add a little more ale.
3 Put a 2 litre (70 fl oz/8 cup) pudding basin (steamed pudding mould) on a trivet or upturned saucer in a large saucepan with a lid, and pour in enough water to come halfway up the side of the basin. Remove the basin and put the water on to boil.

4 Fill the pudding basin with the pudding mixture. To cover the pudding, place a sheet of foil on the bench, top with a piece of baking paper and brush the paper with melted butter. Fold a pleat across the centre of the foil and paper. Put the paper and foil, foil side up, over the basin. Tie a double length of string firmly around the rim of the basin, then tie a double length of string onto that string to form a handle to lower the pudding into the water. If you have a basin with a lid, clip it on at this stage. The paper/foil lid prevents any moisture from getting into the pudding and making it soggy.
5 Use the handle to carefully lower the pudding into the saucepan and reduce the heat until the water is simmering quickly. Cover the saucepan. Steam the pudding for 8 hours, replenishing with boiling water when necessary. If you want to keep your pudding and reheat it later, then steam it for 6 hours and steam it for another 2 hours on the day you would like to eat it. Store in a cool, dry place for up to 3 months. Serve with cream and brandy custard.

NOTE: Buy suet from your butcher.

brandy butter

Use electric beaters to beat 250 g (9 oz) softened butter and 185 g
(6½ oz/1½ cups) sifted icing (confectioners') sugar until smooth and creamy.
Gradually add 60 ml (2 fl oz/¼ cup) brandy, beating thoroughly between each
addition. Refrigerate, or pipe rosettes onto a baking tray lined with baking paper
and refrigerate until required. Serves 8–10.

chocolate pudding

✷ ✷

Preparation time: 20 minutes
Cooking time: 1 hour 25 minutes
Serves 6

125 g (4½ oz) dark chocolate, chopped
90 g (3¼ oz) unsalted butter, at room
   temperature
95 g (3¼ oz/½ cup) soft brown sugar
3 eggs, separated
1 teaspoon natural vanilla extract
125 g (4½ oz/1 cup) self-raising flour
1 tablespoon unsweetened cocoa powder
½ teaspoon bicarbonate of soda
   (baking soda)
60 ml (2 fl oz/¼ cup) milk
2 tablespoons brandy
whipped cream, to serve

CHOCOLATE SAUCE
125 g (4½ oz) dark chocolate, chopped
60 ml (2 fl oz/¼ cup) pouring cream
1 tablespoon brandy

1   Grease a 1.25 litre (44 fl oz/5 cup)
pudding basin (steamed pudding mould)
and line the base with a circle of baking
paper. Preheat the oven to 180°C
(350°F/Gas 4).
2   Put the chocolate in a heatproof bowl.
Half-fill a saucepan with water and bring
to the boil, then remove the pan from the
heat. Sit the bowl over the pan, making
sure the base of the bowl doesn't touch the
water. Stir occasionally until chocolate has
melted. Set aside to cool. Keep the pan of
water for making the chocolate sauce.
3   Beat butter and half the brown sugar
until light and creamy. Beat in egg yolks,
melted chocolate and vanilla. Sift together
the flour, cocoa and bicarbonate of soda.
Fold into the mixture, alternating with
spoonfuls of combined milk and brandy.
4   Whisk the egg whites in a clean,
dry bowl until soft peaks form. Gradually
whisk in the remaining sugar, until
stiff and glossy, then fold into the
chocolate mixture.
5   Pour into the prepared basin. Cover
tightly with foil and secure with string. Put

in a deep ovenproof dish and pour in
enough hot water to come halfway up the
side of the basin. Bake for 1¼ hours, or
until a skewer comes out clean. Unmould
onto a serving plate.
6   To make the chocolate sauce, put
chocolate, cream and brandy in a
heatproof bowl. Reheat the saucepan of
water, bring to the boil, then remove from
the heat. Sit the bowl over the pan,
making sure the bowl doesn't touch the
water. Stir occasionally until chocolate has
melted and the sauce is smooth. Serve the
pudding with the chocolate sauce and
whipped cream.

fig pudding with brandy sauce

✷ ✷

Preparation time: 40 minutes + 2 hours
   standing time
Cooking time: 4 hours
Serves 8–10

240 g (8½ oz) soft dessert figs, chopped
225 g (8 oz) pitted dates, chopped
90 g (3¼ oz) raisins
80 g (2¾ oz) glacé ginger, chopped
2 tablespoons brandy or orange juice
60 g (2¼ oz/⅓ cup) soft brown sugar
240 g (8½ oz/3 cups) fresh white
   breadcrumbs
250 g (9 oz/2 cups) self-raising flour, sifted
160 g (5¾ oz) unsalted butter, melted
3 eggs, lightly beaten
125 ml (4 fl oz/½ cup) milk
2 teaspoons finely grated lemon zest
3 tablespoons lemon juice
figs (optional), sliced, to decorate

BRANDY SAUCE
30 g (1 oz/¼ cup) cornflour (cornstarch)
60 g (2¼ oz/¼ cup) caster (superfine) sugar
500 ml (17 fl oz/2 cups) milk
30 g (1 oz) unsalted butter
80 ml (2½ fl oz/⅓ cup) brandy

1   Combine the figs, dates, raisins and
ginger in a bowl. Stir in the brandy or

orange juice and set aside for at least
2 hours. Grease a 2 litre (70 fl oz/8 cup)
pudding basin (steamed pudding mould)
and line the base with baking paper. Place
the empty basin in a saucepan, on a trivet,
and pour in enough water to come
halfway up the side of the basin. Remove
the basin and put the water on to boil.
Place a sheet of foil on a work surface and
put a sheet of baking paper on top. Grease
the paper. Make a large pleat in the centre
of the foil and paper.
2   Combine brown sugar, breadcrumbs
and sifted flour. Stir in the soaked fruit,
then add butter, eggs, milk, lemon zest
and juice and stir until evenly mixed.
Spoon into the basin and press firmly to
eliminate air bubbles. Smooth the surface,
cover with the foil and paper, foil-side up,
and smooth down the sides. Do not press
onto the top of the pudding. Cover if your
basin has a lid. If not, tie a double piece of
string around the rim, knot tightly and,
using another double piece of string, tie a
handle onto the string so you can lift the
pudding in and out.
3   Gently lower the basin into the pan
of boiling water, reduce to a fast simmer,
cover the pan and cook for 4 hours, or
until a skewer comes out clean. Remove
the basin from the water, remove the
coverings and leave for 5 minutes before
turning out onto a serving plate.
4   To make the sauce, combine cornflour
and sugar in a pan and mix to a smooth
paste with a little milk. Add the remaining
milk and whisk over medium heat for
3–4 minutes, until the sauce boils and
thickens. Stir in the butter and brandy.
Serve with the hot fig pudding. Decorate
with sliced figs, if desired.

steamed upside down mango pudding

✹ ✹ ✹

Preparation time: **35 minutes**
Cooking time: **1 hour 30 minutes**
Serves **4–6**

3 tablespoons sugar
400 g (14 oz) tin mangoes
  in natural juice
100 g (3½ oz) soft unsalted butter
125 g (4½ oz/½ cup) caster (superfine) sugar
½ teaspoon finely grated lime zest
2 eggs
125g (4½ oz/1 cup) self-raising flour
3 tablespoons ground almonds
pinch of crushed cardamom seeds
1 tablespoon lime juice
2 teaspoons arrowroot

1 Grease a 1.5 litre (52 fl oz/6 cup) heatproof glass or ceramic pudding basin (steamed pudding mould) with melted butter or oil. Don't use a metal basin or the pudding will stick. Place the empty basin in a saucepan, on a trivet, and pour in enough water to come halfway up the side of the basin. Remove the basin and put the water on to boil. Line the base with baking paper and grease the paper. Place a sheet of foil on a work surface and put a sheet of baking paper on top. Grease the paper. Make a large pleat in the centre of the foil and paper.
2 Combine the sugar and 60 ml (2 fl oz/ ¼ cup) water in a clean, heavy-based saucepan and stir over low heat, tipping the pan from side to side, until the sugar dissolves. Bring to the boil, reduce the heat and simmer, without stirring, until the mixture turns a golden caramel. (This should take about 6 minutes but watch carefully, as it can burn quickly.) As soon as the mixture is golden, pour it quickly into the pudding basin. Set aside.
3 Drain the mangoes and reserve the juice. Cut 5 long strips of mango, set aside and roughly chop the rest. Beat the butter, sugar and lime zest in a small bowl until light and creamy. Add the eggs one at a

time, beating well after each addition. Transfer to a large bowl. Fold in half the flour and the chopped mango. Add the remaining flour, ground almonds and cardamom and mix well.
4 Arrange the reserved mango in a single layer on the caramel in the base of the basin. Spoon the mixture into the basin. Place the foil and paper over the basin, foil-side-up, and smooth it down the sides. Cover if your basin has a lid. If not, tie a double piece of string around the rim, knot tightly and, using another double piece of string, tie a handle onto the string.
5 Carefully lower the basin into the boiling water, reduce to a fast simmer,

cover the pan and simmer for 1 hour 15 minutes, topping up the water if necessary during cooking. When cooked, the pudding should appear well risen and feel firm.
6 To make the sauce, combine the reserved mango juice in a pan with the lime juice. Whisk in the arrowroot and cook over gentle heat, stirring constantly, until the sauce boils, thickens and becomes clear. Loosen the pudding from the basin by running a knife around the edges before turning out. If any pieces of mango stick, place them on the pudding. Serve with the warm mango sauce.

Arrange the shortcake rolls around the base and side, then fill the centre.

hot lime shortcake pudding

✳ ✳

Preparation time: 1 hour 5 minutes
Cooking time: 1 hour 20 minutes
Serves 6

375 g (13 oz/3 cups) plain (all-purpose) flour, sifted
1½ teaspoons baking powder
200 g (7 oz) unsalted butter, chilled and cubed
45 g (1½ oz/½ cup) desiccated coconut
250–300 ml (9–10½ fl oz) pouring (whipping) cream, plus extra, to serve
160 g (5¾ oz/½ cup) lime marmalade

HOT LIME SYRUP
185 g (6½ oz/¾ cup) caster (superfine) sugar
3 limes, peeled and zest cut into thin strips, and juiced
60 g (2¼ oz) unsalted butter

1 Combine the sifted flour, baking powder and a pinch of salt in a large bowl. Rub in the butter until the mixture resembles fine breadcrumbs, then stir in the coconut. Use a knife to mix in almost all the cream. Add the rest, if necessary, to form a soft dough. Bring the dough together with your hands. Roll the dough out between two sheets of baking paper into a 25 x 40 cm (10 x 16 inch) rectangle. Spread with the marmalade, roll up lengthways and refrigerate for 20 minutes.

2 Preheat the oven to 180°C (350°F/ Gas 4). Grease a 1.5 litre (52 fl oz/6 cup) pudding basin (steamed pudding mould). Cut the roll into 2 cm (¾ inch) thick slices and cover the base and side of the basin. Fill the centre with the remaining slices.

3 To make the hot lime syrup, combine all the ingredients in a small pan with 185 ml (6 fl oz/¾ cup) water and stir over low heat until the sugar dissolves. Bring to the boil and pour over the pudding. Put the basin on a tray, to catch drips, and bake for 1 hour 15 minutes, or until a skewer comes out clean. Leave for 15 minutes before turning out. Serve with the cream.

sweet sauces

What a marriage made in heaven ... deliciously sweet sauces poured over sponge puddings that soak up their syrup and soften into irresistible gooeyness.

butterscotch sauce

Stir 75 g (2½ oz) butter, 185 g (6½ oz/1 cup) soft brown sugar and 185 ml (6 fl oz/¾ cup) pouring (whipping) cream in a small saucepan over low heat until the butter melts and the sugar dissolves. Bring to the boil, reduce the heat and simmer for 2 minutes. Makes 420 ml (14½ fl oz/1⅔ cups).

caramel bar sauce

Chop four Snickers® bars. Put in a saucepan with 60 ml (2 fl oz/¼ cup) milk and 185 ml (6 fl oz/¾ cup) pouring (whipping) cream and stir over low heat until melted. Add 100 g (3½ oz) chopped milk chocolate and stir until melted. Cool to room temperature. Makes 560 ml (19¼ fl oz/2¼ cups).

dark chocolate sauce

Put 150 g (5½ oz) chopped dark chocolate in a bowl. Bring 300 ml (10½ fl oz) pouring (whipping) cream to the boil in a saucepan. Stir in 2 tablespoons caster (superfine) sugar, then pour over the chocolate. Leave for 2 minutes. Stir. Add a spoonful of any liqueur. Serve warm. Makes 500 ml (17 fl oz/2 cups).

chocolate fudge sauce

Put 250 ml (9 fl oz/1 cup) pouring (whipping) cream, 30 g (1 oz) butter, 1 tablespoon golden syrup and 200 g (7 oz) chopped dark chocolate in a pan. Stir over low heat until melted and smooth. Serve hot or warm. Makes 500 ml (17 fl oz/2 cups).

liqueur tokay syrup

Put 250 g (9 oz) sugar and 250 ml (9 fl oz/1 cup) water in a medium saucepan. Slowly bring to the boil, stirring to dissolve the sugar. Add half a vanilla bean and boil, without stirring for 5 minutes. Add 250 ml (9 fl oz/1 cup) liqueur tokay, liqueur muscat or sauterne and stir. Bring to the boil and cook for 15 minutes. Makes 500 ml (17 fl oz/2 cups).

vanilla hazelnut sauce

Pour 300 ml (10½ fl oz) pouring (whipping) cream into a small saucepan. Split 1 vanilla bean and scrape seeds into the cream. Add the pod and bring to the boil. Remove from the heat, cover and leave for 10 minutes, then strain. Put 200 g (7 oz) chopped white chocolate in a bowl, reheat the cream and pour over the chocolate. Leave for 2 minutes, then stir until melted. Stir in 30 g (1 oz) chopped roasted hazelnuts. Makes 500 ml (17 fl oz/2 cups).

rich brandy sauce

Bring 500 ml (17 fl oz/2 cups) pouring (whipping) cream to the boil in a heavy-based saucepan. Whisk 4 egg yolks with 125 g (4½ oz/½ cup) caster (superfine) sugar until creamy. Slowly pour the hot cream in, stirring. Return to the pan and stir over low heat for 5–6 minutes, until slightly thickened; do not boil. Stir in 60 ml (2 fl oz/¼ cup) brandy before serving. Makes 810 ml (28 fl oz/3¼ cups).

citrus syrup

Cut the zest from an orange, a lemon and a lime. Remove the pith. Cut the zest into fine strips. Put in a pan with the juice from the lime and half the juice from the lemon and orange. Add 125 g (4½ oz) sugar and 125 ml (4 fl oz/½ cup) water. Stir over low heat to dissolve. Add half a vanilla bean. Simmer for 10 minutes; do not stir. Makes 250 ml (9 fl oz/1 cup).

pecan and maple syrup pudding

beat in the egg, then the vanilla. Combine the flour, three-quarters of the pecans, cinnamon and zest and fold in, alternating with spoonfuls of milk, until smooth.

2 Grease a 2.25 litre (79 fl oz/9 cup) pudding basin (steamed pudding mould) and line the base with a circle of baking paper. Pour three-quarters of the maple syrup into the basin and add the remaining pecans. Fill with mixture and pour the rest of the syrup over.

3 Cover with foil and put in a large baking dish. Pour enough water into the dish to come halfway up the side of the bowl, then bake for 2 hours. Test with a skewer — it should come out clean. Turn out onto a large serving plate. Serve with cream.

steamed orange pudding

Preparation time: 30 minutes
Cooking time: 1 hour 30 minutes
Serves 4

1 thin-skinned orange
90 g (3¼ oz) butter, softened
1 tablespoon sugar
2 eggs
4 tablespoons chunky marmalade
finely grated zest of 1 orange
250 g (9 oz/2 cups) self-raising flour
80 ml (2½ fl oz/⅓ cup) milk

1 Grease a 1.25 litre (44 fl oz/5 cup) pudding basin (steamed pudding mould) and line the base with a circle of baking paper. Place the empty basin in a saucepan on a trivet and pour in enough cold water to come halfway up the side of the basin. Remove the basin and put the water on to boil. Place a sheet of foil on a work surface and put a sheet of baking paper on top. Grease the paper. Make a pleat in the centre to allow for expansion.

2 Remove the skin and pith from the orange by cutting off the top and bottom and cutting downwards all the way round. Slice the orange thinly, place one slice in

pecan and maple syrup pudding

Preparation time: 20 minutes
Cooking time: 2 hours
Serves 8–10

200 g (7 oz) unsalted butter
250 g (9 oz/1 cup) caster (superfine) sugar
4 eggs, lightly beaten

1 teaspoon natural natural vanilla extract
375 g (13 oz/3 cups) self-raising flour, sifted
200 g (7 oz) pecans, chopped
½ teaspoon ground cinnamon
finely grated zest of 1 lemon
185 ml (6 fl oz/¾ cup) milk
250 ml (9 fl oz/1 cup) maple syrup
pouring (whipping) cream, to serve

1 Preheat the oven to 180°C (350°F/ Gas 4). Beat the butter and sugar with electric beaters until creamy. Gradually

the bottom of the basin and arrange the others around the sides.

3 Beat the butter and sugar until light and creamy. Add the eggs, one at a time, and beat well. Add the marmalade and zest, mix in, then add the sifted flour and a pinch of salt and mix thoroughly. Add the milk and spoon the mixture into the basin without disturbing the orange slices. Place the foil and paper over the basin, foil-side-up, and smooth it down the sides. Cover if your basin has a lid. If not, tie a double piece of string around the rim, knot tightly and, using another double piece of string, tie a handle onto the string. Cover the pan and steam for 1 hour 30 minutes, replenishing the water when necessary. Turn out to serve.

with 435 ml (15¼ fl oz/1¾ cups) water. Bring to the boil, then remove from the heat, add the bicarbonate of soda and ginger and leave to stand for 5 minutes.

2 Beat together the butter, sugar and 1 egg with electric beaters until creamy. Beat in the remaining eggs one at a time, beating well after each addition. Fold in the sifted flour and spice, add the date mixture and stir until well combined. Pour into the tin and bake for 55–60 minutes, or until a skewer comes out clean. Cover

with foil if overbrowning during cooking. Stand for 5 minutes before turning out onto a serving plate.

3 To make the caramel sauce, stir all the ingredients in a saucepan over low heat until the sugar dissolves. Simmer, uncovered, for 3 minutes, or until thickened slightly. Brush some sauce all over the warm pudding. Serve immediately with the remaining sauce and the crème fraîche.

sticky date pudding with caramel sauce

☀

Preparation time: 40 minutes
Cooking time: 1 hour 10 minutes
Serves 6–8

370 g (13 oz) pitted dates
1½ teaspoons bicarbonate of soda (baking soda)
1 teaspoon grated fresh ginger
90 g (3¼ oz) unsalted butter
250 g (9 oz/1 cup) caster (superfine) sugar
3 eggs
185 g (6½ oz/1½ cups) self-raising flour
½ teaspoon mixed (pumpkin pie) spice
crème fraîche, to serve

CARAMEL SAUCE
150 g (5½ oz) unsalted butter
230 g (8½ oz/1¼ cups) soft brown sugar
80 ml (2½ fl oz/⅓ cup) golden syrup
185 ml (6 fl oz/¾ cup) pouring (whipping) cream

1 Preheat the oven to 180°C (350°/ Gas 4). Grease and line the base of a deep 23 cm (9 inch) diameter cake tin. Chop the dates and put them in a saucepan

passionfruit

Native to Brazil, passionfruit were named for their flowers, which the Jesuit missionaries thought were a pictorial representation of the crucifix. There are 350 members of the Passiflora species, three of which are the ones most commonly available. Banana passionfruit have a long yellow fruit with a less acidic pulp and juice. Common passionfruit have a deep-purple, wrinkled skin, a red pith and an orangey pulp with small black seeds. Yellow passionfruit have a smoother skin and yellower colour, but less intense flavour. To use the pulp without the seeds, push it through a sieve.

sticky orange and passionfruit pudding

Preparation time: 55 minutes
Cooking time: 55 minutes
Serves 6

375 g (13 oz/3 cups) plain
   (all-purpose) flour
1½ teaspoons baking powder
200 g (7 oz) unsalted butter,
   chilled and cubed
45 g (1½ oz/½ cup) desiccated coconut
300 ml (10½ fl oz) pouring
   (whipping) cream
160 g (5¾ oz/½ cup) orange marmalade
2 tablespoons passionfruit pulp

PASSIONFRUIT SYRUP
125 ml (4 fl oz/½ cup) orange juice
185 g (6½ oz/¾ cup) caster
   (superfine) sugar
60 g (2¼ oz/¼ cup) passionfruit pulp

1 Sift the flour, baking powder and a pinch of salt into a bowl. Rub in the butter with your fingertips until fine and crumbly. Stir in the coconut. With a flat-bladed knife, mix in most of the cream. Add the rest, if needed, to bring the mixture together. Press into a soft dough and roll between two sheets of baking paper to make a 25 x 40 cm (10 x 16 inch) rectangle.
2 Spread marmalade over the dough and drizzle with passionfruit pulp. Roll up lengthways like a swiss roll. Chill for 20 minutes, or until firm.
3 Preheat the oven to 180°C (350°F/ Gas 4). Brush a deep 20 cm (8 inch) spring-form cake tin with melted butter or oil; line base with baking paper. Cut the rolled dough into 2 cm (¾ inch) thick slices; arrange half over base of tin. Place a second layer over the gaps where the slices join. Place the tin on a baking tray.
4 To make the passionfruit syrup, put all the ingredients with 60 ml (2 fl oz/ ¼ cup) water in a saucepan. Stir over low heat, without boiling, until the sugar

dissolves. Bring to the boil, then pour over the pudding. Bake for 50 minutes, or until a skewer comes out clean. Leave for 15 minutes before turning out.

sago plum pudding with rum butter

✳ ✳

Preparation time: 35 minutes + overnight chilling time
Cooking time: 4 hours
Serves 6–8

65 g (2¼ oz/⅓ cup) sago
250 ml (9 fl oz/1 cup) milk
1 teaspoon bicarbonate of soda (baking soda)
140 g (5 oz/¾ cup) dark brown sugar
160 g (5¾ oz/2 cups) fresh white breadcrumbs
80 g (2¾ oz/½ cup) sultanas (golden raisins)
75 g (2½ oz/½ cup) currants
80 g (2¾ oz/½ cup) dried dates, chopped
2 eggs, lightly beaten
60 g (2¼ oz) unsalted butter, melted and cooled
raspberries, to serve
blueberries, to serve
icing (confectioners') sugar, to dust

RUM BUTTER
125 g (4½ oz) butter, softened
140 g (5 oz/¾ cup) dark brown sugar
80 ml (2½ fl oz/⅓ cup) dark rum

1 Combine the sago and milk in a bowl, cover and refrigerate overnight.
2 Lightly grease a 1.5 litre (52 fl oz/ 6 cup) pudding basin (steamed pudding mould) with butter and line base with baking paper. Place the empty basin in a large saucepan on a trivet or upturned saucer and pour in cold water to come halfway up the side of the basin. Remove the basin and put the water on to boil.
3 Transfer the soaked sago and milk to a large bowl and stir in the bicarbonate of soda until dissolved. Stir in the sugar, breadcrumbs, dried fruit, beaten eggs and melted butter and mix well. Spoon into the basin and smooth the surface with wet hands. Cover the pudding (page 168).
4 Cover the basin with the lid and make a string handle. Gently lower the basin into the boiling water, reduce to a fast simmer and cover the saucepan with a tight-fitting lid. Cook for 3½–4 hours, or until a skewer comes out clean. Check the water level every hour and top up with boiling water as necessary.
5 Carefully remove the pudding basin from the saucepan, remove the coverings and leave for 5 minutes before turning out the pudding onto a large serving plate. Loosen the edges with a palette knife, if necessary. Serve decorated with raspberries and blueberries and lightly dusted with icing sugar. Serve hot with cold rum butter.
6 For the rum butter, beat together the butter and sugar with electric beaters for about 3–4 minutes, or until light and creamy. Gradually beat in the rum, 1 tablespoon at a time. You can add more rum, to taste. Transfer to a serving dish, cover and refrigerate until required.

NOTE: Sago is often called pearl sago and is available from supermarkets or health food stores. It is white when uncooked but goes transparent when cooked.

black rice pudding

Preparation time: 10 minutes + 8 hours
    soaking time
Cooking time: 40 minutes
Serves 6–8

400 g (14 oz/2 cups) black
    glutinous rice
3 fresh pandan leaves
500 ml (17 fl oz/2 cups) coconut milk
80 g (2¾ oz) palm sugar (jaggery), grated
3 tablespoons caster (superfine) sugar
coconut cream, to serve

1 Put the rice in a large glass or ceramic
bowl and cover with water. Soak for
8 hours. Drain and put in a pan with 1 litre
(35 fl oz/4 cups) water. Bring slowly to the
boil, stirring frequently, and cook at a low
boil for 20 minutes, or until tender. Drain.
2 Shred the pandan leaves with your
fingers, then knot them. In a large heavy-
based saucepan, heat the coconut milk
until almost boiling. Add the sugars and
pandan and stir until the sugars dissolve.
3 Add the rice to the pan and cook,
stirring, for 3–4 minutes without boiling.
Turn off the heat, cover and leave for
15 minutes. Remove the leaves. Serve
warm with coconut cream.

NOTE: If you can't find pandan leaves
at an Asian grocer, substitute 1 teaspoon
natural vanilla extract.

golden syrup dumplings

Preparation time: 15 minutes
Cooking time: 30 minutes
Serves 4

125 g (4½ oz/1 cup) self-raising flour
40 g (1¼ oz) unsalted butter, cubed
1 egg
1 tablespoon milk

golden syrup dumplings

SYRUP
250 g (9 oz/1 cup) sugar
40 g (1¼ oz) unsalted butter
2 tablespoons golden syrup or light treacle
60 ml (2 fl oz/¼ cup) lemon juice

1 Sift the flour and a pinch of salt
into a bowl. Rub in the butter until fine
and crumbly, and make a well. Use a
flat-bladed knife to stir in the combined
egg and milk to form a soft dough.
2 Put the syrup ingredients in a saucepan
with 500 ml (17 fl oz/2 cups) water and
stir over medium heat until the sugar
dissolves. Bring to the boil, then gently
drop dessertspoons of dough into the
syrup. Cover and reduce the heat to
simmer for 20 minutes, or until a knife
inserted into a dumpling comes out clean.
Serve dumplings drizzled with syrup.

caramel sticky rice

Preparation time: 40 minutes + 8 hours
    soaking time
Cooking time: 1 hour 15 minutes
Serves 4

400 g (14 oz/2 cups) white glutinous
    rice
250 ml (9 fl oz/1 cup) coconut milk
85 g (3 oz) palm sugar (jaggery), grated

1 Put the rice in a sieve and wash until
the water runs clear. Put in a glass or
ceramic bowl, cover with water and soak
for 8 hours. Drain.
2 Line a bamboo steamer with baking
paper or a damp tea towel (dish towel)
and place over a water-filled wok. Don't let
the base of the steamer touch the water.

Spread the rice over the paper, fold the paper or tea towel over the rice and cover with another sheet of paper or tea towel — tuck it in so the rice is encased. Cover with the bamboo lid and steam over medium heat for 50 minutes, checking the water regularly, until just cooked.

3 Stir the coconut milk, palm sugar and a pinch of salt in a small saucepan until boiling. Reduce the heat and simmer for 15 minutes, or until thick.

4 Pour a quarter of the coconut mixture over the rice, fork it through, cover with the paper and lid and steam for 5 minutes. Repeat with the remaining coconut mixture, cooking until the rice is plump and sticky. Transfer the rice to a metal tray or lamington tin, pressing in lightly, then set aside until firm. Cut into diamonds and serve warm.

coconut sago puddings

☀

Preparation time: **10 minutes + 3 hours chilling time**
Cooking time: **1 hour**
Serves **8**

220 ml (7¾ fl oz) coconut milk
90 g (3¼ oz/¼ cup) grated palm sugar (jaggery)
1 stem lemon grass, bruised
250 g (9 oz) sago
1 teaspoon finely grated lime zest
1 egg white, lightly beaten
4 guavas, thinly sliced

LIME SYRUP
500 g (1 lb 2 oz/2 cups) caster (superfine) sugar
1 tablespoon finely shredded fresh ginger
2 limes, peeled and zest cut into thin strips

1 Lightly grease eight 125 ml (4 fl oz/ ½ cup) dariole moulds. Put the coconut milk, palm sugar and lemon grass in a saucepan with 750 ml (26 fl oz/3 cups) water. Bring just to the boil. Add the sago and zest and cook over low heat, stirring, for 35–40 minutes, until the sago is thick and clear.

2 Remove from the heat and cool slightly. Remove the lemon grass. Whisk the egg white into stiff peaks and fold into the sago. Spoon into the moulds, cover with plastic wrap and refrigerate for 3 hours, or until firm. Stand the moulds in hot water for 20 seconds before turning out.

3 To make the lime syrup, put the sugar and 250 ml (9 fl oz/1 cup) water in a pan and stir over low heat until the sugar is dissolved. Bring to the boil and cook for 10 minutes, without stirring, until the syrup thickens. Add the ginger and lime zest and cook for 5 minutes. Arrange the sliced guava on a plate, pour over the lime syrup and serve with the puddings.

coconut sago puddings

Cook the sago over low heat, stirring until the mixture is thick and clear.

Spoon the mixture into the lightly greased dariole moulds, cover with plastic wrap, then chill for 3 hours.

gateaux & trifles

A gateau is simply a cake with its best frock on. More often than not, layered and drenched with liqueur, then lavishly assembled with peaks of cream, fruit, custard or chocolate, the gateau has taken the simple cake from its humble afternoon tea setting to the dizzy heights of spectacular dessert stardom. How ironic that the trifle, like the fool and the flummery, takes its silly name from a 'thing of little importance', a trifling matter in a world of bullying, rumbustious main courses. Had it been created in today's more enlightened times, the trifle might perhaps have been named the 'importance'.

hazelnut torte

✻ ✻

Preparation time: 1 hour
Cooking time: 35 minutes
Serves 8–10

6 egg whites
280 g (10 oz/1¼ cups) caster
    (superfine) sugar
180 g (6½ oz) ground hazelnuts
2 tablespoons plain (all-purpose) flour,
    sifted
100 ml (3½ fl oz) white rum
chopped roasted hazelnuts, to decorate

CHOCOLATE LEAVES
150 g (5½ oz) white chocolate, chopped
non-toxic leaves (choose leaves with
    prominent veins)

WHITE CHOCOLATE CREAM
125 g (4½ oz) white chocolate, chopped
435 ml (15¼ fl oz/1¾ cups) pouring
    (whipping) cream

DARK CHOCOLATE CREAM
40 g (1½ oz) dark chocolate
125 ml (4 fl oz/½ cup) pouring
    (whipping) cream

1 Lightly grease two 20 cm (8 inch) cake
tins. Line the bases with baking paper and
then grease the paper. Dust the tins lightly
with flour, shaking off any excess. Preheat
the oven to 180°C (350°F/Gas 4).
2 Whisk the egg whites in a clean, dry
bowl with electric beaters until stiff peaks
form. Gradually add the sugar, whisking
until thick and glossy.
3 Gently fold in the ground hazelnuts
and flour. Divide the mixture evenly
between the prepared tins and smooth the
tops with wet fingers. Bake for 15–20
minutes, or until the cakes feel spongy to
touch. Leave in the tins to cool a little
before turning out onto wire racks to cool
completely. Cut each cake in half
horizontally with a long serrated knife.
4 To make the chocolate leaves, put the
white chocolate in a heatproof bowl.
Half-fill a saucepan with water and bring

to the boil, then remove the pan from the
heat. Sit the bowl over the pan, making
sure the base of the bowl doesn't touch
the water. Stir occasionally until the
chocolate melts. Use a fine brush to paint
the chocolate over the underside of the
leaves. Leave to set, then peel away the
leaf. If the coating of chocolate is too thin,
it will break when the leaf is removed.
5 To make the white chocolate cream, put
the chocolate in a heatproof bowl. Half-fill
a saucepan with water and bring to the
boil, then remove the pan from the heat.
Sit the bowl over the pan, making sure the
base of the bowl doesn't touch the water.
Stir occasionally until the chocolate melts,
then allow to cool. Whisk the cream in a

bowl with electric beaters until it begins to
hold its shape. Add the chocolate and
whisk it in, then allow to cool. Make the
dark chocolate cream in the same way.
6 Put a layer of cake on a serving plate,
brush the cut surface with a little rum and
spread with a quarter of the white
chocolate cream. Top with a second cake
layer. Brush with rum and spread with all
the dark chocolate cream. Add another
layer of cake and spread with rum and a
quarter of the white chocolate cream. Top
with the final cake layer and spread the
remaining white chocolate cream over the
top and side of the cake. Decorate the
torte with the chocolate leaves and
chopped hazelnuts.

charlotte malakoff

✳ ✳

Preparation time: 1 hour + 8 hours chilling time
Cooking time: nil
Serves 8–12

250 g (9 oz) savoiardi (lady finger) biscuits
  (cookies)
125 ml (4 fl oz/½ cup) Grand Marnier
500 g (1 lb 2 oz) strawberries, hulled
  and halved
whipped cream and strawberries, to serve

ALMOND CREAM
125 g (4½ oz) unsalted butter
80 g (2¾ oz/⅓ cup) caster (superfine) sugar
60 ml (2 fl oz/¼ cup) Grand Marnier
¼ teaspoon almond essence
185 ml (6 fl oz/¾ cup) pouring (whipping)
  cream, whipped
140 g (5 oz/1⅓ cups) ground almonds

1 Brush a deep 1–1.5 litre (35–52 fl oz/
4–6 cup) soufflé dish with melted butter
or oil. Line the base with baking paper
and grease the paper. Trim the biscuits to
fit the height of the dish.
2 Combine the liqueur with 125 ml
(4 fl oz/½ cup) water. Quickly dip the
biscuits into the liqueur mixture and
arrange upright around the side of the
dish, rounded side down.
3 To make the almond cream, use electric
beaters to beat the butter and sugar until
light and creamy. Add the liqueur and
almond essence. Continue beating until the
mixture is smooth and the sugar dissolves.
Use a metal spoon to fold in the whipped
cream and ground almonds.
4 Place one-third of the strawberry halves,
cut-side-down, in the base of the dish.
Spoon one-third of the almond cream over
the strawberries. Top with a layer of dipped
biscuits. Continue layering, finishing with a
layer of biscuits, then press down.
5 Cover with foil and place a small plate
and weight on top. Refrigerate for 8 hours,
or overnight. Remove the plate and foil
and turn onto a chilled serving plate.
Remove the baking paper. Decorate with
whipped cream and strawberries.

sponge fingers

Sponge finger biscuits (cookies) are available in different sizes and under different names. Sometimes called savoiardi biscuits, lady-fingers or boudoir biscuits, they are served with chilled desserts, ice cream and fruit purées, and are used as a border for various desserts. They are made from a light sponge batter that has been baked to form a firm biscuit.

trifles and zuppa inglese

Trifles were originally flavoured creams eaten by the Elizabethans. They changed gradually: the cream was thickened, biscuits and other ingredients were added and decorations were used. In 1755, Hannah Glasse had a recipe for a 'Grand Trifle', described as 'fit to go on a King's table'. It contained biscuits and ratafias soaked in alcohol, a layer of custard, then syllabub on top. Trifle means 'a thing of little importance' and this is where the dish got its name. Zuppa inglese means 'English soup' in Italian, presumably because the dish resembles the English trifle. Originally, it was baked but modern versions are not cooked.

zuppa inglese

Preparation time: 25 minutes + 3 hours chilling time
Cooking time: 5 minutes
Serves 6

500 ml (17 fl oz/2 cups) milk
1 vanilla bean, split lengthways
4 egg yolks
115 g (4 oz/½ cup) caster (superfine) sugar
2 tablespoons plain (all-purpose) flour

300 g (10½ oz) Madeira cake, cut into 1 cm (½ inch) slices
80 ml (2½ fl oz/⅓ cup) dark rum
50 g (1¾ oz) flaked almonds, toasted
30 g (1 oz) chocolate, grated or shaved

1 Heat the milk and vanilla bean in a saucepan over low heat until bubbles appear around the edge of the pan.
2 Whisk the egg yolks, sugar and flour together in a bowl until thick and pale.
3 Discard the vanilla bean and whisk the warm milk slowly into the egg mixture, then blend well. Return to a clean saucepan and stir over medium heat until the custard boils and thickens. Allow to cool slightly.
4 Line the base of a 1.5 litre (52 fl oz/ 6 cup) serving dish with one-third of the cake slices and brush well with the rum combined with 1 tablespoon water. Spread one-third of the custard over the cake. Repeat this process, finishing with a layer of custard. Cover and refrigerate for 3 hours. Sprinkle with almonds and chocolate just before serving.

tipsy trifle

Preparation time: 25 minutes + 1 hour
chilling time
Cooking time: nil
Serves 6

85 g (3 oz) packet apricot jelly crystals
500 ml (17 fl oz/2 cups) boiling water
20 cm (8 inch) sponge cake
160 g (5¾ oz/½ cup) apricot jam
125 ml (4 fl oz/½ cup) brandy
2 sliced bananas, sprinkled with lemon juice
500 ml (17 fl oz/2 cups) prepared custard
250 ml (9 fl oz/1 cup) pouring (whipping)
cream, whipped
60 g (2 ¼ oz) toasted almonds, chopped
pulp of 2 passionfruit

1   Add the jelly crystals to the boiling water and stir until dissolved. Pour into a 27 x 18 cm (10¾ x 7 inch) rectangular tin. Refrigerate until set, then cut into cubes with a rubber spatula.
2   Cut the sponge into small cubes and put in a large serving bowl, or divide among individual parfait glasses. Combine the jam, brandy and 60 ml (2 fl oz/½ cup) water and sprinkle over the sponge.
3   Put the jelly cubes over the sponge and top with the bananas and custard. Top with cream, almonds and passionfruit. Refrigerate for 1 hour or until required.

english trifle

Preparation time: 25 minutes + 3 hours
chilling time
Cooking time: 10 minutes
Serves 6

4 eggs
2 tablespoons caster (superfine) sugar
2 tablespoons plain (all-purpose) flour
500 ml (17 fl oz/2 cups) milk
¼ teaspoon natural vanilla extract
4 slices Madeira cake or trifle sponges
60 ml (2 fl oz/¼ cup) sweet sherry
or Madeira

250 g (9 oz) raspberries, plus extra,
to serve
125 ml (4 fl oz/½ cup) pouring
(whipping) cream, whipped
25 g (1 oz/¼ cup) flaked almonds, to serve

1   Mix the eggs, sugar and flour in a bowl. Heat the milk in a saucepan and stir into the egg mixture. Pour back into a clean saucepan. Cook over medium heat, stirring constantly, until the custard boils and thickens. Stir in the vanilla.

Cover the surface with plastic wrap and refrigerate for 1 hour or until cool.
2   Put the cake in a serving bowl and sprinkle with the sherry. Scatter the raspberries over the top and crush them gently into the sponge with the back of a spoon, leaving some of them whole.
3   Pour the cooled custard over the raspberries and refrigerate for 2 hours or until firm but not solid. Top with the cream, almonds and raspberries to serve.

english trifle

tiramisu

tiramisu

✹

Preparation time: 30 minutes + 2 hours
   chilling time
Cooking time: nil
Serves 6–8

750 ml (26 fl oz/3 cups) strong black
   coffee, cooled
60 ml (2 fl oz/¼ cup) brandy or Kahlua
2 eggs, separated
3 tablespoons caster (superfine) sugar
250 g (9 oz) mascarpone cheese
250 ml (9 fl oz/1 cup) pouring (whipping)
   cream, whipped
16 large sponge finger (lady finger) biscuits
   (cookies)
2 teaspoons unsweetened cocoa powder,
   plus extra, to dust

1 Put the coffee and liqueur in a bowl.
Use electric beaters to whisk the egg yolks
and sugar in a small bowl for 3 minutes, or
until thick and pale. Add the mascarpone
and whisk until just combined. Fold in the
cream with a metal spoon.
2 Whisk the egg whites until soft peaks
form. Fold quickly and lightly into the
cream mixture with a metal spoon.
3 Quickly dip half the biscuits, one at a
time, into the coffee mixture. Drain off
any excess and arrange the biscuits in the
base of a deep serving dish. Spread half
the cream mixture over the biscuits.
4 Dip the remaining biscuits and repeat
the layers. Smooth the surface and dust
with the cocoa. Refrigerate for 2 hours, or
until firm. Serve dusted with extra cocoa.

Fold the beaten egg whites
into the cream mixture with a
metal spoon.

Dip the biscuits into the coffee
mixture and then arrange in the
serving dish.

flourless chocolate roll

✹ ✹

Preparation time: 20 minutes
Cooking time: 25 minutes
Serves 6

5 eggs, separated
140 g (5 oz) caster (superfine) sugar
225 g (8 oz) good-quality dark cooking
   chocolate, chopped

250 ml (9 fl oz/1 cup) pouring
   (whipping) cream
icing (confectioners') sugar,
   to dust

1 Line a baking tray 20 x 30 cm (8 x 12
inch) with baking paper and sprinkle with
a little caster (superfine) sugar. Preheat
the oven to 200°C (400°F/Gas 6).
2 Place the egg yolks and sugar in a bowl
and whisk with electric beaters until thick
and mousse-like. Put the chocolate in a
small saucepan with 75 ml (2¼ fl oz)
water over low heat and melt slowly. When
melted, stir into the egg yolk mixture.
3 Put the egg whites in a large, clean
glass bowl and whisk until stiff peaks
form. Stir one tablespoon into the
chocolate mixture to loosen it, then fold
in the remainder. Spread into the tin and
bake for 12–15 minutes, or until cooked.
4 Turn onto a cooling rack lined with
baking paper. Remove the baking paper
from the roll and cover with a tea towel
(dish towel). Leave to cool. Whip the
cream to firm peaks. Place the roll on a
work surface and spread the bottom
two-thirds with the cream, leaving a small
border around the edge. Roll up, using
the paper as a guide, and pulling it off as
you roll. Don't worry if the roll cracks a
little. Dust with icing sugar.

strawberry swiss roll

✳ ✳

Preparation time: 45 minutes
Cooking time: 10 minutes
Serves 6–8

145 g (5¼ oz/⅔ cup) caster (superfine)
   sugar
3 eggs, separated
90 g (3¼ oz/¾ cup) self-raising flour, sifted
185 ml (6 fl oz/¾ cup) pouring
   (whipping) cream
160 g (5¾ oz/½ cup) strawberry jam
250 g (9 oz/1⅔ cups) strawberries, hulled
   and quartered
whipped cream and sliced strawberries,
   extra, to serve

1 Preheat the oven to 200°C (400°F/
Gas 6). Sprinkle a tablespoon of the sugar
over a piece of baking paper 30 x 35 cm
(12 x 14 inches), resting on a tea towel
(dish towel). Brush a 25 x 30 cm (10 x 12
inch) Swiss roll (jelly roll) tin with oil or
melted butter and line with baking paper.
Whisk the egg whites in a clean, dry
bowl until soft peaks form. Gradually add
115 g (4 oz/½ cup) of the remaining
sugar and beat until dissolved. Beat in the
lightly beaten egg yolks until thick.
2 Fold in the flour and 2 tablespoons hot
water. Spread into the tin and bake for
8–10 minutes, or until firm and golden.

3 Turn out onto the sugared paper and
peel the paper from the base. Use the tea
towel as a guide to roll up loosely from the
narrow end. Leave for 20 minutes, or until
cooled, then unroll. Whisk the cream and
remaining tablespoon of sugar until soft
peaks form. Spread the roll with the jam
and cream and top with the strawberries.
Re-roll and chill. Top with cream and
strawberries to serve.

spices & herbs

While herbs are the leaves of plants, spices can be the root, bark, bud, seed, fruit or stem. Dried spices and herbs are best bought in small quantities and stored in airtight containers in a cool, dark place.

allspice

Also known as Jamaican pepper and myrtle pepper, allspice is a berry, the size of a baby pea, which can be used whole or ground. Used in Christmas pudding.

bay leaf

A dark, glossy green when fresh, bay leaves respond well to drying, which intensifies their flavour. They go well with desserts such as baked custards. Fresh bay leaves keep for a few days in a plastic bag in the refrigerator (wash before use).

cardamom

Cardamom pods are pale green. The brown variety are not true cardamoms and taste different. Each pod contains black and brown seeds, sometimes sold separately. Seeds and ground cardamom lose flavour quickly so it is best to buy pods and bruise them slightly before use, or extract the seeds. Cardamom goes well with coffee and chocolate.

cinnamon and cassia

These come from the bark of different types of laurel trees. Cassia is coarser and redder than cinnamon, with a stronger flavour. Cinnamon is more subtle. Much of what is sold as cinnamon is actually cassia. Ground cinnamon and cassia do not retain their flavour as well and should not be stored too long. Quills should be stored in an airtight container away from light.

ginger

Ginger is available fresh, dried, ground, pickled, preserved in sugar syrup, glacé or crystallised. Ground ginger is best used in baking in small quantities as it has a slightly harsh flavour.

Crystallised, glacé and preserved ginger need to be kept in a cool, dark place or refrigerated—they are good in desserts and ice creams. Ginger complements rhubarb, apples and melon.

cloves

Cloves have a highly aromatic perfume and flavour, which can taste bitter in large doses. They are used whole or ground in sweet dishes, especially festive food such as Christmas puddings and mincemeat. Don't store cloves longer than 6 months.

nutmeg and mace

Two of the strangest looking spices, these are the fruit of a tree, indigenous to the Spice Islands, that contains a hard, dark brown kernel (nutmeg) surrounded by a lacy red covering that dries to a hard yellowy brown (mace). Mace has a milder flavour and is used in cakes and desserts. Nutmeg has a warm flavour that marries well with stewed fruit, custard, rice puddings and eggnog. Ground nutmeg loses its flavour quickly so grate your own on the fine side of a grater when needed.

star anise

This brown star-shaped pod has eight segments, each containing a seed. The pod contains most of the flavour and aroma and can be used whole or ground. It is an ingredient of five-spice powder, and is used in custards, shortbreads and syrups.

vanilla bean

These beans should be dark and supple. Keep in airtight containers in a dark, cool place. To re-use, rinse and dry out. When buying extract or essence, look for those marked 'natural' or 'pure extract'.

whipping cream

Cream is easier to whip if it is cold. When cream is overwhipped, it turns to butter, which happens much faster if the cream is too warm. Cream for whipping needs to have at least 35% butterfat. Cream whipped to soft peaks can be easily folded into other mixtures. Cream whipped until stiff can be piped and used for decoration, but be very careful not to overwhip it before piping, or it will split when it is handled in the bag.

black forest gateau

✵ ✵ ✵

Preparation time: 1 hour + 30 minutes standing and cooling time
Cooking time: 1 hour
Serves 8–10

125 g (4½ oz) unsalted butter
230 g (8 oz/1 cup) caster (superfine) sugar
2 eggs, lightly beaten
1 teaspoon natural vanilla extract
40 g (1½ oz/⅓ cup) self-raising flour
125 g (4½ oz/1 cup) plain (all-purpose) flour
1 teaspoon bicarbonate of soda (baking soda)
60 g (2¼ oz/½ cup) unsweetened cocoa powder
185 ml (6 fl oz/¾ cup) buttermilk
100 g (3½ oz) dark chocolate
100 g (3½ oz) milk chocolate
cherries with stalks, to decorate

FILLING
60 ml (2 fl oz/¼ cup) Kirsch
750 ml (26 fl oz/3 cups) pouring (whipping) cream, whipped
415 g (14¾ oz) tin pitted morello or black cherries, drained

1   Preheat the oven to 180°C (350°F/Gas 4). Lightly grease a deep, 20 cm (8 inch) round cake tin. Line with baking paper.
2   Use electric beaters to beat the butter and sugar until light and creamy. Add the egg gradually, beating thoroughly after each addition. Add the vanilla and beat until well combined. Transfer to a large bowl. Use a metal spoon to fold in the sifted flours, bicarbonate of soda and cocoa alternately with the buttermilk. Mix until combined and the mixture is smooth.
3   Pour the mixture into the tin and smooth the surface. Bake the cake for 50–60 minutes, or until a skewer inserted into the centre of the cake comes out clean. Leave the cake in the tin for 30 minutes before turning out onto a wire rack to cool.
4   When cold, cut the cake horizontally into three layers, using a long serrated knife. The easiest way to do this is to rest

the palm of one hand lightly on top of the cake while cutting into it. Turn the cake every few strokes so the knife cuts in evenly all the way around the edge. When you have gone the whole way round, cut through the middle. Remove the first layer so it will be easier to see what you are doing while cutting the next one.

5 Meanwhile, leave the dark and milk chocolates in a warm place for 10–15 minutes, or until soft but still firm. With a vegetable peeler, and using long strokes, shave curls of chocolate from the side of the block. If the block is too soft, chill it to firm it up.

6 To assemble, place one cake layer on a serving plate and brush liberally with Kirsch. Spread evenly with one-fifth of the whipped cream. Top with half the cherries. Continue layering with the remaining cake, liqueur, cream and cherries, finishing with the cream on top. Spread the remaining cream evenly on the outside of the cake. Coat the side with the chocolate shavings by laying the shavings on a small piece of baking paper and then gently pressing them into the cream. If you use your hands, they will melt, so the paper acts as a barrier. Decorate the top of the cake with the remaining chocolate shavings and the cherries with stalks.

NOTE: Black forest gateau is one of the world's most famous cakes. It originated in Germany's Black Forest region, where it is known as black forest torte.

peaches and cream trifle

Preparation time: 20 minutes + 1 hour chilling time
Cooking time: nil
Serves 6–8

1 day-old sponge cake, cut into cubes
825 g (1 lb 13 oz) tin sliced peaches
60 ml (2 fl oz/¼ cup) Marsala, peach schnapps liqueur or Grand Marnier
250 ml (9 fl oz/1 cup) pouring (whipping) cream
200 g (7 oz) mascarpone cheese
25 g (1 oz) flaked almonds, toasted

1 Put the cake cubes in a 2 litre (70 fl oz/8 cup) dish and press down firmly. Drain the peaches, reserving 125 ml (4 fl oz/½ cup) of juice. Mix the Marsala with the juice and drizzle over the cake.
2 Arrange the peach slices over the cake. Whisk the cream until soft peaks form. Add the mascarpone and whisk briefly, to just mix. Spread over the peaches. Refrigerate for 1 hour. Sprinkle with almonds just before serving.

cranachan

Preparation time: **30 minutes + 2 hours chilling time**
Cooking time: **10 minutes**
Serves **6**

2 tablespoons oatmeal
250 ml (9 fl oz/1 cup) pouring (whipping) cream
2 tablespoons honey
1 tablespoon whisky
500 g (1 lb 2 oz) raspberries or strawberries, hulled, plus extra, to serve
2 tablespoons rolled (porridge) oats, toasted

1 Put the oatmeal in a small frying pan. Stir over low heat for 5 minutes, or until lightly toasted. Remove from the heat and cool completely.
2 Use electric beaters to whisk the cream in a small bowl until soft peaks form. Add the honey and whisky and whisk until just combined. Fold the cooled, toasted oatmeal into the cream mixture with a metal spoon.
3 Layer the berries and cream into six tall dessert glasses, finishing with cream. Refrigerate for 2 hours and serve sprinkled with toasted oats and extra berries.

orange, lemon and white chocolate gateau

Preparation time: **30 minutes**
Cooking time: **10 minutes**
Serves **8–10**

125 g (4½ oz/1 cup) plain (all-purpose) flour
4 eggs, at room temperature
145 g (5 oz/⅔ cup) caster (superfine) sugar
60 g (2¼ oz) unsalted butter, melted and cooled

FILLING
2 tablespoons cornflour (cornstarch)
80 ml (2½ fl oz/⅓ cup) lemon juice

cranachan

80 ml (2½ fl oz/⅓ cup) orange juice
1 teaspoon finely grated lemon zest
1 teaspoon finely grated orange zest
80 g (2¾ oz/⅓ cup) caster (superfine) sugar
2 egg yolks, at room temperature
20 g (¾ oz) unsalted butter

TOPPING
200 g (7 oz) chopped white chocolate
125 ml (4 fl oz/½ cup) pouring (whipping) cream
60 g (2¼ oz) unsalted butter
white chocolate curls and candied lemon zest, to decorate

1 Preheat the oven to 180°C (350°F/ Gas 4). Grease two shallow 20 cm (8 inch) cake tins and line with baking paper.
2 Sift the flour three times onto a sheet of baking paper. Whisk the eggs and sugar with electric beaters until very thick and pale.

3 Use a metal spoon to fold in the flour in two batches, quickly and lightly until just combined. Add the melted butter with the second batch, discarding any white sediment in the butter. Spread into the tins and bake for 20 minutes, until lightly golden. Leave for 2 minutes before turning out onto a wire rack to cool.
4 To make the filling, blend the cornflour with 1 tablespoon water. Place 60 ml (2 fl oz/⅓ cup) water, the juice, zest and sugar in a small saucepan and stir over medium heat, without boiling, until the sugar dissolves. Add the cornflour and stir until the mixture boils and thickens. Cook, stirring, for another minute. Remove from the heat, add the egg yolks and butter and stir well. Transfer to a bowl, cover the surface with plastic wrap and cool completely.
5 To make the topping, place the chocolate, cream and butter in a small

pan and stir over low heat until melted. Transfer to a bowl, cover with plastic wrap and allow to cool completely. Do not refrigerate. Use electric beaters to beat until fluffy.

6 Use a serrated knife to cut the cakes in half horizontally. Place one cake layer on a serving plate and spread evenly with one-third of the filling. Continue layering cake and filling, ending with a cake layer on top. Spread the top and sides of the cake with the topping. Decorate with chocolate curls and candied zest.

NOTE: To make candied lemon zest, cut each lemon into quarters and pull out the flesh. Put the lemon zest in a saucepan of cold water and bring to the boil. Reduce the heat, simmer for 2 minutes, then discard the water and repeat. This will remove the bitterness from the pith. Drain. Combine 220 g (7¾ oz) sugar and 250 ml (9 fl oz/1 cup) water in a pan and dissolve the sugar over low heat, stirring constantly. When the sugar dissolves, bring to the boil, reduce the heat and simmer. Add a few drops of lemon juice and the pieces of lemon zest and cook over very low heat until the pith and zest look translucent. Leave to cool in the syrup, then remove and drain. Cut out desired shapes, using a cutter or sharp knife. Roll the shapes in caster (superfine) sugar.

chocolate cherry trifle

❄

Preparation time: 30 minutes + 3–4 hours
    chilling time
Cooking time: 10 minutes
Serves 6

350 g (12 oz) chocolate cake
2 x 415 g (14¾ oz) tins pitted
    dark cherries
60 ml (2 fl oz/¼ cup) Kirsch
2 egg yolks, at room temperature
2 tablespoons sugar
1 tablespoon cornflour (cornstarch)

250 ml (9 fl oz/1 cup) milk
1 teaspoon vanilla extract
185 ml (6 fl oz/¾ cup) pouring (whipping)
    cream, whipped
whipped cream, extra, to serve
30 g (1 oz) toasted slivered almonds,
    to serve

1 Cut the cake into thin strips. Line the base of a 1.75 litre (61 fl oz/7 cup) serving bowl with a third of the cake.
2 Drain the cherries, reserving the juice. Combine 250 ml (9 fl oz/1 cup) of the juice with the Kirsch and sprinkle some liberally over the cake. Spoon some cherries over the cake.
3 To make the custard, whisk the egg yolks, sugar and cornflour in a heatproof bowl until thick and pale. Heat the milk in a saucepan and bring almost to the boil. Remove from the heat and add the milk gradually to the egg mixture, whisking constantly. Pour the whole mixture back into the pan and stir over medium heat for 5 minutes, or until the custard boils and thickens. Remove from the heat and add the vanilla. Cover the surface with plastic wrap and allow to cool, then fold in the whipped cream.
4 Spoon a third of the custard over the cherries and cake in the bowl. Top with more cake, syrup, cherries and custard. Continue layering, finishing with custard on top. Cover and refrigerate for 3–4 hours. Top with the extra whipped cream and almonds before serving.

hazelnut roll with raspberry cream

Preparation time: 40 minutes + 2 hours
 chilling time
Cooking time: 15 minutes
Serves 8

100 g (3½ oz) roasted hazelnuts
5 eggs, separated
185 g (6½ oz/¾ cup) sugar
1 teaspoon natural vanilla extract
40 g (1½ oz/⅓ cup) self-raising flour
1 tablespoon plain (all-purpose) flour
thick (double/heavy) cream, raspberries and
 chocolate flakes, to serve

RASPBERRY CREAM
170 ml (5½ fl oz/⅔ cup) pouring
 (whipping) cream
200 g (7 oz) raspberries,
 lightly mashed
1 tablespoon caster (superfine)
 sugar
1 tablespoon brandy

1 Preheat the oven to 180°C (350°F/
Gas 4). Brush a 30 x 25 (12 x 10 inch)
swiss roll (jelly roll) tin with oil. Line
with baking paper and grease the paper.
Sprinkle with a little caster (superfine)
sugar. Chop the hazelnuts in a food
processor for 15 seconds, or until
finely crushed.
2 Whisk the egg yolks and sugar with
electric beaters until thick and pale,
then add the vanilla.
3 In a clean, dry bowl, whisk the egg
whites until stiff peaks form. Use a metal
spoon to fold the whites and sifted flours
into the yolks, one-third at a time. Fold
in the nuts with the last third.
4 Spoon the mixture into the tin and
smooth the surface. Bake for 15 minutes,
or until lightly golden and springy to
touch. Turn onto a dry tea towel (dish
towel) covered with baking paper and
sprinkled with sugar and leave to stand
for 1 minute. Use the tea towel as a guide
to carefully roll the cake up with the
paper, then leave for 15 minutes, or until
cool. Unroll and discard the paper.
5 To make the raspberry cream, whisk
the cream until stiff peaks form. Fold
in the raspberries, sugar and brandy
(cream should have a marbled look).
Spread the cream over the cake, leaving
a 1.5 cm (⅝ inch) border. Gently re-roll
and refrigerate for 2 hours before
serving. Serve with cream, raspberries
and chocolate flakes.

mascarpone trifle

Preparation time: **40 minutes + chilling time**
Cooking time: **10 minutes**
Serves **4–6**

175 g (6 oz) plain sponge cake
125 ml (4 fl oz/½ cup) Tia Maria or Kahlua
70 g (2½ oz) dark chocolate, grated
500 g (1 lb 2 oz) strawberries, hulled
unsweetened cocoa powder and icing
   (confectioners') sugar, to dust

CUSTARD
4 egg yolks
2 tablespoons sugar
2 teaspoons cornflour (cornstarch)
125 ml (4 fl oz/½ cup) pouring
   (whipping) cream
125 ml (4 fl oz/½ cup) milk
2 teaspoons natural vanilla extract
350 ml (12 fl oz) pouring
   (whipping) cream, extra
250 g (9 oz) mascarpone cheese

1 Cut the cake into chunks and put
in the base of a 1.75 litre (61 fl oz/7 cup)
dish. Spoon the liqueur over the cake
and sprinkle with half the grated
chocolate. Slice a third of the strawberries
and sprinkle over the top. Cover and
refrigerate.
2 To make the custard, whisk together
the yolks, sugar and cornflour until thick
and pale. Heat the cream and milk in a
saucepan until almost boiling, then
gradually whisk into the yolk mixture.
Pour into a clean pan and return to low
heat, until the custard thickens and coats
the back of a spoon. Remove from the
heat and stir in the vanilla and remaining
grated chocolate until smooth. Cover the
surface with plastic wrap, to stop a skin
forming, and allow to cool.
3 Whip a third of the extra cream
until soft peaks form and gently fold this
and the mascarpone into the cooled
custard. Spoon over the cake and
strawberries, cover with plastic wrap and
then refrigerate until needed. When you
are ready to serve, whip the remaining

cream until stiff peaks form and spoon
over the trifle. Cut the remaining
strawberries in half and arrange on top.
Dust with a mixture of sifted cocoa
powder and icing sugar to serve.

NOTE: Mascarpone cheese is made with
cream and looks more like cream than
cheese. Slightly sweet with an acidic edge,
it is softer than cream cheese.

show stoppers

It's time to show off, amaze and thrill. There are moments in life when a simple bowl of ice cream just isn't enough ... you need something spectacular, awe inspiring and attention grabbing. You need a SHOW STOPPER. The wonderful thing about this selection of recipes is that they make you look like a master chef when actually, with a little time, patience and enthusiasm, most of our fabulous creations are rather easy to make. Just don't let anyone in on the secret.

chocolate chestnut bliss

✳ ✳ ✳

Preparation time: 1 hour + 20 minutes chilling time
Cooking time: 30 minutes
Serves 6

100 g (3½ oz) unsalted butter, chopped
80 g (2¾ oz) dark chocolate, chopped
125 ml (4 fl oz/½ cup) milk
125 g (4½ oz/½ cup) caster (superfine) sugar
25 g (1 oz/¼ cup) desiccated coconut
30 g (1 oz/¼ cup) unsweetened cocoa powder, sifted
60 g (2¼ oz/½ cup) self-raising flour, sifted
2 eggs, lightly beaten

AMARETTO SYRUP
2 tablespoons caster (superfine) sugar
60 ml (2 fl oz/¼ cup) Amaretto

CHESTNUT FILLING
30 g (1 oz) unsalted butter, softened
260 g (9 ¼ oz/1 cup) unsweetened chestnut purée
30 g (1 oz/¼ cup) icing (confectioners') sugar

CHOCOLATE TOPPING
75 g (2½ oz) unsalted butter
150 g (5½ oz) dark chocolate, chopped
2 tablespoons light corn syrup

RASPBERRY SAUCE
150 g (5½ oz) frozen raspberries, thawed
2 tablespoons caster (superfine) sugar

CHOCOLATE SWIRLS
60 g (2¼ oz) dark chocolate

1 Preheat the oven to 180°C (350°F/ Gas 4). Lightly grease a 30 x 25 cm (12 x 10 inch) swiss roll tin and line with baking paper. Combine the butter, chocolate, milk and sugar in a small saucepan and stir over low heat until the sugar dissolves and the chocolate melts. Remove from the heat and allow to cool slightly. Combine the coconut, cocoa and flour in a bowl, pour in the chocolate mixture and the beaten eggs and mix well. Spread evenly into the tin and bake for 15 minutes, or until just firm to touch. Leave for 5 minutes before turning onto a rack to cool.
2 To make the Amaretto syrup, combine the sugar and 60 ml (2 fl oz/¼ cup) water in a small pan and stir over low heat until the sugar dissolves. Remove from the heat, stir in the Amaretto and allow to cool.
3 To make the chestnut filling, beat the butter, chestnut purée and icing sugar in a bowl until smooth. Cut rounds from the chocolate cake using 3 cm (1¼ inch), 5 cm (2 inch), 7 cm (2¾ inch) cutters, making six of each size. (Any leftover chocolate cake can be frozen.)
4 Reserve 125 ml (4 fl oz/½ cup) of the chestnut cream. Place large rounds of cake on a wire rack over a baking paper-covered tray, brush well with some of the syrup and spread with a layer of the chestnut cream. Top with another round of cake, slightly smaller than the first, brush well with syrup and top with some chestnut cream. Top with the remaining round of cake and brush with remaining syrup. Spread the reserved chestnut cream as thinly and smoothly as possible over the outside of each cake, to form smooth sides. Refrigerate for 1 hour, or until the chestnut cream has firmed slightly.
5 To make the chocolate topping, combine the butter, chocolate and corn syrup in a bowl, place over a pan of simmering water and stir until melted. Lift the cakes onto a wire rack over a baking tray, spoon topping over each cake to completely cover, then refrigerate until just set.
6 Meanwhile, to make the raspberry sauce, combine the raspberries and sugar in a small pan, then simmer for 5 minutes. Strain through a plastic sieve and allow to cool.
7 To make the chocolate swirls, melt the dark chocolate and spoon into a paper piping bag or small plastic bag. Snip off a corner and drizzle chocolate into concentric circles, about 7 cm (2¾ inch) in diameter, on a baking paper-lined baking tray, then refrigerate until firm. Place the chocolate bliss on a serving plate, decorate with the chocolate swirls and spoon raspberry sauce onto the side of the plate.

After brushing the largest rounds of cake with syrup, spread a layer of chestnut cream over them.

Spread the reserved chestnut cream as thinly and smoothly as possible all over the outside of each cake to form smooth sides.

With the cakes on a wire rack over a baking tray, spoon the topping over the cakes to cover completely, then refrigerate until set.

Snip off a corner of the bag and drizzle the melted chocolate into concentric circles onto a baking tray.

licorice allsort ice cream

Preparation time: 1 hour + freezing time
Cooking time: 30 minutes
Serves 6–8

whipped cream, to serve

COCONUT MERINGUE
2 egg whites
125 g (4½ oz/½ cup) caster (superfine) sugar
90 g (3¼ oz/1 cup) desiccated coconut
1 tablespoon cornflour (cornstarch)

RASPBERRY ICE CREAM
200 g (7 oz) fresh or frozen raspberries
170 ml (5½ fl oz/⅔ cup) milk
90 g (3¼ oz/⅓ cup) caster (superfine) sugar
125 ml (4 fl oz/½ cup) pouring (whipping) cream

LICORICE ICE CREAM
60 g (2¼ oz) soft eating licorice, chopped
250 ml (9 fl oz/1 cup) milk
185 ml (6 fl oz/¾ cup) pouring (whipping) cream
60 g (2¼ oz/¼ cup) caster (superfine) sugar
black food colouring (optional)

MANGO ICE CREAM
1 large mango
170 ml (5½ fl oz/⅔ cup) milk
90 g (3¼ oz/⅓ cup) caster (superfine) sugar
125 ml (4 fl oz/½ cup) pouring (whipping) cream

1   Preheat the oven to 150°C (300°F/ Gas 2). Cover two baking trays with baking paper and draw six 25 x 7 cm (10 x 2¾ inch) rectangles. For the coconut meringues, whisk the egg whites in a small bowl, with electric beaters, until stiff peaks form. Gradually add the sugar, whisking well after each addition until the sugar dissolves. Stir in the combined coconut and cornflour. Spread evenly over the rectangles. Bake for 20 minutes, or until just firm to touch. Turn the oven off and leave to cool in the oven with the door slightly ajar.

2   Lightly grease two 25 x 7.5 cm (10 x 3 inch), 4 cm (1½ inches) deep bar tins and line with plastic wrap. Trim the edges of all the meringues to fit into the tins.

3   To make the raspberry ice cream, purée the raspberries and press through a plastic strainer to remove the seeds (do not use a metal strainer or the raspberries will discolour). You will need 170 ml (5½ fl oz/⅔ cup) purée. Combine the milk and sugar in a small saucepan, stir over heat without boiling, until the sugar dissolves, remove from heat, stir in the cream and allow to cool. When cool, stir in the purée, pour into a shallow metal container and freeze until semi-frozen. Chop the mixture and beat in a bowl with electric beaters until thick and creamy. Divide between the prepared tins. Top each with a trimmed coconut meringue. Freeze until firm.

4   To make the licorice ice cream, stir the licorice, milk and cream together in a small pan over low heat, stirring gently until the licorice is soft and melting. Press through a strainer to remove any remaining lumps. Add the sugar, stir until dissolved, then allow to cool. Tint a deeper colour with food colouring if desired. Pour the mixture into a shallow metal container and freeze until firm. Chop the mixture, beat in a large bowl with electric beaters until thick and creamy, then spread over the meringues and top each with another meringue. Freeze until firm.

5   To make the mango ice cream, purée the mango until smooth. You will need 180 ml (6 fl oz) purée. Follow the same method as for the raspberry ice cream. Spread over the meringues, top the mango ice cream with the remaining meringues, cover and freeze until firm. When ready to serve, invert the ice cream onto a cutting board, remove the plastic and cut into slices. Serve with cream.

NOTE: The ice creams can also be made in an ice cream machine.

LICORICE
Licorice, or liquorice, is the root of a small plant. Licorice reached Europe via the Arab spice routes and in the 17th century, ground licorice was used to flavour cakes, desserts and drinks. Now, the most common usage is to extract the juice of the root to flavour a variety of sweets and the Italian liqueur, Sambucca. Licorice is available as a root or as a powder.

chocolate

It was the Aztecs who discovered the delights of the cocoa bean and indulged themselves with chocolate drinks, and sixteenth century Spanish explorers who introduced the bean to Europe.

Good-quality chocolate is glossy and smooth with a slightly reddish colour. It breaks cleanly, melts easily (cocoa butter melts at body temperature) and has a high percentage of cocoa solids and natural vanilla extract as a flavouring. The golden rule for cooking with chocolate is to use the best-quality you can afford.

to melt chocolate
Chocolate needs to be handled carefully. Water will make it seize and go clumpy, as will overheating. Use a clean, dry heatproof bowl and only melt as much chocolate as you need. Chop the chocolate finely, place it in the bowl and set the bowl over a pan with about 4 cm (1½ inches) water that has been boiled and taken off the heat. The bottom of the bowl should not touch the water and should fit the pan tightly. Leave the chocolate to soften, then stir until smooth. Either remove the bowl from the pan to cool the chocolate or leave in place if you want to keep it liquid. Do not overheat chocolate or it will scorch, seize and taste bitter.

things to make
chocolate collars Collars are beautiful decorations for cheesecakes or cakes. Remove the dessert from the tin and put it on a board. Measure the height and add 1 cm (½ inch). Cut a strip of baking paper or mat contact this wide and long enough to easily go round the dessert. Spread a thin even layer of melted chocolate over the paper or shiny side of the contact, allow to set a little and wrap round the cake, paper-side-out. Fix in place and chill until set, then peel off the paper.

chocolate curls Pour melted chocolate onto a marble work surface or a heavy chopping board. When it has cooled and just set, scrape off curls by pulling a knife set at a 45 degree angle across the chocolate. Make striped curls by pouring melted chocolate onto the surface and making ridges through it with a fork or comb scraper. Leave this layer to set, then pour a layer of different coloured melted chocolate over the top. Scrape off curls as above. Or pour lines of different-coloured chocolate side by side and make curls as above. Small chocolate curls or shavings can be made by pulling a potato peeler over a block of chocolate.

chocolate cups Spread a circle of chocolate onto a piece of freezer wrap or plastic wrap and drape it over a mould. Allow it to harden before removing the chocolate cup and pulling out the plastic wrap. The insides of moulds can also be brushed with oil and then with chocolate. The chocolate shrinks as it cools — a few minutes in the refrigerator helps and the chocolate cup should pull away from the inside of the mould.

chocolate boxes Melt chocolate and spread it in a thin, even layer on a piece of baking paper. When it begins to set, cut it into equal squares with a sharp knife (heat the knife if the chocolate has set too much). Use more melted chocolate to glue the squares together to make into a box.

piped shapes Put melted chocolate into a piping bag and pipe shapes onto baking paper. Peel the shapes off the baking paper and stick them together with melted chocolate to give three-dimensional effects, or use them flat to pattern surfaces.

chocolate leaves Wash the underside of non-toxic, unsprayed leaves such as rose or camellia, and dry well. Brush each leaf with a thin layer of melted chocolate, leave until set, then carefully peel the leaf away from the chocolate shape.

charlotte

A charlotte was originally a hot apple pudding baked in a bread- or cake-lined deep mould. It appears in British cookbooks in the 18th century and is possibly named after Queen Charlotte who was apparently an apple enthusiast. The charlotte then transformed into the Charlotte Russe, in which the centre was filled with a cold custard or Bavarian type mixture and chilled. This was supposedly invented by the French chef Antonin Carême in 1802 and originally called charlotte à la parisienne before he renamed it in honour of Czar Alexander.

charlotte russe

Preparation time: 40 minutes + 1 hour chilling time + overnight chilling time
Cooking time: 10 minutes
Serves 8–10

250 g (9 oz) sponge finger (lady finger) biscuits (cookies) (30–35 fingers)
9 egg yolks
185 g (6½ oz/¾ cup) caster (superfine) sugar
500 ml (17 fl oz/2 cups) milk
1 teaspoon natural vanilla extract
5 teaspoons powdered gelatin
125 g (4½ oz/½ cup) sour cream
125 ml (4 fl oz/½ cup) pouring (whipping) cream
cream and berries, to serve

1 Choose a charlotte mould or round cake tin of 2 litre (70 fl oz/8 cup) capacity. Cover base with baking paper. If necessary, cut the biscuits so they are wider at one end than the other, then arrange the biscuits to fit snugly, side by side, round the inside of the mould so that there are no gaps.
2 Whisk the egg yolks until thick, add the sugar and continue beating vigorously until the mixture is thick but still runny. Heat the milk with the vanilla until the first small bubbles appear on the side of the saucepan. Immediately but slowly, pour the milk into the egg mixture, continually beating. Return the mixture to a clean pan. Heat again, stirring constantly, until it thickens, but do not boil. Remove from the heat. Sprinkle the gelatin in an even layer over 60 ml (2 fl oz/¼ cup) water in a small heatproof bowl and leave until spongy. Stand the bowl in a pan of hot water (off the heat) and stir until the gelatin dissolves. Add to the custard and stir well. Cover the surface of the custard with plastic wrap and leave to cool. Whip the creams until thick and stir into the custard.
3 Cover the surface of the custard again and refrigerate for about 1 hour, stirring a few times until the custard is thick but not set (if it is too runny the biscuits may float to the surface). Pour into the biscuit mould and refrigerate overnight.
4 To serve, invert the serving plate on top of the mould and carefully flip both over. The mould should come off easily unless there were cracks in the biscuit mould and custard has stuck to the side. In that case, use a wet knife to ease off any difficult areas. Serve with berries and cream or maybe a fruit purée.

Cut the cake into curved pieces with a sharp knife (or use a template).

If you make a template to dust the cake you may need help holding it in place.

zuccotto

❋ ❋ ❋

Preparation time: 1 hour + 8 hours chilling time
Cooking time: nil
Serves 6–8

1 ready-made sponge cake
80 ml (2½ fl oz/⅓ cup) Kirsch
60 ml (2 fl oz/¼ cup) Cointreau
80 ml (2½ fl oz/⅓ cup) rum, Cognac, Grand Marnier or Maraschino
500 ml (17 fl oz/2 cups) pouring (whipping) cream
90 g (3¼ oz) roasted almond dark chocolate, chopped

175 g (6 oz) finely chopped mixed glacé fruit
100 g (3½ oz) dark chocolate, melted
70 g (2½ oz) hazelnuts, roasted and chopped
unsweetened cocoa powder and icing (confectioners') sugar, to dust

1 Line a 1.5 litre (52 fl oz/6 cup) pudding basin (steamed pudding mould) with damp muslin (cheesecloth). Cut the cake into curved pieces with a knife (you will need about 12 pieces). Work with one strip of cake at a time, brushing it with the combined liqueurs and arranging the pieces closely in the basin. Put the thin ends in the centre so the slices cover the

base and side of the basin. Brush with the remaining liqueur to soak the cake. Chill.
2 Whisk the cream until stiff peaks form, then divide in half. Fold the almond chocolate and glacé fruit into one half and spread evenly over the cake in the basin, leaving a space in the centre.
3 Fold the cooled melted chocolate and hazelnuts into the remaining cream and spoon into the centre cavity, packing it in firmly. Smooth the surface, cover and chill for 8 hours to allow the cream to firm slightly. Turn out onto a plate and dust with sifted cocoa and icing sugar.

raspberry miroire

✳ ✳ ✳

Preparation time: 1 hour + 6 hours
    chilling time
Cooking time: 30 minutes
Serves 8–10

raspberries, to serve
icing (confectioners') sugar, to dust
cream, to serve

SPONGE BASE
1 egg
2 tablespoons caster (superfine) sugar
2 tablespoons self-raising flour
1 tablespoon plain (all-purpose) flour

RASPBERRY MOUSSE
500 g (1 lb 2 oz) fresh or frozen
    raspberries
4 egg yolks
125 g (4½ oz/½ cup) caster (superfine)
    sugar
250 ml (9 fl oz/1 cup) milk
1½ tablespoons powdered gelatin
60 ml (2 fl oz/¼ cup) crème de cassis
    liqueur
250 ml (9 fl oz/1 cup) pouring
    (whipping) cream

RASPBERRY TOPPING
2 teaspoons powdered gelatin
1 tablespoon crème de cassis liqueur

CHOCOLATE BARK
100 g (3½ oz) white chocolate melts,
    melted

1 Preheat the oven to 180°C (350°F/ Gas 4). Lightly grease a 22 cm (8½ inch) springform tin and line base with baking paper. Whisk the egg and sugar in a small bowl with electric beaters, for 5 minutes, or until thick and fluffy. Sift the flours together three times, then fold into the egg mixture with a metal spoon. Spread evenly into the prepared tin and bake for 10–15 minutes, or until lightly browned and shrunk slightly away from the edge. Remove from the tin and leave to cool on a wire rack. Clean the springform tin, fit the base into the tin upside down and lightly oil the pan and line the base and side with plastic wrap.
2 To make the raspberry mousse, blend or process the raspberries in batches until smooth and press through a plastic strainer (not a metallic one or the raspberries may discolour) to remove the seeds. Reserve 125 ml (4 fl oz/ ½ cup) raspberry purée for the topping. Whisk the egg yolks and sugar in a heatproof bowl for 5 minutes, or until thick and pale. Bring the milk to the boil and gradually pour onto the egg mixture, beating continually. Place the bowl over a saucepan of simmering water and stir for about 10 minutes, or until the mixture thickens slightly and coats the back of a spoon. Transfer to a bowl, cover the surface with plastic wrap and refrigerate for 1 hour or until cooled.
3 Sprinkle the gelatin in an even layer over 60 ml (2 fl oz/¼ cup) water in a small heatproof bowl and leave to go spongy. Put a large pan with about 4 cm (1½ inches) water on to boil. When it

boils, remove from the heat and carefully lower the gelatin bowl into the water (it should come halfway up the side of the bowl), then stir until dissolved. Cool slightly. Stir the gelatin mixture, raspberry purée and liqueur into the custard mixture, then refrigerate for 30 minutes or until thick but not set, stirring occasionally. Whisk the cream until soft peaks form and fold into the raspberry mixture with a metal spoon. Place the sponge into the base of the prepared pan and pour the raspberry mixture evenly over the top. Refrigerate for 4 hours, or until firm.
4 For the topping, sprinkle the gelatin in an even layer over 80 ml (2½ fl oz/ ⅓ cup) water in a heatproof bowl and leave to go spongy. Put a large pan filled with about 4 cm (1½ inches) water on to boil. When it boils, remove from the heat and lower the gelatin bowl into the water (it should come halfway up the side of the bowl), then stir until dissolved. Cool slightly. Stir in the reserved raspberry purée and the liqueur, pour evenly over the set mousse, then refrigerate for 30 minutes or until set.
5 To make the chocolate bark, cover a tray with baking paper, spread the chocolate thinly over the paper and allow to set. When set, break into large angular pieces.
6 To serve, remove the miroire from the tin. Place pieces of chocolate around the side and keep in place with a little cream. Top with raspberries and sprinkle with icing sugar. Cut the miroire into slices and serve with cream.

NOTE: Miroire denotes the shiny jelly topping, meaning 'mirror' in French.

white chocolate

White chocolate is a blend of cocoa butter, sugar, milk solids, vanilla and a stabiliser. It contains no cocoa liquor and therefore is not a true chocolate. In America, it cannot be called chocolate and instead is often labelled 'confectionery coating'. White chocolate is softer than other types of chocolate and is not as easy to handle. It seizes more easily on melting and cannot be easily substituted for other chocolates in recipes.

pashka

2 Beat the butter and sugar in a bowl until light and creamy, then beat in the egg yolks one at a time. Add the almonds, zests and lemon juice and mix well. Transfer to a large bowl and fold in the ricotta, sour cream and fruit mixture.
3 Press the ricotta mixture into the basin and fold the edges of the cloth over the top. Cover the top with plastic wrap, place a saucer on top and weigh down with a tin placed on top of the saucer. Place the bowl on a plate and refrigerate overnight. Turn out onto a serving plate and peel away the muslin. Decorate with glacé fruits and almonds and serve in small wedges.

NOTE: Pashka is a Russian Easter dish, traditionally made in a cone or four-sided pyramid-shaped mould. This dessert will keep for up to 2 days in the refrigerator.

chocolate tart with espresso cones

✻ ✻ ✻

Preparation time: 1 hour + 3 hours chilling
    and overnight freezing time
Cooking time: 5–10 minutes
Serves 8

15 g (½ oz/¼ cup) instant coffee granules
1 litre (35 fl oz/4 cups) good-quality vanilla
    ice cream, softened
unsweetened cocoa powder, to dust

TART BASE
100 g (3½ oz) pecans
100 g (3½ oz) dark chocolate-flavoured
    biscuits (cookies)
1 tablespoon unsweetened cocoa powder
3 teaspoons soft brown sugar
1 tablespoon overproof dark rum
30 g (1 oz) unsalted butter, melted
40 g (1½ oz) good-quality dark
    chocolate, melted

FILLING
200 g (7 oz) good-quality dark chocolate
30 g (1 oz) unsalted butter

pashka

✻ ✻

Preparation time: 30 minutes + overnight
    draining and 2 hours soaking and overnight
    chilling time
Cooking time: nil
Serves 8–10

750 g (1 lb 10 oz) ricotta cheese
100 g (3½ oz) glacé pineapple, chopped
100 g (3½ oz) glacé ginger, chopped
60 g (2¼ oz) mixed peel
    (mixed candied citrus peel)
60 g (2¼ oz) sultanas (golden raisins)
2 tablespoons white or dark rum
100 g (3½ oz) unsalted butter, softened

125 g (4½ oz/½ cup) caster (superfine) sugar
2 egg yolks
60 g (2¼ oz) slivered almonds, toasted
2 teaspoons finely grated lemon zest
2 teaspoons finely grated orange zest
2 tablespoons lemon juice
125 g (4½ oz/½ cup) sour cream
glacé fruits and slivered almonds, to serve

1 Drain the ricotta overnight in a sieve in the refrigerator. In a bowl, soak pineapple, ginger, mixed peel and sultanas in rum for 2 hours. Thoroughly wet a piece of muslin (cheesecloth) in boiling water, wring out the excess water and use to line a 2 litre (70 fl oz/8 cup) pudding basin (steamed pudding mould) or charlotte mould.

125 ml (4 fl oz/½ cup) pouring
    (whipping) cream
3 egg yolks, lightly beaten
250 ml (9 fl oz/1 cup) pouring
    (whipping) cream, whipped

1 To mould the ice cream into shape for the espresso cones, first prepare the moulds. Cover eight large cream horn moulds with baking paper and secure with sticky tape. Pull the paper off the moulds and transfer the paper cones to the inside of the moulds. Stand the lined cream horn moulds, points down, in mugs to make it easier to spoon in the ice cream.

2 Use a metal spoon to dissolve the coffee in 1 tablespoon hot water and then fold through the ice cream in a bowl. Stir until smooth, then spoon into the paper inside the moulds, before freezing overnight.

3 To make the tart base, grease a shallow, 23 cm (9 inch) round fluted flan (tart) tin. Process all the ingredients in short bursts in a food processor for 30 seconds, or until even and crumbly. Press into the base and side of the tin. Refrigerate for 1 hour or until firm.

4 To make the filling, stir the chocolate, butter and cream together in a heavy-based pan over low heat until melted and smooth. Remove from the heat, whisk in the egg yolks and transfer to a bowl. Cool slightly. Use a metal spoon to fold in the cream. Stir until smooth, pour into the tart base, then refrigerate for 2 hours or until set.

5 Serve a wedge of chocolate tart with each espresso cone. Dust the tart with sifted cocoa.

dark chocolate

The seeds from the beans of the cacao tree, native to Central America, are fermented, dried, roasted and then formed into a solidified paste known as bitter unsweetened chocolate. The more bitter the chocolate, the more intense the flavour. Bitter-sweet and semi-sweet chocolates have some sugar added. Couverture chocolate, though very expensive, is considered the best baking chocolate as it is very high quality due to its high cocoa butter content.

caramel

For creating real show-stopping desserts, caramel is an invaluable and delicious accessory. Glaze, dip, or spin it into golden threads, set nuts in caramel to make praline, or let it harden into a toffee topping.

There are two different ways to make caramel. The wet method involves dissolving the sugar in water and then boiling the sugar syrup; the dry method means melting the sugar on its own. The wet method is more complicated as the syrup can crystallise, but it is easier to keep an eye on as it starts to darken. The dry method needs a bit more practice to avoid burning the sugar as it melts. Always use a heavy-based saucepan that gives an even heat all over the base. Non-stick pans and those with dark linings are harder to use as you cannot easily see the colour of the caramel. Use a coarser grade of sugar so you get less scum — granulated sugar is good as it dissolves easily.

wet method

Put the water and sugar in a heavy-based saucepan and stir over low heat until all the sugar has dissolved, then bring to the boil. If you boil before the sugar has completely dissolved, it will crystallise. Do not stir the syrup as it boils or crystals will form on the spoon. Do not allow any crystals to form on the side of the pan from splashes — if they do, dip a clean dry pastry brush in cold water and brush down the side of the pan.

As the water evaporates off the syrup, the temperature will start to rise. Be very careful as the hot syrup can cause serious burns. Once the syrup reaches 160°C–175°C (315°F–335°F), all the water will have evaporated and the molten sugar which is left will start to caramelise. The syrup will be thicker and the bubbles will be bigger and break more slowly. At this point, the sugar will start to colour quite quickly, so keep an eye on it and remove from the heat the moment it reaches the colour you want. Swirl the pan to keep the colour of the caramel even, otherwise patches may darken and burn before the rest has

coloured. To stop the caramel continuing to cook in the pan after you've removed it from the heat, plunge the base of the pan into a sink of cold water. You can then re-melt the caramel over low heat as you need it.

dry method

Sprinkle the sugar in an even layer over the base of a heavy-based saucepan and place over low heat. Melt the sugar slowly, tipping the pan from side to side so that it melts evenly — keep the sugar moving or it might start to colour on one side before the other side has melted. When the caramel starts to colour, keep swirling until you have an even colour and then remove the pan from the heat. Stop the cooking by plunging the base of the pan into a sink of cold water.

caramel tips

If you find your caramel isn't dark enough, simply re-melt it and cook until it reaches the colour you want — if it gets too dark, there is no magic remedy and you will have to start again, so be careful. The darkest stage of caramel is known as black jack — this has a strong flavour and is used in very small amounts as a colouring for desserts, but is inedible on its own.

If the sugar syrup starts to crystallise, you can rescue it by adding a tablespoon of honey, a squeeze of lemon juice or a pinch of cream of tartar — these all slow down the process of crystallisation by breaking down the sucrose into fructose and glucose. If you only have a few crystals, take your pan off the stove to allow it to cool a little, then add some more water and redissolve the crystals. If you are worried about crystallisation occurring, you can add a few drops of lemon juice to the sugar at the beginning.

caramel decoration

Caramel decorations must be made and used quickly — soften in humidity and become sticky if refrigerated. The sugar in caramel will liquefy when it comes into contact with cream, ice creams and custard, so add decorations just before serving.

Make your caramel as described on the previous page. When it reaches the colour you want, stop it cooking and colouring further; keep liquid by reheating gently when necessary.

caramel sheets
If you are making sheets of caramel, pour it onto an oiled baking tray and leave to cool (be careful as the baking tray will become extremely hot). The sheets of caramel can then be broken into different shapes and sizes for decoration. You can also pour the caramel into freeform threads or shapes, or use a template cut from modelling clay brushed with a little oil. The caramel can be coloured with food colouring to create whole pictures.

spun sugar
Caramel can be spun into fine threads using two forks or a balloon whisk with the ends cut off. Keep the caramel liquid by standing the pan in hot water while you work. It will need to be thick enough to run in continuous streams. Oil the handle of a broom or long-handled wooden spoon and place it between two chairs. Lay newspaper on the floor under the handle. Hold two forks back to back and dip them in the caramel. Flick them backwards and forwards across the handle — sugar threads will form across the handle and hang down on each side. Re-dip the forks as necessary until you have enough threads. Gently form the threads into shapes with your hands. Use immediately.

caramel baskets
Make caramel baskets by drizzling the caramel backwards and forwards across the bowl of a well-oiled ladle or mould. Leave to harden before carefully sliding the basket off the ladle. Lines or crisscross patterns for decoration can be made by drizzling the caramel in patterns on a well-oiled baking tray or any metal mould. The thicker the threads, the less likely they are to break.

praline
Add toasted whole, flaked or slivered blanched almonds (or other nuts) to a golden caramel made with an equal quantity of sugar to the weight of the nuts. Mix, tip out onto a marble surface or oiled baking sheet, spread out into a layer and cool. The praline can then either be broken into pieces or crushed in a plastic bag with a rolling pin or in a food processor. Store in an airtight container.

lining a mould
Pour the liquid caramel into the bases of moulds used for desserts such as crème caramel and swirl them to coat the mould evenly. Be careful as the mould will get hot.

toffeed fruit and nuts
Whole fruit or nuts can be dipped in pale caramel to give a glossy sheen. Use a fork or skewer or hold the fruit by its stalk. Place on baking paper until completely cool.

caramel bark
Sprinkle a foil-lined baking tray with a thin layer of sugar and place under a hot preheated grill (broiler). Watch carefully until the sugar melts and turns to caramel. Leave to set then carefully lift the caramel off the foil and break into pieces.

toffee glazes
Pour liquid caramel onto crème brulées and other similar desserts to make a hard toffee topping. Pour the caramel over the surface and tip from side to side to coat evenly.

tuile cones with nougat mousse and blackberry sauce

✳ ✳ ✳

Preparation time: 1 hour 45 minutes + 2 hours chilling time
Cooking time: 1 hour 15 minutes
Serves 6

NOUGAT MOUSSE
200 g (7 oz) soft nougat
125 ml (4 fl oz/½ cup) milk
1 teaspoon finely grated orange zest
310 ml (10¾ fl oz/1¼ cups) thick (double/heavy) cream

BLACKBERRY SAUCE
150 g (5½ oz) fresh or frozen blackberries
80 ml (2½ fl oz/⅓ cup) quality red wine
2 tablespoons caster (superfine) sugar
1 teaspoon cornflour (cornstarch)

TUILE CONES
40 g (1½ oz) unsalted butter
1 tablespoon honey
30 g (1 oz/¼ cup) plain (all-purpose) flour
1 egg white
60 g (2¼ oz/¼ cup) caster (superfine) sugar

SPUN TOFFEE
250 g (9 oz/1 cup) caster (superfine) sugar

1 Chop the nougat into small pieces, combine with the milk in a saucepan and stir constantly over low heat until the nougat melts. Remove from the heat, stir in the zest and refrigerate for 2 hours or until chilled, stirring occasionally. Whisk the cream until just thick, stir in the cold nougat mixture, then whisk until thickened. Refrigerate until required.
2 For the sauce, combine blackberries, wine and sugar in a small pan. Stir over medium heat until the sugar dissolves, pressing the berries with the back of a spoon, then simmer for 2 minutes. Blend the cornflour with 2 teaspoons water, add to the pan and stir until the mixture boils and thickens. Strain and allow to cool, stirring occasionally.
3 To make the tuile cones, preheat the oven to 180°C (350°F/Gas 4). Draw a 17 cm (6½ inch) circle on baking paper, turn the paper over and place on a baking tray. Combine all the ingredients in a blender for 2 minutes, then spread 3 teaspoons of the mixture thinly and evenly over the circle to the edge.
4 Bake each tuile for 5–6 minutes, or until lightly golden. Working quickly, trim a piece the shape of a new moon off one side, then wrap firmly around a large metal horn mould, placing the point of the mould at the rounded edge of the tuile, opposite the trimmed edge (this will enable the tuile to stand up straight when filled). Repeat with the remaining tuile mixture. Store the tuiles in an airtight container as they will soften if left out.
5 To make the spun toffee, prepare the area you will be working in by first spreading a couple of sheets of newspaper on the floor underneath where you will be spinning the toffee. Then, place a wooden spoon on a work bench with the handle extending over the edge, above the newspaper. Place a chopping board or similar heavy object on top to weigh it down. Lightly oil the handle and remember to oil it each time. Place a heavy-based saucepan over medium heat, gradually sprinkle with sugar and as it melts, sprinkle with the remaining sugar. Stir to melt any lumps and prevent the sugar from burning. When the toffee is golden brown, remove from the heat and place the base of the pan in a large dish of cold water, to quickly cool the toffee and prevent it burning. This also will make the toffee thicken.
6 Dip two forks in the hot toffee and use a flicking motion to carefully flick the toffee backwards and forwards over the handle of the wooden spoon, dipping the forks in the toffee again as often as necessary. If the toffee gets too thick, warm again slightly over low heat. You will need to do this three or four times. Before the toffee sets, quickly lift the toffee off the spoon handle and form into a nest shape. Store in an airtight container. Repeat with the remaining toffee to form six nest shapes. This may take some practice.
7 To assemble, spoon the nougat mousse into a piping bag fitted with a large plain nozzle. Pipe the mousse into the cones and invert onto a serving plate. Spoon the blackberry sauce around the cone and top with a nest of spun toffee.

NOTE: The cones, sauce and mousse can be made a day ahead. The mousse may need to be beaten to thicken. The toffee should be made on the day of serving; store in an airtight container.

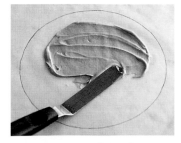
Spread 3 teaspoons of the tuile cone mixture thinly and evenly over the circle, to reach the edge.

Remove the tuile from the oven when golden and immediately trim off a piece shaped like a new moon.

Wrap the tuile firmly around a large metal horn mould, placing the point of the mould at the rounded edge of tuile.

Dip two forks in the hot toffee and carefully flick backwards and forwards over the handle of the wooden spoon.

paper piping bags

To make a paper piping bag
to use with melted chocolate,
cut a 25 cm (10 inch) square of
baking paper. Fold it in half
diagonally to form a triangle.
Working with the longest side
closest to you, curl the left
point in to meet the top point.
Hold in place while wrapping
the other side around tightly
to form a cone shape. Secure
with tape or a staple. Tuck
the upstanding ends into the
cone. Fill with the melted
chocolate and fold the top
edges to seal. Snip off the tip
and gently apply pressure from
the top of the bag.

chocolate roulade

❈ ❈

Preparation time: **35 minutes + 30 minutes
chilling time**
Cooking time: **12 minutes**
Serves **6–8**

3 eggs
125 g (4½ oz/½ cup) caster (superfine) sugar
30 g (1 oz/¼ cup) plain (all-purpose) flour
2 tablespoons unsweetened cocoa powder
250 ml (9 fl oz/1 cup) pouring
  (whipping) cream
1 tablespoon icing (confectioners') sugar,
  plus extra, to dust
½ teaspoon natural vanilla extract

1 Preheat the oven to 200°F (400°F/
Gas 6). Lightly grease the base and sides
of a 25 x 30 cm (10 x 12 inch) swiss roll
tin. Line base with paper and grease the
paper. Place the eggs in a small bowl with
90 g (3¼ oz/⅓ cup) of the caster sugar.
Whisk with electric beaters for about
8 minutes, or until thick and pale.
2 Sift the flour and cocoa together and
gently fold into the egg mixture with a
metal spoon. Spread the mixture evenly
into the prepared tin. Bake for about
12 minutes, or until the cake is just set.
3 Meanwhile, place a clean tea towel
(dish towel) on a work surface, top with a
sheet of baking paper and sprinkle with
the remaining caster sugar. When the cake

is cooked, turn it out immediately onto the prepared paper and sugar. Trim off any crispy edges. Roll the cake up from the long side, rolling the paper inside the roll and using the tea towel as a guide. Stand the rolled cake on a wire cake rack for 5 minutes, then carefully unroll the cake and cool to room temperature.

4 Whisk the cream, icing sugar and vanilla until stiff peaks form. Spread the cream over the cooled cake, leaving a 1 cm (½ inch) border around each edge. Roll the cake again, using the paper as a guide. Place the roll, seam-side-down, on a tray and refrigerate, covered, for about 30 minutes. Dust with icing sugar then carefully cut into slices to serve.

chocolate mud cake

✺ ✺

Preparation time: 30 minutes
Cooking time: 1 hour 55 minutes
Serves 8–10

250 g (9 oz) unsalted butter
250 g (9 oz) dark chocolate, broken
2 tablespoons instant coffee granules
150 g (5½ oz) self-raising flour
155 g (5½ oz/1¼ cups) plain
    (all-purpose) flour
60 g (2¼ oz/½ cup) unsweetened cocoa
    powder
½ teaspoon bicarbonate of soda
    (baking soda)
550 g (1 lb 4 oz/2½ cups) sugar
4 eggs
2 tablespoons oil
125 ml (4 fl oz/½ cup) buttermilk
milk and white chocolate curls (page 208),
    to decorate

GLAZE
250 g (9 oz) dark chocolate, chopped
125 ml (4 fl oz/½ cup) pouring (whipping)
    cream
145 g (5 oz/⅔ cup) caster (superfine) sugar

1 Preheat the oven to 160°C (315°F/ Gas 2–3). Brush a deep 24 cm (9 inch) round cake tin with melted butter or oil.
Line with baking paper, extending at least 5 cm (2 inches) above the rim.
2 Stir the butter, chocolate, coffee and 185 ml (6 fl oz/¾ cup) hot water in a saucepan, over low heat, until melted and smooth. Remove from the heat.
3 Sift the flours, cocoa and bicarbonate of soda into a large bowl. Stir in the sugar and make a well in the centre. Add the combined eggs, oil and buttermilk. Use a large metal spoon to slowly stir in the dry ingredients, then the melted chocolate mixture until combined. Spoon the mixture into the tin and bake for 1 hour 45 minutes. Test the centre with

a skewer — it may be slightly wet. Remove the cake from the oven. If the top of the cake looks raw, bake for another 5–10 minutes, then remove. Cool in the tin.
4 To make the glaze, stir all the ingredients in a saucepan over low heat until melted. Bring to the boil, reduce the heat and simmer for 4–5 minutes. Remove from the heat and cool slightly. Put a wire rack on a baking tray. Remove the cake from the tin and place on the rack. Pour the glaze over the cake, making sure the sides are evenly covered. Served topped with the chocolate curls.

ice cream

Ice cream, as one of our most modern desserts, has enjoyed a spectacularly meteoric rise to become one of the most popular. It is not until relatively recent times, of course, that we learnt to make ice and freeze at will. So, while fire and hot food has been familiar to us since the days when we lived in caves, cold food has been treated with suspicion and even fear. Rumour has it that when custards, served at an American society ball in 1831, were found to be still frozen, the cry of 'poison' went up. The hostess herself, with no little bravado, polished one off and declared it 'delicious'. It was a somewhat inauspicious episode in the history of one of our modern favourites.

ice cream tips

The temperature of your freezer should be -18°C (0°F) to ensure proper freezing. The freezer should also be free from ice build-up and not too full. Cover the surface of your ice cream with baking paper or plastic wrap to stop ice crystals forming on the surface. For full flavour, ice cream should not be eaten while rock hard, but slightly softened.

vanilla ice cream

☀ ☀

Preparation time: 30 minutes + 2 hours
    freezing and 30 minutes softening time
Cooking time: 15 minutes
Serves 4

250 ml (9 fl oz/1 cup) milk
250 ml (9 fl oz/1 cup) pouring (whipping)
    cream
1 vanilla bean, split lengthways
6 egg yolks
125 g (4½ oz/½ cup) caster
    (superfine) sugar

1 Combine the milk and cream in a saucepan and add the vanilla bean. Bring to the boil, then remove from the heat and set aside for 10 minutes.
2 Use a wire whisk to whisk the yolks and sugar together in a bowl for 2–3 minutes, until thick and pale, then whisk in the warm milk mixture. Scrape the seeds from the vanilla bean into the mixture. Discard the bean.
3 Wash the saucepan, and pour the mixture into it. Stir over very low heat until thickened. This will take about 5–10 minutes. To test, run a finger through the mixture across the back of the wooden spoon — if it leaves a clear line, the custard is ready.
4 Pour the custard into a bowl and cool to room temperature, stirring frequently to hasten cooling.

To test the custard, run a finger through the mixture, across the back of a wooden spoon. It should leave a clear line.

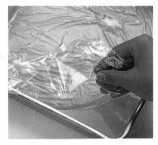

Cover the surface of the custard with plastic wrap and freeze for 2 hours.

Beat the semi-frozen ice cream with electric beaters to break up any large ice crystals. Each time you beat the mixture, the ice crystals will get smaller and the mixture smoother.

5 Pour into a shallow metal container, cover the surface of the custard with plastic wrap or baking paper and freeze for about 2 hours, until almost frozen. Scoop into a chilled bowl and beat with electric beaters until smooth, then return to the tray and freeze again. Repeat this step twice more before transferring to a storage container. Cover the surface with baking paper or plastic wrap to stop ice crystals forming on the surface, then a lid.
6 Soften in the fridge for 30 minutes before serving. Ice cream will keep, well sealed, in the freezer for up to 1 month.

NOTE: This recipe can also be made using an ice cream machine.

VARIATIONS
To make strawberry ice cream, chop 250 g (9 oz) strawberries in a food processor just until smooth. Stir into the custard mixture when it is well chilled (end of step 4). Freeze the ice cream as directed.

To make banana ice cream, thoroughly mash 3 ripe bananas (or for a finer texture, purée in a food processor). Stir into the custard mixture when it is well chilled, along with 1 tablespoon lemon juice. Freeze as directed. Makes 1.5 litres (52 fl oz/6 cups).

chocolate and cinnamon ice cream

✳ ✳

Preparation time: 20 minutes + 1 hour chilling and 5 hours freezing and 30 minutes softening time
Cooking time: 30 minutes
Serves 6–8

500 ml (17 fl oz/2 cups) milk
200 g (7 oz) good-quality dark chocolate, chopped
4 cinnamon sticks
185 g (6½ oz) caster (superfine) sugar

1½ teaspoons ground cinnamon
4 egg yolks
500 ml (17 fl oz/2 cups) pouring (whipping) cream

1 Heat milk, chocolate and cinnamon sticks in a heavy-based saucepan, stirring occasionally, over low heat for 15 minutes, or until the chocolate melts and the ingredients are well mixed. Do not allow to boil. Remove the cinnamon sticks.
2 Mix the sugar and cinnamon in a large heatproof bowl. Add the yolks and place the bowl over a saucepan of simmering water. Whisk until thick and pale.

3 Gradually whisk the chocolate mixture into the eggs and sugar. Cook, whisking all the time, for 5 minutes or until the mixture coats the back of a spoon. Chill for 30 minutes in the refrigerator, then strain and slowly stir in the cream.
4 Transfer to an ice cream machine and freeze according to the manufacturer's instructions. Alternatively, transfer to a shallow metal tray and freeze, whisking every couple of hours until frozen and creamy. Freeze for 5 hours or overnight. Soften in the fridge for 30 minutes before serving.

lemon ice cream

✳ ✳

Preparation time: 20 minutes +
    freezing time
Cooking time: 15 minutes
Serves 4–6

6 egg yolks
250 g (9 oz/1 cup) caster (superfine) sugar
2 teaspoons finely grated lemon zest
80 ml (2½ fl oz/⅓ cup) lemon juice
500 ml (17 fl oz/2 cups) pouring (whipping)
    cream, lightly whipped

1 Whisk or beat the egg yolks in a heatproof bowl. Stand the bowl over a pan of steaming water, off the heat, and whisk until light and fluffy and increased in volume. Add the sugar, lemon zest and juice, and continue whisking until thick and pale. Allow to cool.

2 Use a metal spoon to fold the cream into the lemon mixture. Pour into a 1.25 litre (44 fl oz/5 cup) capacity shallow metal container and freeze for 2 hours, or until firm. When half frozen around the edges, beat well, then freeze again. Repeat the beating and freezing twice more. Serve in scoops.

lemon ice cream

mocha ice cream

✳ ✳

Preparation time: 20 minutes + freezing time
Cooking time: 10–15 minutes
Serves 4–6

40 g (1½ oz/½ cup) espresso coffee
    beans
750 ml (26 fl oz/3 cups) pouring
    (whipping) cream
250 g (9 oz) good-quality dark chocolate,
    chopped
185 g (6½ oz/¾ cup) caster (superfine)
    sugar
6 egg yolks
250 ml (9 fl oz/1 cup) milk

1 Line a rectangular tin with plastic wrap and freeze. Combine the coffee beans and cream in a pan. Stir over medium heat until the mixture just starts to boil. Add the chocolate, remove from the heat and set aside for 1 minute before stirring.

2 Combine the sugar and egg yolks in a large bowl, whisk until slightly thickened, then whisk in the milk. Gradually add the coffee mixture with the beans and whisk until smooth. Strain the mixture and discard the beans.

3 Return the mixture to the pan and stir over low heat until the mixture thickens and coats the back of a spoon. Do not boil. Remove from the heat and set aside to cool.

4 Put the mixture into the prepared tin and freeze until just firm. Transfer to a large chilled bowl and beat with electric beaters until thick. Return to the tin and cover with plastic wrap and freeze again until firm. Repeat, beating once more before transferring to a container for storage in the freezer. Cover the surface with plastic wrap or baking paper. Serve in scoops with frosted rose petals (see Note) or store in the freezer for up to 7 days.

NOTE: To frost rose petals, lightly whisk 1 egg white, dip clean dry petals in egg white (or brush lightly with a paintbrush), then sprinkle with sugar. Shake off excess sugar. Place on a paper-lined tray to dry.

ice cream and alcohol

The addition of alcohol to ice creams lowers the freezing point, sometimes to a stage where it will not freeze at all. Spirits lower the freezing point of ice cream by approximately 1°C (33°F) per tablespoon and sorbets by 6°C (42°F).

chocolate whisky loaf

 ✺ ✺

Preparation time: 20 minutes + 2–3 hours freezing time
Cooking time: 5 minutes
Serves 6

250 g (9 oz/1⅔ cups) chopped dark chocolate
60 g (2¼ oz) unsalted butter, softened
4 egg yolks
310 ml (10¾ fl oz/1¼ cups) pouring (whipping) cream
2 teaspoons natural vanilla extract
2 tablespoons whisky
cream, to serve

1 Line a 21 x 14 x 7 cm (9 x 5 x 3 inch) loaf (bar) tin with plastic wrap. Put the chocolate in a heatproof bowl. Half-fill a saucepan with water and bring to the boil, then remove the pan from the heat. Sit the bowl over the pan, making sure the base of the bowl doesn't touch the water. Stir occasionally until the chocolate melts. Allow to cool.
2 Beat the butter and egg yolks in a small bowl until thick and creamy, then beat in the cooled chocolate. Whisk the cream and vanilla in another bowl until soft peaks form, then fold in the whisky. Using a metal spoon, fold the cream and chocolate mixtures together until just combined.

3 Pour the mixture into the prepared tin, cover the surface with plastic wrap and freeze for 2–3 hours or overnight, until firm. Remove from the freezer, unmould and carefully peel away the plastic wrap. Smooth the wrinkles on the surface of the loaf using a flat-bladed knife. Place on a serving plate. If not serving immediately, return to the freezer for up to 1 week. Cut into slices and serve with cream.

ice cream cassata

※ ※

Preparation time: 1 hour + freezing
   + overnight freezing time
Cooking time: nil
Serves 10

FIRST LAYER
2 eggs, separated
40 g (1½ oz/⅓ cup) icing (confectioners')
   sugar
185 ml (6 fl oz/¾ cup) pouring
   (whipping) cream
50 g (1¾ oz) flaked almonds, toasted

SECOND LAYER
130 g (4¾ oz) dark chocolate, chopped
1 tablespoon unsweetened cocoa powder
2 eggs, separated
40 g (1½ oz/⅓ cup) icing
   (confectioners') sugar
185 ml (6 fl oz/¾ cup) pouring
   (whipping) cream

THIRD LAYER
2 eggs, separated
30 g (1 oz/¼ cup) icing
   (confectioners') sugar
60 ml (2 fl oz/¼ cup) pouring
   (whipping) cream
125 g (4½ oz/½ cup) ricotta cheese
250 g (9 oz) glacé fruit (pineapple,
   apricot, cherries, fig and peach),
   finely chopped
1 teaspoon natural vanilla extract

1 Line the base and sides of a deep
20 cm (8 inch) square tin with foil.
2 To make the first layer, whisk the
egg whites with electric beaters until
soft peaks form. Add the icing sugar
gradually, whisking well after each
addition. In a separate bowl, whisk the
cream until firm peaks form. Use a
metal spoon to fold the yolks and beaten
egg whites into the cream. Stir in the
almonds. Spoon into the tin and smooth
the surface. Tap the tin gently on the
bench to level the surface, then freeze
for 1 hour or until firm but not
completely set.

cassata

Originating in Naples, cassata
is traditionally composed of
flavoured ice cream layered
around a filling of ricotta
cheese and candied fruit in an
oblong mould. Cassata means
'little case'. Cassata Siciliana
is a traditional Sicilian dessert
set in a dome-shaped mould
and made with cake, green
marzipan, crystallised fruit,
ricotta cheese and chocolate.
Cassata Gelata alla Siciliana
is an ice cream based on this.
Vanilla and pistachio ice creams
are layered with cake, then
whipped egg whites, cream,
chocolate and candied fruit and
finally the two ice cream layers
are repeated.

3 To make the second layer, melt the chocolate by stirring in a heatproof bowl over a saucepan of steaming water, off the heat. Make sure the base of the bowl does not touch the water. Stir in the cocoa until smooth. Cool slightly, then proceed as for step 1, whisking the egg whites and icing sugar and then the cream. Use a metal spoon to fold the chocolate into the cream. Fold in the yolks and whisked egg whites and stir until smooth. Spoon over the frozen first layer. Tap the tin on the bench to smooth the surface. Freeze for 1 hour or until firm but not completely set.
4 To make the third layer, proceed as for the first layer, whisking the egg whites with the icing sugar and then the cream. Stir the ricotta into the cream. With a metal spoon, fold the yolks and egg white into the cream, then stir in the fruit and natural vanilla extract. Spoon over the chocolate layer, cover the surface with baking paper, then freeze overnight. Slice to serve.

ice cream christmas pudding

✹ ✹

Preparation time: 1 hour + several overnight freezing times
Cooking time: nil
Serves 10

50 g (1¾ oz/⅓ cup) toasted almonds, chopped
45 g (1½ oz/¼ cup) mixed peel (mixed candied citrus peel)
80 g (2¾ oz/½ cup) raisins, chopped
80 g (2¾ oz/½ cup) sultanas (golden raisins)
50 g (1¾ oz/⅓ cup) currants
80 ml (2½ fl oz/⅓ cup) dark rum
1 litre (35 fl oz/4 cups) good-quality vanilla ice cream
105 g (3½ oz/½ cup) red and green glacé (candied) cherries, quartered
1 teaspoon mixed (pumpkin pie) spice
1 teaspoon ground cinnamon
½ teaspoon freshly grated nutmeg
1 litre (35 fl oz/4 cups) chocolate ice cream

1 Mix the almonds, peel, raisins, sultanas, currants and rum in a bowl, cover with plastic wrap and leave overnight. Chill a 2 litre (70 fl oz/8 cup) pudding basin (steamed pudding mould) in the freezer overnight.
2 Soften the vanilla ice cream slightly and mix in the glacé cherries. Working quickly, press the ice cream around the inside of the chilled basin, spreading it evenly to cover the base and side of the basin. Return the basin to the freezer and leave overnight. Check the ice cream a couple of times and spread it evenly to the top if necessary.
3 The next day, mix the spices and chocolate ice cream with the fruit mixture. Spoon it into the centre of the pudding bowl and smooth the top. Freeze overnight, or until very firm. Turn out the pudding onto a chilled plate. Cut into wedges, to serve.

praline ice cream with caramel bark

✿ ✿ ✿

Preparation time: 25 minutes + 6 hours
  freezing time
Cooking time: 10 minutes
Serves 4

70 g (2½ oz) blanched almonds,
  toasted
55 g (2 oz/¼ cup) caster (superfine) sugar
125 g (4½ oz) white chocolate, chopped
185 ml (6 fl oz/¾ cup) pouring
  (whipping) cream

250 g (9 oz) mascarpone cheese
2 tablespoons sugar

1 To make the praline, line a baking tray
with foil, brush the foil lightly with oil
and put the almonds on the foil.
2 Put the caster sugar in a small
saucepan over low heat. Tilt the saucepan
slightly, but do not stir, and watch until
the sugar melts and turns golden —
this should take 3–5 minutes. Pour the
caramel over the almonds and leave until
set and cold. Break into chunks, put in a
plastic bag and crush with a rolling pin,
or process briefly in a food processor until
it is crumbly.

3 Put the white chocolate in a heatproof
bowl. Half-fill a saucepan with water and
bring to the boil, then remove the pan
from the heat. Sit the bowl over the pan,
making sure the base of the bowl doesn't
touch the water. Stir occasionally until the
chocolate melts. Set aside to cool.
4 Whip the cream until firm peaks form.
Stir the mascarpone and melted chocolate
in a large bowl to combine. Use a metal
spoon to fold in the cream and crushed
praline. Transfer to a 1 litre (35 fl oz/
4 cup) metal tin, cover the surface with
baking paper and freeze for 6 hours, or
overnight. Remove from the freezer
15 minutes before serving, to soften.
5 To make the caramel bark, line a baking
tray with foil and brush lightly with oil.
Sprinkle the sugar evenly onto the tray
and place under a hot grill (broiler) for
2 minutes, until the sugar melts and is
golden. Check frequently towards the end
of cooking time, as the sugar may burn
quickly. Remove from the heat, leave until
set and completely cold, then break into
shards. Serve with the ice cream.

brown bread ice cream

✿

Preparation time: 25 minutes + 1 hour
  freezing time
Cooking time: 15–20 minutes
Serves 6

2 egg yolks
60 g (2¼ oz/¼ cup) caster (superfine) sugar
125 ml (4 fl oz/½ cup) milk
125 g (4½ oz/1½ cups) fine fresh brown
  breadcrumbs
55 g (2 oz) butter, melted
2 tablespoons soft brown sugar
310 ml (10¾ fl oz/1¼ cups) pouring
  (whipping) cream
1 tablespoon dark rum
strips of orange zest, to serve

1 Preheat the oven to 200°F (400°F/
Gas 6). Whisk the egg yolks and sugar in
a bowl until thick and pale. Heat the milk
in a saucepan until simmering, but not

praline ice cream with caramel bark

boiling, and pour over the yolk mixture, whisking constantly.

2 Return the mixture to a clean pan and cook gently over low heat, stirring constantly, until the mixture lightly coats the back of a wooden spoon. Remove from the heat. (Do not boil or it will curdle.) Transfer to a bowl. Cover the surface with plastic wrap and set aside to cool.

3 Mix the breadcrumbs with the butter and brown sugar. Spread on a tray and bake for about 15 minutes. Stir and turn once or twice during cooking. Cool, then crumble.

4 Beat the cream until soft peaks form, then stir in the rum. Carefully fold the cream into the cold custard. Freeze for 1 hour in a metal or plastic container, stir in the breadcrumbs and freeze until firm. Serve with orange zest.

triple chocolate terrine

✳ ✳

Preparation time: **1 hour + freezing time**
Cooking time: **15–20 minutes**
Serves **8–10**

150 g (5½ oz) milk chocolate, chopped
6 eggs
90 g (3¼ oz/¾ cup) icing (confectioners')
   sugar
60 g (2¼ oz) unsalted butter
500 ml (17 fl oz/2 cups) pouring (whipping)
   cream
150 g (5½ oz) white chocolate, chopped
2 teaspoons instant coffee granules
3–4 teaspoons dark rum
150 g (5½ oz) good-quality dark chocolate,
   chopped

1 Line a 10 x 23 cm (4 x 9 inch) loaf tin with baking paper, extending above the top of the tin. Melt the milk chocolate in a small heatproof bowl, over a saucepan of steaming water, off the heat, making sure the bottom of the bowl does not touch the water, until smooth. Separate two of the eggs and whisk the whites until soft peaks form. Gradually whisk in 30 g (1 oz/ ¼ cup) of the icing sugar, until thick and glossy. Whisk in the 2 egg yolks and the cooled melted chocolate. Melt 20 g (¾ oz) of the butter and whisk in. Whip 170 ml (5½ fl oz/⅔ cup) of the cream into soft peaks. Fold into the egg white mixture and then spoon into the tin, with the tin tilted on one side lengthways. Put in the freezer on this angle and leave for 1–2 hours, until just firm.

2 Repeat the same method with 2 of the remaining eggs, 30 g (1 oz/¼ cup) of the icing sugar, the white chocolate, 20 g (¾ oz) of the butter, and 170 ml (5½ fl oz/⅔ cup) of the cream. Spoon this mixture into the other side of the tin so that the terrine becomes level. Put the tin flat in the freezer to set.

3 Repeat the same method with the remaining ingredients, folding in the coffee dissolved in 1 tablespoon of water, and rum, with the dark chocolate. Spoon into the tin and smooth the surface. Freeze for several hours. Turn out onto a plate, then cut into thin slices to serve. Garnish with chocolate leaves (page 208).

fruit sauces

Fresh fruits, herbs and spices can be used to make sublime sauces that transform a bowl of ice cream or simple dessert into something quite out of the ordinary.

rhubarb sauce

Chop 350 g (12 oz) rhubarb and place in a saucepan with 95 g (3¼ oz/½ cup) soft brown sugar, 250 ml (9 fl oz/1 cup) water and ¼ teaspoon ground mixed (pumpkin pie) spice. Slowly bring to the boil, stirring. Simmer for 10 minutes, stirring. Push through a sieve. Serve hot or cold. Makes 375 ml (13 fl oz/1½ cups).

lemongrass, lime and coriander syrup

Finely grate 250 g (9 oz) palm sugar (jaggery) and place in a small saucepan with 250 ml (9 fl oz/1 cup) water. Stir over low heat until the sugar dissolves. Add 2 finely sliced stems lemongrass (white part only), 1 teaspoon crushed coriander seeds, 1 teaspoon lime zest and 2 teaspoons lime juice. Bring to the boil and simmer for 15–20 minutes, or until syrupy. Strain, if desired. Makes 250 ml (9 fl oz/1 cup).

mango coulis

Chop 2 small mangoes. Blend in a food processor with 60 ml (2 fl oz/¼ cup) orange juice and 2 teaspoons Cointreau (optional), until smooth. Makes 350 ml (12 fl oz/1⅓ cups).

passionfruit coulis

Put 125 ml (4 fl oz/½ cup) fresh passionfruit pulp (tinned is not suitable), 125 ml (4 fl oz/½ cup) water and 2 tablespoons caster (superfine) sugar in a small saucepan. Slowly bring to the boil, stirring. Simmer, without stirring, for 5 minutes. Makes 250 ml (9 fl oz/1 cup).

hot blueberry sauce

In a non-metallic bowl, combine 500 g (1 lb 2 oz) blueberries, 60 g (2¼ oz/¼ cup) sugar and 1 tablespoon balsamic vinegar. Set aside for 30 minutes. Place in a saucepan with 2 tablespoons water and stir over low heat. Bring to the boil and simmer for 5 minutes. Serve warm. Delicious on ice cream, ricotta cheese or warm chocolate cake. Makes 500 ml (17 fl oz/2 cups).

strawberry coulis

Hull 250 g (9 oz) strawberries and place in a food processor with 2 tablespoons icing (confectioners') sugar, 2 teaspoons lemon juice and 1–2 teaspoons Grand Marnier (optional). Process until smooth and strain through a fine sieve, if desired. Makes 250 ml (9 fl oz/1 cup).

bumbleberry coulis

Place 300 g (10½ oz) fresh or thawed frozen berries (any combination of raspberry, strawberry, blueberry, blackberry) and 2 tablespoons icing (confectioners') sugar in a food processor. Blend in short bursts until smooth and glossy. Strain in a fine sieve to remove the seeds. Add 2 teaspoons lemon juice and 3 teaspoons Cassis liqueur (optional) and mix well. Makes 250 ml (9 fl oz/1 cup).

spicy peach sauce

Place 500 g (1 lb 2 oz) peaches in a bowl, cover with boiling water and leave for 20 seconds. Drain, peel and chop, then put in a saucepan with 250 ml (9 fl oz/1 cup) water, ½ vanilla bean, 2 cloves and a cinnamon stick. Bring to the boil, reduce the heat and simmer for 15–20 minutes, or until tender. Add 3 tablespoons sugar and stir over low heat until dissolved. Increase the heat and simmer for 5 minutes. Remove the vanilla and spices and cool slightly. Blend in a food processor or blender. Push through a fine sieve. Makes 435 ml (15¼ fl oz/1¾ cups).

ice cream safety

Ice creams, if wrongly handled, can be a perfect breeding ground for bacteria. Bacteria are normally killed when heated to a high enough temperature, and made inactive when cooled down enough or frozen. It is the temperatures between these points which are a problem, especially blood temperature. Custards should be cooled as quickly as possible and dairy products kept well chilled until used. Ice cream, if thawed completely, should be thrown away. All equipment should be thoroughly washed and the ice cream machine may benefit from being sterilised.

chocolate ice cream

Preparation time: 1 hour + overnight freezing
 + 15–20 minutes softening time
Cooking time: 30 minutes
Serves 4

8 egg yolks
125 g (4½ oz/½ cup) caster (superfine) sugar
2 tablespoons unsweetened cocoa powder
500 ml (17 fl oz/2 cups) milk
250 ml (9 fl oz/1 cup) pouring
   (whipping) cream
1 vanilla bean, split lengthways
250 g (9 oz) good-quality dark chocolate,
   chopped

1 Put the egg yolks in a large heatproof bowl and gradually whisk in the sugar.

Continue to whisk until the sugar dissolves and the mixture is thick and pale. (Do not use an electric mixer as this will incorporate too much air into the mixture.) Stir in the sifted cocoa.
2 Combine the milk, cream and vanilla bean in a pan. Bring to the boil, scrape the seeds out of the vanilla bean into the milk, and discard the empty bean. Gently whisk the hot milk into the egg yolk mixture. Place the bowl over a saucepan of simmering water, and stir constantly over low heat until the custard coats the back of a wooden spoon. (This will take about 20 minutes.) Do not allow the mixture to boil, or the eggs will curdle. Remove from the heat, strain and pour into a clean bowl. Chill a deep 20 cm (8 inch) square cake tin in the freezer.

3 Put the chocolate in a heatproof bowl. Half fill a saucepan with water and bring to the boil. Remove from the heat and place the bowl over the pan, making sure it is not touching the water. Stir occasionally until the chocolate melts. Add the warm chocolate to the warm custard and stir constantly until the chocolate mixes through. Allow to cool. Pour the cooled mixture into the chilled container, cover and freeze until the ice cream just sets. Remove from the freezer and spoon into a large bowl. Beat with a wooden spoon or electric beaters until smooth and thick, then return to the container. Repeat the freezing and beating twice more, then cover with a layer of baking paper and freeze overnight, or until completely set. Soften in the fridge for 15–20 minutes before serving.

frozen chocolate parfait

✹ ✹

Preparation time: 40 minutes + 30 minutes
   freezing + overnight freezing time
Cooking time: 25 minutes
Serves 8

6 egg yolks
125 g (4½ oz/½ cup) caster (superfine) sugar
150 g (5½ oz) dark chocolate, finely
   chopped
150 g (5½ oz) milk chocolate, finely
   chopped
1 vanilla bean, split lengthways
250 ml (9 fl oz/1 cup) milk
350 ml (12 fl oz/1⅓ cups) pouring
   (whipping) cream

1 Lightly grease a 1.25 litre (44 fl oz/ 5 cup) terrine mould and line the entire mould with two layers of plastic wrap, allowing the plastic to extend over the sides. (This will help when removing the parfait once it has set.) Place the egg yolks in a bowl and gradually whisk in the sugar. Continue to whisk until the sugar dissolves and the mixture is thick and pale. Place the chopped dark and milk chocolate in separate bowls and set aside.
2 Put the vanilla bean in a small saucepan with the milk. Slowly bring to the boil, then remove from the heat and scrape the seeds out of the vanilla bean and into the milk. Discard the empty bean. Gently pour the milk onto the egg yolks, whisking constantly. Return the mixture to a clean pan and cook over low heat, stirring constantly, until the custard coats the back of a wooden spoon. This

will take about 20 minutes. Do not overcook or the egg will curdle.
3 Divide the hot custard evenly between the bowls of chocolate. Use a wooden spoon to quickly mix in the custard, stirring until the chocolate completely melts. Allow to cool completely. Whisk the cream with electric beaters until soft peaks form. Divide evenly between the cooled chocolate mixtures, and gently fold in. Carefully pour the dark chocolate mixture into the base of the terrine dish. Freeze for 30 minutes, or until firm. Pour the milk chocolate mixture over the back of a spoon to form an even layer, and smooth the top with the back of a spoon. Cover with baking paper and freeze overnight.
4 Just before serving, carefully remove the plastic wrap and parfait from the dish. Slice the parfait and immediately return the remaining portion to the freezer.

Divide the hot custard evenly between the bowls of dark and milk chocolate.

Pour the milk chocolate mixture over the firm dark chocolate layer.

peanut brittle parfait

✹ ✹

Preparation time: 40 minutes
    + freezing time
Cooking time: 15 minutes
Serves 8

375 g (13 oz/1½ cups) caster
    (superfine) sugar
500 ml (17 fl oz/2 cups) milk
6 egg yolks
1 tablespoon instant coffee
    granules
600 ml (21 fl oz/2½ cups) pouring
    (whipping) cream
120 g (4¼ oz) chocolate-coated
    peanut brittle, roughly chopped
caramel bark (page 218), to serve

1 Stir 250 g (9 oz/1 cup) sugar with
80 ml (2½ fl oz/⅓ cup) water in a
saucepan over low heat, without boiling,
until the sugar dissolves. Brush down the
sides of the pan with water to dissolve the
sugar crystals. Bring to the boil, reduce
the heat and simmer without stirring for
4 minutes, or until caramel. Remove from
the heat and allow to cool slightly before
stirring in the milk. Be careful as the
mixture will splutter. Return to the heat
and stir until the toffee dissolves.
2 Line a 15 x 23 cm (6 x 9 inch) loaf tin
with plastic wrap. Whisk the remaining
sugar with the egg yolks in a metal or
heatproof bowl. Whisk in the milk mixture
and the coffee blended with 1 teaspoon
water. Stand the bowl over a pan of
simmering water (or mix in the top of a

double boiler). Whisk until the mixture
thickens and coats the back of a spoon.
3 Cool the mixture, then add the cream.
Pour into a large shallow tin and freeze
until just firm. Transfer to a large bowl.
Use electric beaters to beat until light and
fluffy. Return to the tin and freeze until
just firm. Repeat the beating process twice
more. Fold the chopped peanut brittle
through, spread the mixture into the loaf
tin, cover the surface with a piece of
baking paper, then freeze until firm. Cut
into slices and serve with caramel bark.

espresso parfait

✹ ✹

Preparation time: 10 minutes + 2 hours
    freezing time
Cooking time: 20 minutes
Serves 4–6

45 g (1½ oz/½ cup) ground coffee
185 g (6½ oz/¾ cup) sugar
4 egg yolks
250 ml (9 fl oz/1 cup) thick (double) cream

1 Put the coffee, sugar and 185 ml
(6 fl oz/¾ cup) water in a saucepan, bring
to the boil, remove from the heat and leave
for 3 minutes. Strain through a filter paper
or muslin-lined (cheesecloth-lined) sieve.
Pour back into the rinsed pan. Keep warm.
2 Place the egg yolks in a heatproof bowl
and whisk until pale and light. Whisk in
the coffee syrup a little at a time. Place the
bowl over a pan of simmering water and
cook, stirring until the mixture thickens
enough to coat the back of a spoon — do
not boil or it will curdle. Remove from the
heat and whisk with electric beaters until
doubled in volume. The mixture will hold
a trail when it is allowed to run off the
beaters. Chill until cold.
3 Whip the cream until soft peaks form,
then fold into the egg mixture. Pour the
mixture into a loaf tin lined with plastic
wrap, cover the surface with baking paper
and freeze for at least 2 hours. Transfer
the parfait to the fridge for 10 minutes
before turning out and cutting into slices.

peanut brittle parfait

cappuccino ice cream cakes

☀ ☀

Preparation time: 1 hour 45 minutes
+ freezing time
Cooking time: 30 minutes
Serves 10

1 tablespoon instant coffee granules
1 litre (35 fl oz/4 cups) vanilla ice cream, softened
250 ml (9 fl oz/1 cup) thick (double) cream
1 tablespoon icing (confectioners') sugar
125 g (4½ oz) dark chocolate melts, melted
unsweetened cocoa powder, to dust

CHOCOLATE CAKES
185 g (6½ oz) unsalted butter
330 g (11¾ oz/1½ cups) caster (superfine) sugar
2½ teaspoons natural vanilla extract
3 eggs
75 g (2½ oz/½ cup) self-raising flour
225 g (8 oz/1½ cups) plain (all-purpose) flour
1½ teaspoons bicarbonate of soda (baking soda)
90 g (3¼ oz/¾ cup) unsweetened cocoa powder
280 ml (9½ fl oz) buttermilk

1 Lightly grease ten muffin holes (with 250 ml/9 fl oz/1 cup capacity). Preheat the oven to 180°C (350°F/Gas 4).
2 To make the cakes, beat the butter and sugar with electric beaters until light and creamy. Beat in the vanilla. Add the eggs, one at a time, beating well after each addition.
3 Use a metal spoon to fold in the combined sifted flours, bicarbonate of soda and cocoa powder alternately with the buttermilk. Stir until the mixture is just combined.
4 Divide the mixture evenly among the muffin holes and bake for 25 minutes, or until a skewer comes out clean. Cool in the tins for 5 minutes before turning onto a wire cake rack to cool.

5 Dissolve the coffee powder in 2 tablespoons boiling water, then cool. Roughly break up the ice cream in a large bowl and stir until smooth. Stir in the coffee mixture and freeze until required.
6 Beat the cream and icing sugar together in a small bowl with an electric mixer until soft peaks form. Refrigerate until ready to use.
7 Draw the outline of a small spoon, 10 times, on a piece of baking paper, then turn the paper over. Spoon the melted chocolate into a paper piping bag. Snip the end off the bag and draw a chocolate outline around the spoons, then fill in with melted chocolate. Allow to set.

8 Cut the top off each cake, leaving a 1 cm (½ inch) border around the top edge of each cake. Reserve the tops. Use a spoon to scoop out some of the cake, leaving a 1 cm (½ inch) shell. (Leftover cake can be frozen for another use.)
9 Soften the coffee ice cream with a spoon and pile into the cakes so it comes slightly above the top. Replace the tops and press gently. Spread cream mixture roughly over the top of each cake to represent the froth. Dust the tops with sifted cocoa and serve with a chocolate spoon tucked into the cream.

green tea

A favourite in Japan, green tea is served with meals and is believed to aid digestion. It is always made weak: only 1 teaspoon of tea for the whole pot. Sugar and milk are never added. Japanese green tea is usually sencha tea, with a delicate, light flavour and pale colour.

green tea ice cream

green tea ice cream

❊ ❊

Preparation time: 15 minutes + overnight freezing time
Cooking time: 30 minutes
Serves 4

4 tablespoons Japanese green tea leaves
500 ml (17 fl oz/2 cups) milk
6 egg yolks
115 g (4 oz/½ cup) caster (superfine) sugar
500 ml (17 fl oz/2 cups) pouring (whipping) cream

1 Combine the green tea leaves with the milk in a saucepan and slowly bring to simmering point. This step should not be rushed — the longer the milk takes to come to a simmer, the better the infusion of flavour. Set aside for 5 minutes before straining.
2 Whisk the egg yolks and sugar in a heatproof bowl until thick and pale, then whisk in the infused milk. Place the bowl over a saucepan of simmering water, making sure that the base of the bowl does not touch the water. Stir the custard until it is thick enough to coat the back of spoon, then remove from the heat and

allow to cool slightly before stirring through the cream.
3 Transfer to an ice cream machine and freeze according to manufacturer's instructions. Alternatively, transfer to a shallow metal tray and freeze, whisking every couple of hours until frozen and creamy. Freeze overnight.

NOTE: Add a few drops of green food colouring for pale green ice cream.

mango ice cream

❄

Preparation time: 20 minutes + freezing
  + 30 minutes softening time
Cooking time: nil
Serves 6

400 g (14 oz) fresh mango flesh
125 g (4½ oz/½ cup) caster
  (superfine) sugar
60 ml (2 fl oz/¼ cup) mango or
  apricot nectar
250 ml (9 fl oz/1 cup) pouring
  (whipping) cream
mango slices, extra (optional), to serve

1 Put the mango in a food processor and process until smooth. Transfer the mango purée to a bowl and add the sugar and nectar. Stir until the sugar dissolves.
2 Beat the cream in a small bowl until stiff peaks form and then gently fold it through the mango mixture.
3 Transfer to an ice cream machine and freeze according to manufacturer's instructions. Alternatively, transfer to a shallow metal tray and freeze, whisking every couple of hours until frozen and creamy. Freeze for 5 hours or overnight. Soften in the fridge for 30 minutes before serving with mango slices, if desired.

NOTE: Frozen or tinned mango can be used.

raspberry ripple

❄

Preparation time: 30 minutes + freezing
  and overnight freezing time
Cooking time: nil
Serves 8–10

250 g (9 oz) raspberries
1 litre (35 fl oz/4 cups) good-quality
  vanilla ice cream
250 ml (9 fl oz/1 cup) pouring (whipping)
  cream
extra raspberries and cream,
  to serve

1 Line the base and sides of a 1.75 litre (61 fl oz/7 cup) loaf tin with plastic wrap or foil.
2 Purée the raspberries in a food processor until smooth. Remove the ice cream from the freezer and allow to soften. Whisk the cream until soft peaks form. Use a metal spoon to gently fold the cream into the raspberry purée. Pour the mixture into a metal freezer tray and put in the freezer until cool but not frozen solid. Stir occasionally until thick. When half frozen, remove from the freezer and beat well.

3 Spoon blobs of softened vanilla ice cream over the base of the prepared loaf tin. Spoon the raspberry mixture between the vanilla blobs. Use a sharp knife or skewer to swirl the two together, being careful not to dig into the foil.
4 Freeze for 2 hours, or until half frozen, then smooth the top of the ice cream. Freeze overnight. When ready, it may be served in scoops or removed from the tin and cut in slices. Serve with extra raspberries and cream.

raspberry ripple

parfaits

These are American-style parfaits with layers of ice cream, fruit and sauces made to classic 'soda fountain' formulae. The original French parfait was a type of ice cream made with eggs, sugar and cream.

vanilla and caramel parfait

Heat 90 g (3¼ oz) unsalted butter in a heavy-based pan. Add 140 g (5 oz/¾ cup) soft brown sugar and stir over low heat, without boiling, until the sugar dissolves. Increase the heat and simmer, without boiling, for 3 minutes, or until golden. Remove from the heat and cool slightly. Stir in 170 ml (5½ fl oz/⅔ cup) pouring (whipping) cream, allow to cool, then whisk until smooth. Layer vanilla ice cream, halved chocolate-coated malt balls and the caramel sauce into four parfait glasses and top with some more halved malt balls. Serve immediately. Serves 4.

strawberry and raspberry parfait

Stir an 85 g (3 oz) packet strawberry-flavoured jelly crystals in 500 ml (17 fl oz/2 cups) boiling water until the crystals dissolve, then refrigerate until set. Process 125 g (4½ oz) chopped strawberries in a food processor for 30 seconds. Layer 500 ml (17 fl oz/2 cups) vanilla ice cream, the jelly, 125 g (4½ oz) chopped strawberries, 100 g (3½ oz) raspberries and the strawberry purée in six parfait glasses. Serve immediately. Serves 6.

spiced cherry brandy parfait

Place 3 tablespoons sugar, 2 tablespoons soft brown sugar, 1 teaspoon mixed (pumpkin pie) spice and 60 ml (2 fl oz/¼ cup) brandy in a pan with 250 ml (9 fl oz/1 cup) of water and stir without boiling until all the sugar dissolves, then bring to the boil. Add 500 g (1 lb 2 oz) pitted cherries and reduce the heat, simmer for 10 minutes, remove from the heat and cool. Layer cherries with 1 litre (35 fl oz/4 cups) vanilla ice cream in tall glasses and top with cherry syrup. Serve with brandy snaps. Serves 6.

chocolate kahlua parfait

Combine 125 g (4½ oz) chopped chocolate and vanilla cream biscuits (cookies) with 2 tablespoons Kahlua in a bowl. Set aside for 5 minutes. Layer 500 ml (17 fl oz/2 cups) chocolate ice cream, the biscuit mixture, 250 ml (9 fl oz/1 cup) pouring (whipping) cream, whipped, and 60 g (2¼ oz) chocolate chips, alternately, in four parfait glasses. Finish with whipped cream and sprinkle with choc chips. Serves 4.

caramel nut parfait

Put 100 g (3½ oz) butter, 2 tablespoons golden syrup or light treacle, 95 g (3 oz/½ cup) soft brown sugar and 250 ml (9 fl oz/1 cup) pouring (whipping) cream in a saucepan and stir over low heat until dissolved. Do not boil. Cool slightly. Layer 1 litre (35 fl oz/4 cups) vanilla ice cream and the warm sauce in parfait glasses. Sprinkle with chopped nuts. Serves 4–6.

banana split

Put 200 g (7 oz) good-quality dark chocolate, 185 ml (6 fl oz/¾ cup) pouring (whipping) cream and 30 g (1 oz) butter in a saucepan and stir over low heat until smooth. Cool slightly. Split 4 ripe bananas lengthways, and place the halves on a glass serving plate or bowl. Place 3 small scoops of ice cream on each plate and pour the chocolate sauce over the top. Sprinkle chopped nuts over the banana splits. Serves 4.

strawberry granita

Preparation time: 30 minutes + 5-6 hours
    freezing time
Cooking time: 10 minutes
Serves 4

125 g (4½ oz/½ cup) sugar
500 g (1 lb 2 oz) strawberries
2 tablespoons lemon juice

1 Stir the sugar and 125 ml (4 fl oz/
½ cup) water in a saucepan over low heat
until the sugar dissolves. Bring to the boil
and simmer for 5 minutes. Leave to cool.
2 Hull the strawberries and chop in a food
processor or blender with the lemon juice
for 30 seconds, or until smooth. Add the
cooled sugar syrup. Process to combine.

3 Sieve the purée to remove the seeds.
Pour into a shallow metal container,
cover and freeze for 2 hours, or until the
granita around the edge of the tray is
frozen. Stir with a fork to break up the
ice crystals. Return to the freezer for
1 hour and stir again with a fork. Repeat
this until the mixture is a smooth
consistency of ice crystals, then pour into
a storage container, cover with baking
paper and return to the freezer for
3–4 hours, or until set.
4 To serve, soften the frozen mixture in
the refrigerator for 15–20 minutes and
stir again with a fork to evenly break up
the ice crystals.

NOTE: If you have stored the granita for a
few days, you may need to fork and freeze
it again more than once until you to get it

to the correct consistency to serve. It is
delicious with a dollop of cream.

coffee granita

Preparation time: 20 minutes + 6-7 hours
    freezing time
Cooking time: 5 minutes
Serves 6

185 g (6½ oz/¾ cup) caster (superfine)
    sugar
1½ tablespoons unsweetened cocoa powder
1.25 litres (44 fl oz/5 cups) strong
    espresso coffee

1 Put the sugar and sifted cocoa in a
large saucepan, gradually add 125 ml

strawberry granita

Chop the strawberries until
smooth, then add the cooled sugar
syrup and process to combine.

Pout the strained purée into a
metal container then cover and
freeze, until the granita around
the edge of the tray is frozen.

(4 fl oz/½ cup) water and stir over low heat until the sugar dissolves. Bring to the boil, then reduce the heat and simmer for 3 minutes.

2 Remove from the heat and add the fresh coffee. Pour into a shallow metal container or tray and cool completely. Freeze for 2 hours or until partially set, then stir with a fork to distribute the ice crystals evenly. Freeze again for 3–4 hours or until set.

3 Use a fork to work the granita into fine crystals and return to the freezer for 1 hour before serving. Spoon into glasses to serve.

NOTE: This granita is very hard when frozen, so put it into a shallow tray and break it up when only partially frozen. It is difficult to break up if frozen in a deep container.

bellini sorbet

Preparation time: 20 minutes + 6 hours
    freezing time
Cooking time: 25 minutes
Serves 6

500 g (1 lb 2 oz/2 cups) caster (superfine)
    sugar
5 large peaches
185 ml (6 fl oz/¾ cup) Champagne
2 egg whites, lightly beaten
sliced fresh peaches and dessert wafers,
    to serve

1 Combine the sugar with 1 litre (35 fl oz/4 cups) water in a large saucepan and stir over low heat until the sugar dissolves. Bring to the boil, add the peaches and simmer for 20 minutes. Remove the peaches with a slotted spoon and cool completely. Reserve 250 ml (9 fl oz/1 cup) of the poaching liquid.

2 Peel the peaches, remove the stones and cut the flesh into chunks. Purée in a food processor until smooth, add the reserved liquid and the Champagne and process briefly until combined. Pour into a shallow metal tray and freeze for about 6 hours,

orange sorbet

until just firm. Transfer to a large bowl and beat until smooth with electric beaters.

3 Refreeze and repeat this step twice more, adding the egg white on the final beating. Place in a storage container, cover the surface with baking paper and freeze until firm. Serve in scoops, with sliced peaches and dessert wafers.

orange sorbet

Preparation time: 20 minutes + 1 hour freezing
    time and overnight freezing time
Cooking time: nil
Serves 6

10–12 oranges
90 g (3¼ oz/¾ cup) icing (confectioners')
    sugar
2 teaspoons lemon juice

1 Cut the oranges in half and carefully squeeze out the juice, taking care not to damage the skins. Dissolve the icing sugar in the orange juice, add the lemon juice and pour into a metal freezer container. Cover the surface with baking paper and freeze for 1 hour.

2 Scrape the remaining flesh and membrane out of six of the orange halves, cover the six skin halves with plastic wrap and refrigerate.

3 After 1 hour, stir any frozen juice that has formed around the edge of the sorbet into the centre and return to the freezer. Repeat every hour, or until nearly frozen. Freeze overnight.

4 Divide the sorbet among the orange skins and freeze until ready to serve. This sorbet may seem very hard when it has frozen overnight but it will melt quickly, so work fast.

kulfi

kulfi

❈ ❈

Preparation time: 20 minutes + overnight
    freezing time
Cooking time: 50 minutes
Serves 6

1.5 litres (52 fl oz/6 cups) milk
8 cardamom pods
4 tablespoons caster (superfine) sugar
20 g (¾ oz) blanched almonds, finely chopped
20 g (¾ oz) pistachio nuts, chopped,
    plus extra, to garnish
vegetable oil, for greasing

1 Put the milk and cardamom pods in
a large heavy-based saucepan, bring to
the boil then reduce the heat and simmer,
stirring often until it has reduced by
about one-third, to 1 litre (35 fl oz/
4 cups) — this will take some time. Keep
stirring or it will stick.
2 Add the caster sugar and cook for
2–3 minutes. Strain out the cardamom and
add the nuts. Pour the kulfi into a shallow
metal or plastic container, cover the surface
with a sheet of baking paper and freeze for
1 hour. Remove from the freezer and beat
to break up any ice crystals, freeze again
and repeat twice more.
3 Lightly brush six 250 ml (9 fl oz/1 cup)
ramekins or dariole moulds with the oil
and divide the kulfi among them, then
freeze overnight. To serve, unmould each
kulfi and cut a cross ½ cm (¼ inch) deep
in the top. Serve sprinkled with extra
chopped pistachio nuts.

kulfi and semifreddo

Kulfi is a traditional Indian ice
cream made by boiling milk
until it reduces in volume. It is
a time consuming procedure
but one which gives a unique
flavour. Kulfi has a dense icy
texture and is traditionally set
in cone shaped moulds. If you
can't find any moulds, you can
use cream horn moulds or any
other shape. They are usually
served with a cross cut in the
top to make them easier to eat.
Quick kulfis can be made using
evaporated or condensed milk
instead of boiling fresh milk.

Semifreddo means 'half
frozen' in Italian. It does not
freeze as hard as other ice
creams due to its alcohol and
sugar content. It is also known
as perfetti in Italy and is set in a
mould without churning.

deep-fried ice cream
in coconut

❈ ❈

Preparation time: 20 minutes + several days
    freezing time
Cooking time: 10 minutes
Serves 6

2 litres (70 fl oz/8 cups) vanilla ice cream
1 egg

125 g (4½ oz/1 cup) plain (all-purpose) flour
150 g (5½ oz/1½ cups) fine dry breadcrumbs
2 tablespoons desiccated coconut
oil, for deep-frying

1 Make six large scoops of ice cream and place them on a baking tray and return to the freezer.
2 Mix the egg, flour and 185 ml (6 fl oz/¾ cup) water in a bowl and stir thoroughly to make a thick batter. Coat the ice cream balls with the batter, then roll in the breadcrumbs and coconut to coat thickly. Return to the freezer and freeze for several days.
3 Fill a deep-fryer or large heavy-based saucepan one-third full of oil and heat to 180ºC (350ºF), or until a cube of bread dropped into the oil browns in 15 seconds. Slide in one ice-cream ball at a time and cook for a few seconds until the surface is golden. Take care not to melt the ice cream. Remove and serve immediately.

semifreddo

✳ ✳

Preparation time: **20 minutes + 6 hours freezing time**
Cooking time: **30 minutes**
Serves **8**

9 egg yolks
250 g (9 oz/1 cup) caster (superfine) sugar
80 ml (2½ fl oz/⅓ cup) Marsala
375 ml (13 fl oz/1½ cups) thick (double/ heavy) cream, whipped
finely grated zest of 2 oranges

CARAMEL ORANGES
2 oranges
125 g (4½ oz/½ cup) sugar

1 Combine the egg yolks, sugar and Marsala in a heatproof bowl. Set the bowl over a saucepan of steaming water, off the heat (make sure the bottom of the bowl does not touch the water). Beat with a balloon whisk or electric beaters until very thick and pale and doubled in volume (make sure the sugar has dissolved).

Remove from the heat and beat over ice until cooled. Fold in the cream and freeze for 2 hours or until partially frozen, but still soft. Fold in the zest. Spoon into a 1.5 litre (52 fl oz/6 cup) mould or loaf tin lined with plastic wrap. Freeze for 4 hours, or overnight.
2 To make the caramel oranges, cut the bases off the oranges and place, cut-side-down, on a board. Slicing downwards and following the curve of the oranges, trim off the skin and pith. Slice the oranges into rounds and place in a heatproof dish.

3 Melt the sugar gradually in a small saucepan over low heat. When melted, turn the heat up a little until the sugar caramelises. Tip the pan from side to side so the sugar caramelises evenly. When it turns golden brown, add 80 ml (2½ fl oz/ ⅓ cup) water, being careful as it may splutter, re-melt the caramel and pour it over the oranges. Cover with plastic wrap and stand until set.
4 Cut the semifreddo into slices and serve with caramel oranges.

index

Page numbers in *italics* refer to photographs. Page numbers in **bold** type refer to margin notes.